E. J. H. Greene

EIGHTEENTH-CENTURY FRENCH THEATRE

ASPECTS AND CONTEXTS

Studies presented to
E. J. H. Greene

Edited by
Magdy Gabriel Badir and David J. Langdon

Published by the
Departments of Romance Languages and Comparative Literature
of the University of Alberta
1986

Canadian Cataloguing in Publication Data

Main entry under title:
Eighteenth-century French theatre: aspects and contexts

ISBN 0-88864-956-8

1. French drama - 18th century - History and criticism.
2. Theater - France - History - 18th century. 3. Greene,
E. J. H. (Edward Joseph Hollingsworth), 1913-   I. Badir,
Magdy Gabriel. II. Langdon, David J. (David Jeffrey),
1935-   III. Greene, E. J. H. (Edward Joseph
Hollingsworth), 1913-   IV. University of Alberta.
Dept. of Romance Languages.   V. University of Alberta.
Dept. of Comparative Literature.
PQ537.E43 1986   842'.5'09   C87-091007-8

56, 398

Printed by P.S.

Contents

Preface

In publishing this collection of essays in honor of Professor Emeritus E. J. H. Greene, the Departments of Romance Languages and Comparative Literature of the University of Alberta are responding to the wish expressed by many of his colleagues and former students that such a tribute be paid to an eminent scholar, respected colleague and dear friend.

Greene's own fields of interest as teacher and researcher are too extensive to be reflected adequately in any limited theme, but certainly eighteenth-century French theatre has been one of his happiest hunting-grounds. It is also appropriate, in view of Greene's work in comparative literature and his interest in the evolution of French drama, that some of the present essays look beyond the frontiers of France, while others illuminate the relations of eighteenth-century theatre with that of the previous period.

The editors wish to express their gratitude to the University of Alberta and its Faculty of Arts for financial support which has made the undertaking possible. Special thanks are due for their advice and assistance to Professors Jo Ann Creore and Milan V. Dimić and Mrs. June Panteluk of the University of Alberta, President Roseann Runte of the Université Sainte-Anne, Professor Harold Knutson of the University of British Columbia, and the staff of the University of Alberta Printing Services.

M.G.B.
D.J.L.

The Right Man in the Right Place

To Ed Greene, with feeling.

One of the many lapidary entries in the University of Alberta 1986-87 Calendar reads: GREENE, Edward Joseph Hollingsworth, MA (Alberta), DU (Paris), Professor Emeritus of Romance Languages (1938, 1978). Clear and evocative as these facts are, they can only hint at the contributions E. J. H. Greene, as he is better known by the profession, has made to the University with which he was associated before retirement for well over forty years, to French and international literary history, and to the development of Comparative Literature as a discipline in Alberta and Canada. And his friends and collegues, who usually call him Ed Greene or simply Ed, will want to remember many events and anecdotes, whether they are related or not to his teaching and administration, research and honors.

When I arrived in Edmonton, most punctually, for a contract beginning on July 1, 1966, I was totally unaware of Canadian academic customs. Professor Ernest Reinhold, Head of the Department of Germanic Languages and Linguistics, who had offered me the opportunity to come to Canada and who most kindly chaperoned me and my family during the early weeks, presented me to the few new colleagues who were in town during the summer. Among the important persons to meet, especially for a comparatist, was the Head of Romance Languages, who had done much to promote the discipline and who, it was suggested to me, for this reason had favored my appointment. I cannot visualize fully this first, rather brief meeting, but do recall my surprise at two of Dr. Greene's gestures. After the usual presentations, and a few words in French, he told me abruptly, "You should call me Head," or at least, this is how I heard it, and it did not seem to fit the otherwise very cordial and matter of fact behavior of this person. It took me quite a while (and longer exposure to North American Academe) to understand that with my poor English and with German experiences just behind me (everybody was then still *Herr Professor* Dr.) I had mistaken "Ed" for "Head." The other peculiarity was that a few minutes later, as soon as the conversation had begun drifting towards polite banalities, Ed Greene visibly lost interest in it, started looking around and, after another minute or two, rose from behind his neatly organized desk and turned half way towards the window. I gathered that my time was up and bade a hasty farewell. It was much later, when I complained to him about administrative chores and the loss of time because of chatty visitors, that he explained to me his working habits: rising at ungodly hours, he would first do his research and writing (*nulla dies sine linea*), then keep his administrative appointments before lunch, and reserve the afternoon for other duties; and that he shared with me his technique of limiting conversations: one introductory sentence, to put the visitor at ease, about three or four minutes of intense listening, then a prompt, clear and final answer; if the visitor continued, covering the same ground again, visible signs of impatience, followed by standing up and turning half way to the window; if this was still not enough, full turn towards the window. The present words are mine, but the principles his, and after twenty years of experience, I must subscribe to their wisdom — although not to their practicality. Trying to emulate the lofty example, I for one acquired a solid reputation of rudeness, but have yet to improve my dead-lines.

Needless to say, before getting to know Ed Greene in his family circle, surrounded by friends and with a glass of Irish whisky, or Scotch, or wine in his hand (as in all things spiritual, he has broad, catholic tastes), we all at that time not only respected this distinguished Canadian scholar, but were careful when dealing with a serious administrator who had so much common sense and such an obvious dislike of fools. I never forgot how Ed Green reacted to the confused thinking of a colleague, who in a long-winded way exposed complex social theories which clearly belonged to the proverbial "vue de l'esprit" category, by saying, "If this is how you are teaching literature, I am not surprised any more at the results of your students' questionnaires." Or how he quipped, stepping out of another administrator's office, with a heavy load of books under his arm, "Some people have summer plans for gardening, I have a list of books which I must read." What we all appreciated, even at such an early stage of acquaintanceship, was Greene's forthrightness and absolute trustworthiness; whether administratively expedient and politically popular or not, for him a spade was a spade and a case had the merit it had, neither more nor less. And privately, we learned to appreciate a generous host, a very kind and warm human being, full of witty observations (which did not spare pompous pundits and Parisians — "France would be the loveliest country and Paris the most wonderful city in the world, without its inhabitants") and, from time to time, ready to share reminiscences about his student days abroad, his fleeing on a bicycle to Tours in the middle of the exodus before the advancing Germans, his leaving behind the only copy of manuscripts and notes for his dissertation and how he recovered them safely after the war because of a friend's fidelity, about his early years at the University of Alberta and colleagues "hauts en couleurs," about rip-roaring parties ("those were the days!"), about foreign appointees, their background and particularities, about his children and their teachers, about the only time he exploited the full array of his Christian names to impress a snotty attendant and secure visiting privileges at the exclusive golf course of the Banff Springs Hotel . . . All this and much more he narrated with humor, brevity and an eye for the human, all too human in others and himself.

But let us proceed in a more orderly fashion, and as traditional historians, *ab ovo*. Born 1913 in Edmonton, Alberta, to an Irish protestant family, Greene married in 1941 Joan Wood, of Welsh descent, and with her raised three children, two sons, John and Peter, and a daughter, Moira. In the fullness of time, John became Associate Professor and Chairman of French at the University of Victoria and Peter Manager of the School of Management at the Banff Centre — so as to illustrate the old saying about the sins of the fathers being visited upon the children. Moira specialized in early childhood education and is now bringing up her three young children and very actively participating in volunteer community work. Ed Greene went to school and university in Edmonton and completed his B.A. Honors in French and German in 1935 and his M.A. in French in 1936. Following a year at the Sorbonne in Paris on a French Government Bursary, he returned to the University of Alberta in 1938 as a sessional lecturer in the Department of Modern Languages. Another year in France and two more as lecturer were followed by service in the Royal Canadian Naval Volunteer Reserve and Naval Operational Intelligence from 1942 to 1945. He was appointed Assistant Professor in 1945, completed his doctorate in Comparative Literature under the supervision of the great Jean-Marie Carré, at the Sorbonne in 1948, and became Full Professor in 1954. From 1953 to 1964 he was Head of the Department of Modern Languages. In 1964-65 this Department was succeeded by the Departments of Germanic Languages and Linguistics, Slavic Languages, and Romance Languages; he continued as Head of Romance Languages until 1967 and served from 1967 to 1972 as Associate Dean of Arts for the Humanities and Fine Arts. From 1973 until his retirement on 31 December 1978 he held a joint appointment with the Departments of Romance Languages and Comparative Literature; he is now a Professor Emeritus, a term which, as he once commented, is not very precise, the *Oxford English Dictionary* informing us that the first meaning of the word *emeritus* is "honourably discharged from service" and that it is the past participle of the Latin verb *emereri* (earn).

Ed Greene served on the Advisory Academic Panel of the Canada Council from 1967-72 and he was the first Western Canadian to chair this body for a year. From 1974 to 1977 he chaired the Western Region Selection Committee for the Canada Council Special M.A. Fellowship; in 1974-75 he chaired the University of Alberta task force for the Canada Council-sponsored Healy Commission, and was the President of the Canadian Association of University Professors of French from 1960 to 1962, of the Canadian Comparative Literature Association from 1977 to 1979, and of the Canadian Society for Eighteenth-Century Studies in 1981-82, a Society he helped to found in 1968. During his life-long association with the University of Alberta, he was granted three sabbaticals (but spent without pay the academic year 1947-48 in Paris to finish his doctorate), held a Senior Research Fellowship of the Canada Council in 1959-60, obtained one publication grant from the same Council (for his book on Marivaux), two publication grants from the Humanities Research Council of Canada (the present Canadian Federation for the Humanities — for the books on T. S. Eliot and about Comedy), and one grant from Alberta Culture (also for the study about a comic structure). In 1972 he was given, by the Government of Alberta, the Alberta Achievement Award.

According to my bibliographic lights, which are limited, Ed Greene contributed book reviews, usually on eighteenth-century topics in French and Comparative Literature, to such journals as *L'Esprit Créateur*, *Humanities Association Bulletin*, *University of Toronto Quarterly*, *Romanic Review*, and *Canadian Review of Comparative Literature/Revue Canadienne de Littérature Comparée*. He published articles in Canadian, American, and French periodicals and proceedings of conferences, with topics ranging from Marivaux and Voltaire to Laforgue and Eliot. He co-authored two French language manuals; the first, *Eléments de langue française*, was written with the late Dennis M. Healy, then also at the University of Alberta; the second, *Reflex French*, first published in 1960 and reprinted many times, was prepared with the late Manoël Faucher and Dennis M. Healy, and the technical help of Edward Marxheimer. Ed Greene published also three books of literary scholarship: *T. S. Eliot et la France* (1951), *Marivaux* (1965) and *Menander to Marivaux: The History of a Comic Structure* (1977). The reader will find further information in the Bibliography of E. J. H. Greene's writings in the present volume.

I mentioned earlier three main aspects of Greene's work: his service to the University of Alberta, his role in the development of Comparative Literature as a discipline and profession in Canada, and his contribution to French and international literary history. Although these activities are intertwined by their very nature and are united in the same person, it is convenient to maintain this division and offer comments about each type separately.

Throughout his years with the University of Alberta, Greene taught undergraduate and graduate courses, in French and, from 1973 until his retirement, also in Comparative Literature, on the genre of comedy and on the eighteenth century, mainly in French, English, German, and Spanish. Despite heavy administrative responsibilities and the burden of numerous committees (which ranged from those usual for heads and deans to the General Faculties Council, the University of Alberta Press, as well as the chairmanship of the Arts Faculty Curriculum Committee), he taught every year between four and nine weekly hours, with an average of six; in certain years, because of staffing problems, he accepted exceptional teaching loads, for instance thirteen weekly hours in 1965-66, notwithstanding his regular duties. When he returned to full time teaching and research ("and never felt happier or healthier," as he put it), he agreed to serve as his department's graduate advisor and in the last year of service even acted for eight months as Associate Chairman (*mirabile visu*). His teaching was usually evaluated as good to excellent, and the most modest "grade" of satisfactory was given by himself, in a self-assessment prepared for the Dean of Arts. As soon as the University had established a significant graduate program, Greene became one of the most sought-after supervisors in French and, later on, in Comparative Literature. Under his erudite, fatherly, but firm guidance, candidates tended to finish their theses and to do so quite promptly (*mirabile dictu*). His M.A. students frequently entered other schools in pursuit of the Ph.D., and of those who obtained the Ph.D. with him some are now pursuing successful academic careers. He was, for example, the "Doktorvater" of one of the editors of this "Festschrift." His name attracted bright students and his advice — as lecturer, examiner, assessor — was asked for by other departments and other universities. It should be remembered that Greene's headship and deanship coincided with the most rapid expansion (from 1959 to 1969 the enrollment rose from approximately 5,000 to 17,500) and the most fundamental change so far in this University's history, and that he has been one of the engineers of its transformation from a provincial into an international institution of higher learning. Moreover, he was always realistic and optimistic in his basic attitudes, an indefatigable promoter of the study of French before this language became a Canadian political necessity, of literature and the humanities before the province of Alberta had any reputation in the arts. To advance such goals, he worked with CKUA, the Alumni Players, the Alliance Française, and other local bodies and groups; he was also unwavering in the support and defense of the University's accomplishments and image whenever the occasion for this arose: in Edmonton and Ottawa, in the hallowed halls of older eastern establishments, or in Paris.

The University of Alberta knows how much it owes to him, and to his family for the indispensable support and encouragement he has received from his spouse and children; it has shown him the confidence, respect and gratitude he deserves.

Nevertheless, a scholar of probity and unwilling to "sell himself in the academic marketplace" will be taken for granted at times by an emerging multiversity which is by necessity both impersonal and sensitive to institutional politics. Behind my own desk as an administrator, I had occasion to peruse Greene's personal file. It is the slimmest and trimmest ("le dossier le plus épuré") I have seen so far, with only one personal request in it: after retirement, he had to plead, at the highest level, for the privilege of a library card. (In this respect, we still seem to lack policies and attitudes which would permit the University to honor more meaningfully and pragmatically the really eminent emeriti who desire to continue their research and certain relationships with the school.) But I do hope that, many years ago, the "powers that be" at least marked with a white pebble the day (*albo lapillo notare diem*) when Greene declined an invitation by the University of Toronto and decided to spend his life with his Alma Mater, in his city and province.

In Canada, Comparative Literature became an academic discipline quite late. This can be attributed, in all probability, to the conservative mood of the land and the influence of British universities, which only reluctantly found a place for the systematic teaching of international aspects of literature. In his 1970 overview of the teaching of French Canadian literature, the well-known classical scholar and distinguished administrator from Laval, Maurice Lebel, was still deploring the fact that "Beaucoup d'universitaires sont versés, bien sûr, en littérature comparée, dirigent même parfois des thèses en ce domaine. Mais fait inouï et paradoxal, c'est seulement à l'Université de l'Alberta, à Edmonton, qu'il existe un véritable département de littérature comparée au Canada."[1] In fact, while there was little systematic teaching of this discipline until the late 1960's, Canadian universities did grant many Master's and doctoral degrees based on international topics, scholars such as Northrop Frye did publish theoretical and historical works of very great distinction, and comparative studies of the French and East European type were pursued by others, for instance Eugène Joliat, Victor Graham, and Zbigniew Folejewski. In that generation, Ed Greene was among the foremost, and his *T. S. Eliot et la France* was the first of the eight books sponsored between 1951 and 1969 by the Canada Council and the Humanities Research Council of Canada under the category of "littérature comparée." At the University of Alberta isolated honors and graduate courses, initiated by Greene, had been taught since the late Fifties. The heading "Comparative Literature" appeared for the first time in the calendar for 1961-62, a Master's program was sponsored in 1964 and a doctoral one in 1965 by the foreign language departments, by English, and by Classics. The first chairman of this interdepartmental program was Charles H. Moore, with a doctorate in Comparative Literature from the Sorbonne, a colleague and friend of Greene; the first courses in literary theory were taught by Juan Ferraté, professor of Spanish and later Comparative Literature, who came to Alberta at Greene's invitation. In 1969, a Department was established, with the full range of graduate, postgraduate and undergraduate activities. These developments, which have given this discipline an institutional and material basis which is still the strongest in Canada, have been facilitated and often made possible by his championship. Without his authority, the program and the Department would have had even more difficulty in overcoming intellectual distrust and bureaucratic resistance to changes in the *status quo.* I remember with emotion how he stood steadfast in our darkest hours of need. As officer of the Canadian Comparative Literature Association/Association Canadienne de Littérature Comparée and its President, as one of the founding members of the editorial committee and at times acting editor of the *Canadian Review of Comparative Literature/Revue Canadienne de Littérature Comparée* and the journal's book series, Greene had participated in the rapid development of the discipline from coast to coast, and well beyond the boundaries of Canada. It is a happy coincidence indeed that the Association's Executive received under his presidency the following telegram, signed by Northrop Frye: "Congratulations to the Canadian Comparative Literature Association for having made so remarkable an achievement in having brought the study of comparative literature to the centre of the humanities stage in such a short time."

Other accomplishments notwithstanding, I should like to single out Greene's publications. Both of the language manuals are still popular with students (I checked the loan records of the library) and the second one was a considerable publishing success. Revised by the authors at least four times, *Reflex French* was an experimental text, which embodied a structural approach and invited the student to adopt an active attitude; it integrated its lessons with specially prepared tapes and suggested the use of audio-visual adjuncts at a time when the "language laboratory" was much less prominent at universities.

In literature, his substantive early article on Laforgue and Eliot became a classic, frequently quoted in the voluminous scholarship about the great English modernist poet. Referring in 1960 to his book *T. S. Eliot et la France*, Greene stated with characteristic sobriety: "My doctoral dissertation is still selling at the rate of one copy per month, and has been my passport to the approved learned bodies in Europe and North America." In reality, it was much more. The fruit of diligent labor spanning a period of twelve years, the book brought the author into contact with Eliot's elder brother, Henry Ware Eliot, Jr., who opened to the young scholar the collections of Eliot House at Harvard; more importantly, the research resulted in an intensive and useful correspondence with the artist himself and in three personal encounters in London, as well as Eliot's critical reading of the manuscript before publication. The poet liked the study very much, preferred it in fact to all others published so far. The same favorable stance was adopted by critics, publishing their comments in at least six leading periodicals.[2] For Robert Finch

> This book is probably the most fundamental contribution yet made to Eliot literature . . . It examines clearly, impartially, and most readably a subject which has . . . cried out for adequate treatment . . . The whole vexed and exciting question of Eliot's indebtedness to French writers is here at last thoroughly and skilfully dealt with . . . An excellent bibliography . . . throw[s] new light on Eliot . . . and on modern poetry in general, but for Eliot readers and critics of whatever persuasion or experience it furnishes a henceforth indispensable guide.

Finch offers also a precise indication of the book's contents:

The first two-thirds of the book, a detailed examination of the influence, upon Eliot the poet, of such poets as Rimbaud, Tailhade, Corbière, Gautier, Baudelaire, and Mallarmé, reaches the conclusion that Eliot's debt to these is above all a technical one, involving the assimilation and transformation of new poetic manners and their eventual fusion into a newer manner still. The remainder of the volume evaluates the influence, upon Eliot the critic, of critics such as Baudelaire, de Gourmont, Benda, Maurras, and Maritain, and analyses Eliot's progressive realization of new critical principles and a new method of criticism, not imitating from but expanding and perfecting theirs.

Jean-Marie Carré pointed out the delicate nature of the task, the fact that the Sorbonne had accepted the topic in spite of its usual prohibition of dissertations about living authors, and praised Greene for very successfully combining erudition, judgment and subtlety, and expressing himself with rare precision and elegance: ". . . rien de plus suggestif, de plus stimulant que son livre." For M. C. Bradbrook, the "evidence has been admirably done"; for Albert Baiwir, "il convient de féliciter l'auteur non seulement de la compétence parfaite, mais aussi de la probité et du tact qu'il a apportés à sa brillante démonstration." Even for George Boas, who openly decried all influence studies, "Mr. Green with amazing patience has gone through the poetry and prose of Eliot line by line, indeed word by word . . . He has done the job with such thoroughness that it will never have to be done again." And in 1969, Jacques Voisine, in his review of another publication about Eliot, lauds *T. S. Eliot et la France*, "qui reste sur la question l'ouvrage essentiel."[3]

Greene's next book was the first full-length and methodical presentation of Marivaux in English; with the possible exception of Frédéric Deloffre's *Marivaux et le marivaudage*, it stood quite alone in French criticism too. In ten chapters, *all* the works of Marivaux are analyzed and discussed in chronological order and related to the writer's life, insofar as it was known at the time of Greene's research. Five other chapters trace the fortunes of Marivaux after his death, show the reasons for the hostility of his contemporaries and the roots of his present popularity. I was able to find eleven reviews of the book, in prominent learned journals, signed by some of the great names of Marivaux studies and French literary history, such as Frédéric Deloffre, Christoph Miething and Henri Peyre.[4] All critics praised the clarity of exposition, the completeness of the treatment, the judicious critical stance, the excellent bibliography, the vigorous style, and the interpretations of lesser known texts by Marivaux, but also the analyses of *Les Fausses Confidences* and *La Vie de Marianne*, as well as the more profound understanding of the real meaning of "marivaudage." Some of the recurring terms are "sanity" and "masterly." For a monography in English, the book had the unusual distinction of being recommended in the printed program of Marivaux' plays performed by the Comédie-Française.

Menander to Marivaux: The History of a Comic Structure, which inaugurated the Bibliothèque de la Revue Canadienne de Littérature Comparée, studies 693 comedies, covering the period between Greek New Comedy and eighteenth-century French *drame*, i.e., from Menander, Plautus and Terence, by the way of the Commedia Umanistica, the Commedia Erudita, the Commedia dell'arte, and French Renaissance comedy, until Beaumarchais, against the backdrop of the comic structure or formula ('F') which enjoyed its steep rise, immense popularity and relative downfall in France from about 1660 to 1759: "The spontaneous loves of the Young, traversed by the Old, are aided and abetted by the Servants." This structure, stated independently by N. Frye in the *Anatomy of Criticism*, hinted at by R. Barthes in *Sur Racine*, and interpreted by Charles Mauron and other psychoanalysts, is fully explored here for the first time: Greene read all extant French comedies from the century in question. At least thirteen reviews greeted the book[5] and while certain critics regretted the author's aversion to orthodox structuralism and reluctance to pursue a sociological analysis, they all stressed the thoroughness of the monograph and the lively style. They praised, in their individual way, particular aspects, too. So, for example, Edith Kern, author of the *The Absolute Comic*, stated: "It seems to me laudable, indeed, that Professor Greene — in contrast to Northrop Frye — dwells on the growing importance of the servant — both male and female — in the French comedies of the decades he discusses." Others singled out the pages devoted to Marivaux's original use of 'F' (David A. Trott), the book's empirical nature and the continuity it establishes between eighteenth-century comedy and its classical predecessors (Harold C. Knutson), the author's thoroughness and originality (Donald C. Spinelli), his table of French comedies written during the period under scrutiny (Elizabeth M. Tilton), his phenomenal amount of reading (Ronald C. Rosbottom) and knowledge of forgotten pages of theatrical history (Manfred Schmeling), his ability "de nous présenter un panorama où les auteurs mineurs ne sont pas sacrifiés, et qui, en nous donnant une vue générale d'un théâtre souvent mal connu, permet non seulement d'en saisir les structures et les modes, mais d'en dégager l'esprit et de percevoir comment, acceptant le corset de règles étroites, il essaie néanmoins de renouveler constamment l'expression des caractères et des mœurs de son temps" (André Blanc).

Ed Greene is now working on a book-length study of the impact of the "adventures of Telemachus" theme on French and English literature from the early seventeenth to the early twentieth century, without neglecting classical antecedents and including both serious and burlesque treatments (Homer, Vergil, Scarron, Fénelon, Marivaux, Aragon, etc.). The first two chapters are typed already and the manuscript is advancing at a steady pace. Once it is ready, I hope as an editor to make the author an offer he cannot refuse.

For those who have the privilege of knowing Ed Greene and his family personally, he has always been one of their favorite contemporaries, truly the right man in the right place. May he continue to enjoy health, happiness and a productive life and may we hope that he will take a kind view of this "hommage" and, indeed, of the whole book. Supported by the University of Alberta, written and edited by colleagues and friends from here and afar, it is a belated but sincere "coup de chapeau."[6]

Milan V. Dimić
University of Alberta

Laughter, Comedy, Catharsis:
The French Contribution

Of the three terms included in the title, catharsis has been the most contro-versial. Fortunately, the controversy concerning the notion of catharsis has been amply treated in the past, and more particularly by Leon Golden in a series of articles.[1] This makes it unnecessary for me to become involved in the theoretical complexities of the question and enables me to move more or less directly into the domain of French comedy. So for the purposes of this short essay, I am accepting as my main working hypothesis the idea of catharsis as intellectual clarification (rather than moral and emotional purgation), and I should like to suggest that there are three distinct levels on which this clarification may be considered to take place: a) the level of spectator-observation, b) the level of spectator/character identification, c) the level of character-perception.

There is much brilliant comic narrative in French literature, from Voltaire's *Candide* to Jules Romain's *Les Copains*, André Gide's *Les Caves du Vatican*, or Montherlant's *Les Célibataires*, but I shall restrict myself here to the relatively distinct type of comic catharsis involved in theatrical writing and staging. In spite of this restriction, there is still a great deal of material to cover, if one could treat the subject thoroughly. The inevitable key figure must of course be Molière, to whose name I should like to add that of Marivaux for the specific purposes of this essay. Besides Molière and Marivaux, French theatre includes medieval farce and the work of writers like Lesage, Regnard, Dufresny. There are also im-portant contributions by Beaumarchais, Jules Romains, Ionesco and others.

On the theoretical level, Bergson's essay is well known, so before discussing individual plays and writers, I should like to mention in passing a recent French contribution to the theory of comic catharsis.

Laughter: its nature and function:—In a lecture given at Florida State University a few years ago, René Girard proposed what he termed "a mini-theory of laughter." How does it relate to previous theories? The most traditional interpretation of Aristotle's notion of catharsis is that based on moral and emotional purgation. I have already mentioned another view, developed by schol-ars like Leon Golden, also now well established, which sees catharsis as intellec-tual clarification. With René Girard, we add yet another possible interpretation: to the emotional and the intellectual he adds the physiological, which seems to be somewhat related to a third position on catharsis known as the medical.

Girard emphasizes the similarity between tears and laughter, tragedy and comedy, the difference depending on tragedy's stress on heroic individualism and comedy's stress on structural patterns. According to Girard, Bergson fails to understand this essential difference, and that "the comic is rooted in the ultimate failure of all individualism." Girard emphasizes the incorporation of tears into laughter: in successful farce, the audience will "laugh till it cries"; in sentimental comedy (*comédie larmoyante*), the audience will "weep tears of joy." He sees tears as providing a metaphorical physiological accompaniment to a medical process of evacuation and a religious process of scapegoating designed to expel both the scapegoat and the danger of endless reciprocal violence.

1

Comedy: its nature and function:—Leon Golden gives us three categories of comedy, one of which is the expression of the superego (reflected in the Meredith/Bergson view of Molière) while the other two are both expressions of the Id (Freud's view of Aristophanes, Segal's view of Plautus). Charles Mauron, another Freudian, sees comic theatre as based on a fantasy of triumph linked to subconscious drives: recovery of the mother and triumph of the pleasure principle (Eros) over the father — for example, by a love-marriage in ancient comedy (Plautus), by cuckoldry in modern comedy (Molière).

To these I should like to add a mention of the myth-and-ritual perspective suggested by Harold Watts. According to this perspective, a cyclical view of existence is proposed by myths of the Jesus type and by tragedy, essentially pessimistic. Watts remarks: "The linear assertion is, I believe, a record of a later, a more subtle, and certainly a more intimate reading of man's position in the world since it sees that man as a person, an individual."[2] Comedy is thus related to a more primitive view of man, now to be found only in such Eastern religions as Buddhism, which deny the significance ot the individual and the unique.

If we are to look, within the French tradition, for examples which would follow closely Aristotle's definition of comedy and of comic catharsis as elaborated by Leon Golden, then the name of Molière is the first that comes to mind. *L'Avare*, *Le Misanthrope*, *Le Tartuffe*, *Don Juan*, and even less serious and more farcical plays such as *L'Ecole des femmes*, *Le Malade imaginaire* and *Le Bourgeois gentilhomme*, involve, to put it in Aristotelian terms, an action which is complete, has magnitude, is represented by means of language that has been adorned, and more importantly they exemplify the Aristotelian notions of *phaulos*, *geloios*, *hamartema* and *aischos*.

A great number of Molière's plays can be said to be a mimesis of actions, situations, and incidents which frequently arouse a certain kind of "indignation" — one, however, which does not cause pain and is not destructive. For example, the "indignation" or "negative reaction" in *L'Avare* aroused by Harpagon's behavior persists, for Harpagon is no less a miser at the end than at the beginning of the play, but it is compensated for and counteracted by the resolution provided by the *deus ex machina* (in the person of the father) which ensures the reward and happiness of the two young couples (Cléante-Marianne, Valère-Elise).

The characters of Dom Juan, Tartuffe and to a lesser extent Arnolphe in *L'Ecole des femmes* would also arouse "indignation" in varying degrees of intensity, but again this negative feeling is "purged" at the end of the plays: Dom Juan, confounded by the statue (which represents divine justice), is struck by lightning and swallowed up by the earth; Tartuffe is carried off to prison, and Arnolphe's elaborate plot to have Agnès is finally blocked by another *deus ex machina*, the girl's father.

All these plays, and many others by Molière, involve a recognition of a *phaulos* or *geloios*; indignation at their behavior; and a final purgation of that feeling, mainly by means of the neutralization of the *phaulos*.

There are some plays in which catharsis falls less within the notion of purgation and more within that of intellectual clarification, sometimes successfully brought to term, sometimes less clearly so. For example, in *Le Misan-*

thrope, the gradual revelation and proof of Célimène's true character to Alceste can clearly be seen as a kind of intellectual clarification, a process in which the spectator sometimes precedes Alceste, by means of scenes in which the latter is not present. This clarification has not, however, been totally painless since the Romantic period, as the spectator may identify with Alceste's disillusionment regarding the woman he loves as well as the whole of society, provided, of course, we tend a little towards Rousseau's view of Alceste rather than that of Molière himself.

It could, of course, also be argued that the process of intellectual clarification concerns Alceste himself more directly in a twofold manner: either (a) he fails to recognize his own faults and blames everything on the others — in which case there is no clarification, as with Oedipus; or (b) he realizes his failings but prefers to isolate himself rather than admit he is guilty of lack of tolerance, his own kind of hubris.

The cases of Orgon in *Le Tartuffe* and of Philaminte in *Les Femmes savantes*, both infatuated with false figures to the point of wanting to give them their daughters in marriage (accompanied by a sizeable dowry), likewise culminate in *anagnorisis* and "clarification." Philaminte finally understands the materialistic motives of the man she had chosen as son-in-law. Here, the character finally arrives at the truth which the spectator knew throughout the play. In other words, in terms of the categories I mentioned earlier, the character-perception follows chronologically the spectator-observation. There is no indication that either Orgon or Philaminte will be wiser in the future, but unhappiness has been avoided, and the action of the *geloios* exorcised and purged of its potential harm to others.

The best-known French comic dramatist is, of course, Molière. But the comic theatre which provides the best support and illustration for the view of catharsis as intellectual clarification is, in my opinion, that of Marivaux. His comedies would fit less well in the Aristotelian definition, although there are comic and at times even farcical situations and incidents. However, the notions of *phaulos* and *geloios* are so attenuated as to be almost non-existent, and so is the spectator's "indignation" or "negative reaction." Furthermore, Marivaux's theatre is "smiling" comedy rather than "laughing" comedy. It is interesting to note at this point that Meredith draws most of his examples from Molière to illustrate a conception of smiling rather than laughing comedy. Such a view of Molière is highly debatable — and is indeed implicitly contradicted by T. S. Eliot, who declares that Molière's comedy is always farce, even in *Le Misanthrope*. I am inclined to agree with Eliot rather than Meredith: in the context of French comedy at least, Molière clearly represents "laughing" comedy, while Marivaux represents "smiling" comedy and would have illustrated Meredith's view much better. This is confirmed by Meredith's other examples — Congreve's *The Way of the World*, Pope's *The Rape of the Lock*. These belong, like the works of Marivaux, to the rococo aesthetic, whose contempt for laughing as vulgar is well expressed by Chesterfield and Fontenelle.[3] This view of the difference between Molière and Marivaux is clearly reflected in the traditional view of Beaumarchais, who is seen as returning French comedy, after decades of comedy of psychology and manners and sentimental comedy (*comédie larmoyante*), to the frank laughter (*le franc rire*) of a Molière.

In many Marivaux plays, the principal characters are seen to follow a slow process of clarification, almost exclusively related to their feelings and emotions towards the other sex and which culminates in their recognition of being in love. The examples are too numerous and the situations too complex to be given here in detail. But my previous investigation of this author[4] has led me to formulate the hypothesis that, in many cases, the so-called "truth" the characters (and with them the inattentive spectator) arrive at is often distorted and interfered with by the numerous mirrors, masks and illusions they use in order to attain that perception. Two examples from the two best-known Marivaux plays should suffice to make my point. In *Le Jeu de l'amour et du hasard*, the two-fold disguise of the hero and heroine (they both change places with their servants in order to observe each other) causes them to be so surprised, delighted and impressed with each other's looks, poise, language and sensibility as to fall in love. They are then torn between their feelings and the social pressures which they imagine to be real, but the unmasking occurs and all ends well: they will marry and live happily ever after — or at least so it appears.

On the level of character-perception, there is catharsis in the sense of clarification, i.e., they gradually come to recognize their feelings as love. There is also catharsis in the sense of purgation, i.e., the relief of a very real tension and emotion. But the astute spectator is the beneficiary of a further degree of intellectual clarification not attained by the characters. He can see well before them that they are in love, but he can also see that ultimately the person with whom they have fallen in love does not really exist. Dorante, for instance, cannot separate the Silvia he discovers after the unmasking takes place from the servant-Silvia with whom he fell in love. A further step of *anagnorisis* would be to adjust his criteria and to ask himself how *exceptional* is Silvia, now that he knows she is not a servant? And inversely, Dorante's wit, subtlety, politeness and refinement would be less striking if he were judged by standards appropriate to his real station. It is too late for the characters, but this kind of intellectual clarification is available to the spectator or reader.

Similarly, at the very end of *Les Fausses Confidences*, the heroine, a rich and beautiful widow, arrives at the truth about her own feelings for her young and handsome (but poor) financial adviser, aided by an elaborate scheme of carefully planned circumstances and incidents. Dorante is genuinely in love with Araminte, however, and he does confess at the end that most of the events were really stratagems, but the spectator has a much more complete grasp of the number and nature of the lies told in the course of the play than Araminte. In any case, as in *Le Jeu*, it is too late for her to adjust her criteria to the new information. As Dorante's master-minding servant Dubois exclaims triumphantly: "Il est trop tard . . . l'heure du courage est passée, il faut qu'elle nous épouse."

In conclusion, perhaps I might venture the following general formulation. Three distinct stages may be perceived in the process of *anagnorisis* and clarification in French comedy. First there is the moment at which the spectator becomes aware of the truth; then there is a period of tension during which the spectator is torn between amused superiority and detachment on the one hand and sympathetic anxiety on the other (in the sense that we want the character to

4

reach the truth mainly for the sake of the people around him, rather than for his own sake); and finally we have the moment at which the protagonist attains to awareness of the truth, although this is not always as complete or as philosophical a truth as that posessed by the spectator.

Valentini Brady-Papadopoulou
University of Houston

Notes

[1] "Catharsis," *Transactions and Proceedings of the American Philological Association*, 93 (1962), 51-60; "Is Tragedy the 'Imitation of a *Serious* Action'?" *Greek, Roman, and Byzantine Studies*, 6, No. 4 (Winter 1965), 283-89; "*Mimesis* and *Katharsis*," *Classical Philology*, 64, No. 3 (July 1969), 145-53; "*Katharsis* as Clarification: An Objection Answered," *The Classical Quarterly*, 23, No. 1 (May 1973), 45-46; "The Clarification Theory of *Katharsis*," *Hermes*, 104, No. 4 (1976), 437-52; "*Hamartia, Ate,* and Oedipus," *The Classical World*, 72, No.1 (September 1978), 3-12.

[2] H. Watts, "Myth and Drama," in *Myth and Literature: Contemporary Theory and Practice*, ed. J. B. Vickery (Lincoln: Nebraska Univ. Press, 1966), p. 81.

[3] Fontenelle was described in his old age by Madame Geoffrin as "une petite machine bien délicate, qui durerait éternellement si on la posait dans un coin, et qu'on ne la frottât ni ne la froissât jamais . . . Il n'avait jamais pleuré, il ne s'était jamais mis en colère, il n'avait jamais couru. Je lui disais un jour: 'Monsieur de Fontenelle, vous n'avez jamais ri? — Non, je n'ai jamais fait, ah! ah!' Voilà l'idée qu'il se faisait du rire" (reported in *Nouveaux Mélanges* of Madame Necker; see P. M. H. de Ségur, *Le Royaume de la rue Saint-Honoré* [Paris: Calmann-Lévy, 1925], pp. 44-45). As for Chesterfield, this is what he wrote to his son regarding laughter: "Having mentioned laughing, I must particularly warn you against it: and I could heartily wish that you may often be seen to smile, but never heard to laugh while you live. Frequent and loud laughter is the characteristic of folly and ill manners: it is the manner in which the mob express their silly joy at silly things; and they call it being merry. In my mind there is nothing so illiberal and so ill bred, as audible laughter . . . I am neither of a melancholy, nor a cynical disposition, and am as willing, and as apt, to be pleased, as anybody; but I am sure that, since I had the full use of reason, nobody has ever heard me laugh" (*Letters*, ed. Bonamy Dobrée [London: Eyre and Spottiswood, 1932], III, 1115 *et seq.*).

[4] V. Brady, *Love in the Theatre of Marivaux* (Geneva: Droz, 1970), Part IV: "The Mask."

The Role of Greek Tragedy
in the Search for Legitimate Authority
under the Ancien Régime

Richelieu understood authority and how to impose it better than most men, and he devoted his life with single-minded brilliance to thinking up and implementing a variety of schemes to increase the authority of the monarch of France. It would be misguided to assume that his interest in the theatre was unconnected with this search for authority — that it was a relaxation from the cares of state, or that he was driven by the emotions of a "tragique manqué." On the contrary, "as with all other institutions on which Richelieu exerted his influence, it may be said that the Cardinal regarded the theatre primarily as a means of pursuing his political ends."[1] "Les théoriciens de l'Etat avaient bien vu que si la politique est affaire de forces analysées et calculées, la littérature doit être considérée comme l'une de ces forces et utilisée en conséquence. Richelieu poussa très loin cette idée";[2] "from 1631 onwards he mentioned on numerous occasions that he intended to control the further development of French drama himself."[3]

As well as being a shrewd tactician Richelieu had considerable ability as a strategist, and we should be as careful not to underestimate this ability as his contemporaries learned to be. The Greek tragic tradition was a long one and it had come down to seventeenth-century France via the Romans and the learned medieval commentators as a set of static and immutable rules. (Richelieu did not realize that the very essence of Greek tragedy made it an unsuitable vehicle for the promotion of authoritarian views and a static society, but neither did the contemporary learned commentators or practitioners.) If this set of "classical" — hence "reasonable" — rules could be grafted onto the French theatrical tradition and the results made authoritative, a victory would have been gained in the struggle to make a turbulent society accept other sets of authoritative rules based on "reason" — or "raison d'Etat". Since this is what indeed happened, and since Richelieu's actions were largely instrumental in establishing the conditions which made it happen, it seems reasonable to assume that this was his strategy; he did not normally cause things to happen unless they were part of a strategy. We shall examine briefly how effective this strategy was, and how it received support from an unexpected quarter in the eighteenth century.

To modern eyes which have learned to see tragedy and the myths on which it is based as expressions of the collective consciousness of nations, the idea of appropriating another nation's myths and public rituals may seem odd. The Romans had done so when they conquered Greece, but this was clearly a case of a poorly-developed culture appropriating a highly-developed culture, and the appropriation had been close to total — religion, mythology, and the thought and value system that went with them. Whatever may have been Richelieu's opinion of French culture in the 1630's, he knew that it was impossible, and in terms of his ultimate goals undesirable, for France to adopt the religious beliefs and value systems which underpinned Greek mythology and Greek tragedy. These were indeed so foreign to the Christian tradition that they were incomprehensible and inexplicable even to sympathetic scholars.[4] Until Thucydides the Greeks made no clear distinction between their history and their myths, and Bossuet's *Histoire universelle* of 1681 shows biblical and Christian history and mythology still being treated in that same fashion. Greek mythology and the tragedies which were one of the emanations of it were the foreign affectation of the privileged classes, and they remained so. Consequently they lacked the authority which comes from being an integral part of the nation's value system (as Christianity was), and any authority people might wish to give them had to come from an external source.

For Richelieu's scheme this external source was to be the *Poetics* of Aristotle as viewed through the latinized optic of the learned commentators.[5] Aristotelian logic and thought formed the basis of scholasticism and the theology of the Catholic Church, and thus Aristotle's name enjoyed great authority in Catholic countries. It is not by chance that the lessons of the *Poetics* were rejected by the boisterous Elizabethan tragedy of Protestant England and accepted in Catholic France. Until Richelieu's intervention, however, they had no more authority in France than in England: Hardy took no more notice of them than had Shakespeare. To put an end to this state of affairs Richelieu hired a coterie of dramatists to write plays under his supervision and authority and on themes he proposed.[6] The success of Corneille's *Le Cid* posed a problem, since it was essentially an example of tragi-comedy (a genre which was enjoying a brief and final revival of popularity among authors and audiences), and clearly did not fit the current interpretation of the Aristotelian model. Richelieu ordered Chapelain and the Académie française, which he had recently created,[7] to criticize the play, but even here the results were not entirely to his liking. After a long gestation the *Sentiments de l'Académie sur le Cid* essentially forgave the irregularities noted in the play because of its other qualities, rather than condemning them. However all was not lost, since an authoritative tradition had been established which insisted that deviations from the accepted Aristotelian model had to be justified or excused. The lesson was well learned by Corneille whose return to the stage was marked by a series of much more "regular" tragedies. Here, as in so many other areas, Richelieu's initial success was less than total, but laid the basis for future consolidation of what had been gained.

A second move by Richelieu which helped to appropriate the tradition of Aristotle's *Poetics* and to create an authorized form of French drama, was his request that D'Aubignac produce an up-to-date presentation of the rules of drama. Following Richelieu's death two or three years later (in 1642), D'Aubignac dropped his project[8] (though he continued to attend the theatre and observe carefully), so that we have no means of knowing how closely the final product met the requirements Richelieu undoubtedly laid down. When D'Aubignac eventually made up his mind to publish his *Pratique du théâtre* in 1657, readers found in it a large number of examples drawn from French tragedy — over 120 as against about 150 from Greek tragedy.[9] The two traditions were with this work firmly joined together. Though he quotes Aristotle sixty times,[9] D'Aubignac devotes a whole chapter to his claim to have based his work not on the authority of the Ancients (or anyone else) but on reason.[10] Like Scaliger before him, his real interest was "la vraisemblance," which was the result of the application of reason to theatrical praxis. To us, this reason and "vraisemblance" were clearly culture-based and valid only within fairly strict limits of time and space, but D'Aubignac had the "classical" view that both were eternal and not subject to change or appeal.[11]

The connection in D'Aubignac's mind between the authority of this reason and the authority of the State is clear from his text. When he began his work — while Richelieu was still alive — "Toutes les Regles des Anciens dont je pretendois qu'il falloit suivre la conduite pour faire éclatter toutes les beautés du Theatre, estoient rejettées, comme des nouveautez que l'on voudrait introduire dans le gouvernement de l'Estat, ou dans les mystères de la Religion." And later: "En tout ce qui dépend de la raison et du sens commun, comme sont les regles du Theatre, la licence est un crime qui n'est jamais permis." He goes on to say that "Euripide a preferé dans les *Suppliantes* la gloire de son païs à celle de son Art" and that this sort of *raison d'Etat* alone can justify the breaking of the rules of the theatre.[12]

Regardless of the validity of its prescriptions, D'Aubignac's work is a remarkable achievement in its fusion of the Greek and French dramatic traditions, its successful (at least in its time) attempt to establish their joint authority on reason and to link this authority with that of the State. By the time it was published, many of its prescriptions were being more or less generally obeyed, and even Corneille had felt the need to start to compose *ex post facto Examens* to justify and rationalize his breaking of the rules.[13]

After the initial criticisms of the work died down, it remained for generations as the standard work on what had now become the French classical tradition. Racine had a copy in which he made marginal notes, and Boileau praised it. When it was republished in 1715, the *Mémoires de Trévoux* noted: "On peut dire qu'il [D'Aubignac] rendit [la scène] en France si régulière que l'antiquité sur laquelle il la réforma, pourrait nous envier sa perfection."[14] It is impossible to pin-point the time at which obedience to these rules became generally recognized as an end in itself, rather than a means to an end, just as it is impossible to pin-point the time at which the total authority of the rule of Louis XIV was generally recognized, but the increasing enforcement of written and unwritten rules in all phases of court life, including the King's bedroom, was paralleled by the increasing authority of the D'Aubignacian rules in the French theatre.[15]

By 1692, when André Dacier published his translations of Aristotle's *Poetics*, and of the *Oedipus tyrannus* and *Electra* of Sophocles, the authority of both the King and the dramatic rules seemed total. But just as the royal power was starting to crumble unseen, so the authority of the tragic rules was being weakened, especially the bonds between the French and Greek traditions. Perrault's *Siècle de Louis XIV* of 1687 and the *Parallèles des Anciens et des Modernes* which he began to publish in 1688 led to claims, not that French tragedy was an inferior form of Greek tragedy — the classical idea of decadence and imitation — but that it was superior, or at least equal, to its Greek sources. This idea of progress was inconsistent with the static world view that formed the basis of the authority of tradition, and the case of tragedy was particularly difficult, because a comparison of Racine and Corneille with Euripides and Sophocles was universally admitted to be valid. The best of the Modern tragic dramatists could not be attacked, especially since Racine was a sincere admirer of the Ancients, but yet the authority of the Greek tradition had to be upheld. This could only be done by again separating the Greek and French tragic traditions, and asserting the superiority of the Greek. This is what Dacier set out to do, as he makes very clear in the Preface to his translation of the *Poetics*.

D'Aubignac's style and manner were authoritarian in parts, especially where his arguments were weakest, but were more often persuasive and reasonable. With Dacier the style and manner are aggressive and peremptory, a sign of changed times as well as of a different kind of man. On the first page, after a reference to "le désordre où nôtre théatre est tombé depuis quelque temps"[16] (Racine having stopped writing for the public theatre in 1677, this could not be seen as an attack on him), Dacier, too, compares the authority of the rules in the theatre with those of the laws of the State: "Comme l'injustice des hommes a donné lieu aux Loix, la décadence des Arts, et les fautes qu'on y a faites ont donné lieu aux regles et obligent de les renouveller." But, "pour prévenir les objections de certains esprits ennemis des regles et qui ne veulent que leur caprice pour guide" — this is a red herring; nobody in 1692 seriously wanted to abandon the rules; the real enemies of Dacier were Perrault and the Moderns who wanted to look to French rather than Greek examples for guidance — "je croy qu'il est nécessaire d'établir non seulement que la Poësie est un art, mais que cet art est trouvé et que ses regles sont si certainement celles qu'Aristote nous donne, qu'il est impossible d'y réüssir par un autre chemin." He will also prove that "les regles et ce qui plaît ne sont jamais deux choses contraires" and that "la Poësie étant un art, elle ne peut être nuisible aux hommes et . . . n'a été inventée ni cultivée que pour leur utilité."

Behind this mixture of pomposity, hyperbole and dogmatism which pervades the work, it is clear that Dacier is changing the terms of the discussion by giving the moral equal prominence with the practical. Indeed, the picture he paints of the origins of tragedy shows it as a process not of progress but of moral decadence, with the rules literally compared to a medicine. Briefly, poetry "fut d'abord la fille de la Religion . . . elle s'abandonna ensuite à la dissolution et à la débauche, et . . . enfin elle se soumit aux regles de l'art, qui vint au secours de la Nature dont il corrigea les égaremens." It was the gift of the Christian God, and was kept in its pure form by the "peuple de Dieu," but it degenerated in the hands of the pagans and its "desordre" could only be corrected by "des instructions déguisées sous l'apast du plaisir." Here it is evidently the authority of the altar rather than that of the throne which is being invoked in Aristotle's favor, though after the Revocation of 1685 there was no need for a distinction, especially to a recent convert like Dacier. He rarely feels a need to back up his assertions and deductive reasoning by any evidence, and the authority of "la droite raison," which he refers to as being, like "le bon sens," "de tous les païs et de tous les siècles," appears to be only the reason of authority. "Jamais Loix n'ont eu tant de force, tant d'autorité, tant de poids. Les Loix des hommes meurent ou changent le plus souvent après la mort de leurs auteurs; mais [les regles de la poësie] prennent toujours une nouvelle vigueur, parce que ce sont les loix de la Nature." Some improvement is possible, and "si nous n'avons pu rien ajouter *au sujet* et *au moyen*, nous avons ajôûté quelque chose *à la manière.*" Not only are the laws of poetry stronger than the laws of any state, but tragedy is, according to Dacier, the only acceptable form of entertainment and the only thing standing between civilized society and anarchy.[17] The moral purpose of tragedy is belabored at length, and Dacier gives a clear explanation of his view of the role of tragedy in the State: "Disons encore que l'unique but de la véritable Politique étant de procurer aux peuples la vertu, la paix et le plaisir, ce but ne sçauroit être contraire à celuy de la Religion, pourveu que parmy les plaisirs on n'en choisisse pas qui détruisent les deux premieres. La Tragedie, bien loin de les détruire, ne travaille qu'à leur conservation, puisque c'est le seul plaisir qui dispose les hommes à reduire les passions à une mediocrité parfaite, laquelle contribuë plus que toute autre chose à l'entretien de la paix, et à l'acquisition de la vertu." From being a means, among others, of bringing order into the State, of getting people accustomed to abiding by rules in all aspects of life and thus helping to establish the authority of the monarchy, as tragedy had been in the time of Richelieu and D'Aubignac, tragedy had become the third pillar of the State, along with the throne and the altar. Richelieu would no doubt have rejected such a preposterous idea, which was so clearly inconsistent with observed reality: the spectators leaving even the most moral modern tragedy were evidently not purged even temporarily of the moral blemishes they had when entering the theatre. But Dacier, like most of the Ancients,[18] — for he was not an exception either in his ideas or in his expression of them — rarely allowed reality to interfere with his theorizing.

By the time Dacier wrote this, his style of language and argument was no longer generally acceptable where the subject was literary, and his attempts to tie Greek tragic forms to the preservation of Church and State in late seventeenth-century France were unconvincing. By making exaggerated claims as to the importance of Greek tragedy, Dacier undermined his credibility with the relatively uncultured public for whom he was writing. His attempt to distinguish between Greek tragedy, which was good, and French tragedy which was not good either in theory[19] or in practice,[20] on the basis of unsubstantiated assertions about the role of tragedy, may have preserved what Dacier saw as the pristine purity of Greek tragedy, but it meant that the tradition of scholarly critical commentary on the Greek theatre, being separated from the mainstream of critical commentaries on the French theatre, which no longer needed external support, lapsed into an irrelevancy which lasted nearly a century. Finally, the shifting of the arguments for Greek tragedy to moral grounds through an insistence on its purgative qualities, which were deemed necessary to the preservation of civilization, suffered from two major faults — apart from its evident divorce from reality. The more obvious is that there was no agreement then, as now, as to exactly what was supposed to be purged, or how, or why.[21] The second problem is that the Church had been carrying on a running battle against the theatre as a school of immorality for centuries, and this flared up again in 1694. The thunders unleashed against the morality of the theatre in general and French theatre in particular by Bossuet, the most authoritative defender of Church and State, in his *Maximes et réflexions sur la comédie* were far more persuasive, and reached a far wider audience, than Dacier's commentaries. By attacking the authority of the Greek and Aristotelian tradition which the Church had, by and large, adopted as its own, in the name of an entirely different but equally Church-centered tradition, and by demolishing the moral foundations on which Dacier had established his claim that tragedy was a vital constituent of the authority of both Church and State, Bossuet, as he so frequently did, was also unintentionally sapping the foundations of the very authority he was trying to uphold, and wrecking Richelieu's dream of reuniting Church authority and his regularized theatre, and of uniting the country under the authority of its king.

Perhaps it is a fatal flaw of authoritarian mentalities such as Bossuet's that the urge to fight any opposing point of view frequently blinds their judgment as to where the real enemies lie, what the position is that should be defended, and what the most effective defense strategy would be.

By 1700 the French tragic tradition had been separated again from the Greek tragic tradition and was standing on its own merits. The scholarly tradition, represented by Le Bossu and especially Dacier, had lost much of its credibility and relevance, and Greek tragedy had become merely a source of plots, rather than a body of doctrine to be imitated by aspiring dramatists. The dreary series of tragedies on Greek subjects performed at the Comédie-Française between 1700 and 1715, the extraordinary changes made to the Electra myth by Crébillon in composing his *Electre*, and the fact that Longepierre's *Electre*, much closer to Sophocles (though not a good play), was not performed at the Comédie-Française until twenty years after it was performed privately, are convincing evidence that this was indeed the state of affairs. Richelieu's scheme to establish an authorized form of French tragedy on the authority of the Greek tragic tradition and to use the result to reinforce the authority of the State had in the end been ony partially successful.

Voltaire, meanwhile, was growing up in a school system in which the study of things Greek, including tragedy, was in theory important, but in fact probably little and poorly practiced.[22] We know virtually nothing about what the approach to Greek tragedy was, though Porée, one of Voltaire's favorite teachers, much later (1729) composed a very curious Latin discourse in which he attacked the French tragic theatre of his day as a danger to religion and the State: "La scène française souffle aujourd'hui dans les cœurs un double poison, que nous devons regarder comme également funeste à la religion et à l'Etat: la vengeance et l'amour."[23] Again Greek tragedy was being held up as morally good and an aid to religion and the State, while French tragedy was said to be morally bad and a threat to religion and the State. Porée is here only widening the split that Dacier had created.

There is little doubt that this was the sort of thing that Porée taught the young Voltaire and his fellow students. We have even clearer evidence of what Porée taught them about the Greek and French political systems. Another of Porée's discourses had the title: "Sous quelle forme de gouvernement, monarchie ou république, peuvent le mieux se former de grands hommes de guerre" — an interesting sense of priorities. In it he concluded: "Gardez-vous, enfants, d'envier la destinée des républicains soit anciens, soit modernes. Ce que n'aurait pu, ou ne pourrait jamais vous donner aucune République, vous le trouverez dans ce Royaume."[24] There is no doubt that Voltaire was deeply influenced by his Jesuit mentors, and especially by Porée. Indeed, it was immediately following Porée's 1729 discourse attacking French tragedy that Voltaire began his long campaign to throw the responsibility for the love interest in his *Œdipe* onto the actors. It may well have been the case also that his life-long commitment to the monarchy, ambivalent though it sometimes was, was influenced by the examples of the evils of democracy that were fed him in his youth. Certainly, in his first tragedy, *Œdipe*, Voltaire was working out his position with respect to these questions of

11

authority and the rights of the individual in the State, and his central character, Œdipe, already presents, intentionally or not, the image of the ideal king which remained consistent throughout Voltaire's works and life.

We shall never know why Voltaire chose to compose his first tragedy on the subject of Oedipus, but it was a natural thing to do if, as seems likely, he wished to rival both Racine and Corneille and to make over existing French tragedy into something closer to what the Daciers and Brumoys were recommending, to take the French tragedy of his period, which was generally (and wrongly) considered to have the basic form of Greek tragedy, and, by giving it also the substance of Greek tragedy, to establish an authoritative tradition of French tragedy as it *should* be written.[25] He would be completing the work that Richelieu had set out to do seventy-five years before, though in a different way. Given Voltaire's life-long love for all kinds of scheming, his rather pathetic attempts to be a secret diplomat for Louis XV, and his close life-long personal and financial links with *le grand Richelieu*'s grand-nephew, as well as his dedication to the task of purifying and preserving French tragedy, it is intriguing to speculate on whether one of the roles Voltaire saw for himself was as another Richelieu.

Voltaire studied Dacier's translations of the *Poetics* and Sophocles' *Oedipus tyrannus* and *Electra* when working on his *Œdipe*. Dacier's moral, religious and political views pervade these works and must have made clear to Voltaire the intimate connection between the theatre and attitudes to authority. When the Creon of Sophocles refuses to obey an unjust king, Dacier adds a note: "Il n'y a que la véritable religion qui ait enseigné aux hommes à obéir non seulement aux bons princes, mais aussi aux plus injustes et à ceux qui abusent de leur autorité; car il n'y a qu'elle qui ait donné l'idée de la véritable justice. Assujettir les rois à rendre raison de leurs actions, c'est la plus grande des injustices: car c'est faire des rois des sujets, et des sujets des rois." And after rendering a strong attack on oracles by a much milder French equivalent, he adds the note: "Sophocle n'a voulu dire que ce que j'ai dit."[27] Though Voltaire's *Œdipe* is not a *tragédie philosophique*, it is not unreasonable to suggest that the seed of the idea of the theatre as a means of propaganda was planted in Voltaire's mind by Dacier's works. Since Voltaire used the theatre to attack most of the things Dacier stood for, this is indeed ironic.

Voltaire wrote Dacier for advice on certain points after he had completed the first draft of what became the last two acts of *Œdipe*, and may have sent him a detailed plan of the play. Dacier's reply is extant,[28] though Voltaire's original letter is not, and Voltaire, having consulted the authoritative voice of tradition, ignored every piece of advice he received from this source. In this he was acting sensibly, since he was trying to write a successful play and some of Dacier's suggestions were clearly unworkable on the stage of the Comédie-Française. In particular, Voltaire rejected the use of the chorus as a vehicle for overt moralizing — a cornerstone of Dacier's view of tragedy's purpose. Any moralizing in Voltaire's *Œdipe* is built into the characterization, presumably because Voltaire realized that Paris audiences did not go to the theatre to be preached at or purged — emotionally, spiritually or physically.

The *Lettres sur Œdipe*, published with the first edition of the play in 1719, have never received the careful analysis they deserve.[29] *Œdipe* was the occasion of a public reconciliation between Voltaire and the authority of the State as represented in the figure of the Regent, after Voltaire had been twice punished for scurrilous verses about him. The carefully chosen and curious terms used in the first of the *Lettres*, which deals at length with these matters, and a careful analysis of what it actually says and does not say, make the whole thing seem like a *mystification*, or a hoax played on the general public with the tacit permission of the Regent, who knew that Voltaire, having shown France how tragedies should be written, was busy composing his *Henriade* — about the Regent's favorite ancestor — to show France how an epic poem should be written.

The letters dealing with the versions of the Oedipus myth by Sophocles, Corneille and Voltaire himself have a very practical orientation, designed to prove that all three plays form part of the continuum of the same dramatic tradition (with Voltaire's version being, by implication, the best). Voltaire deliberately rejects the learned tradition represented by Dacier, which interpreted all modern tragedy in the light of Aristotle's *Poetics* and the original Greek tragedy, and substitutes the modern approach of interpreting Sophocles in the light of Racine. To accomplish this he systematically misquotes Dacier and misrepresents Sophocles, so much so that Claude Capperonnier, who was soon to become Professor of Greek at the Collège de France, wrote a pamphlet to defend Sophocles, not because Voltaire had found fault with this Greek predecessor, but "à cause du peu de conformité qu'il y a entre l'analyse française de M. de Voltaire, et l'*Œdipe* grec de Sophocle."[30] Dacier had tried to pry Sophocles away from French classical tragedy and reestablish him as the authoritative model that the French had failed to equal. Voltaire snatched him back, but only as the founder of a dramatic tradition, and not as a model. Voltaire was telling the world that his *Œdipe*, using the rules of Aristotle's Poetics as they evolved in the D'Aubignacian tradition, was what Sophocles would have written if he had been fortunate enough to live in Regency Paris. Sophocles was a brilliant genius, but only as a precursor, Corneille's *Œdipe* was not even good (which is true), and Voltaire had succeeded where Corneille had failed, in rendering the greatness of Greek tragedy in a French form. Voltaire rejected the learned tradition as wrong and irrelevant (which is also largely true) not only by his "refutation" of Dacier in the third of the *Lettres*, but in his comments on the chorus in the sixth. Here it is not only Dacier's interpretation of the physical role of the chorus which Voltaire rejects, it is the whole idea that the major function of tragedy is to moralize and not to entertain, with the chorus as the origin of most of the moralizing — a view Dacier expressed as clearly in the letter he wrote to Voltaire as in his translations of Aristotle and Sophocles. Consequently Voltaire also rejects Dacier's view of tragedy as being of equal importance to the authority of the State as the altar and the throne. While tragedy was no longer to be a hand-maiden of the authority of the State — in Voltaire's hands it later came to be a battering-ram employed against it — it was still to be authoritative in its own right, and the Greek tragic tradition — as interpreted by Voltaire, rather than by the learned commentators — was to be the basis of that tradition.

One way of interpreting Voltaire's first thirty years as a tragic dramatist is that he made successive more or less successful attempts to show France how various kinds of tragedy should be written: after *Œdipe*, *Brutus*, for example, showed how a republican tragedy without love should be written; *Alzire*, how a tragedy about an exotic country should be written; *Jules César*, how Shakespeare should be written; *Zaïre*, how a love tragedy should be written; *Mahomet*, how fanaticism should be treated in tragedy — an anti-*Athalie*, etc. By the late 1740's the threat of the *comédie larmoyante* and the *drame* was clear, and Voltaire began to turn his attention to the need to reestablish the authority of the true tragic tradition — that is, the Greek tragic tradition as Voltaire understood it. He did this first with the *Dissertation sur la tragédie ancienne et moderne*, published with *Sémiramis* in 1748, then with his *Oreste* of 1750 and the *Epître à la duchesse du Maine*, published with it. This was also one of the reasons why Voltaire rewrote and expanded Dumolard's *Dissertation sur les principales tragédies . . . sur le sujet d'Electre . . .*[31] Voltaire's writings on dramaturgy were always *œuvres de circonstance* and served more than one purpose, with the ostensible purpose not necessarily the most important one. All must, therefore, be treated with caution and not accepted without question as Voltaire's true ideas and beliefs at the time they were published. It is clear from the Correspondence of this period[32] that Voltaire's decision to write a tragedy on the subject of Orestes was also part of a conscious campaign to crush any vestiges of reputation that Crébillon might have had. But this was to be done by showing Crébillon and France how Crébillon's play on the subject of Electra should have been written.

When the initial run of *Oreste* was not as successful as it was supposed to be, Voltaire insisted plaintively for a decade that his tragedy be revived.[33] Its successful revival in 1761 gratified him immensely, and seems to have convinced him that his authority in the French tragic theatre was unchallenged.[34] As he had hoped, he had *forced* the audience to applaud what he had decided was good for them — that this was his intent is evident from the Correspondence. But he had imposed his authority, and the authority of Greek tragedy, on a moribund genre. This time it was the genre of French tragedy itself which was dying, while interest in Greek tragedy was beginning to revive, with a new and much more open-minded approach being taken to it.[35] As Richelieu's scheme had essentially been thwarted by the arrival on the scene of the Moderns, so Voltaire's revival of it was destroyed by the growth of new genres and a change in public sensibilities. In both cases a reasonable measure of success had been achieved over a period of close to forty years, and the causes of eventual failure could not have been foreseen or countered.

David H. Jory
University of New Brunswick
Saint John Campus

14

Notes

[1] Carl Burckhardt, *Richelieu*, trans. B. Hoy (London: Allen and Unwin, 1971), III, 375.

[2] Antoine Adam, *L'Age classique I: 1624-1660* (Paris: Arthaud, 1968), p.14.

[3] Burckhardt, p. 374.

[4] Writing of Greek ideas of destiny, Brumoy states: "Si nous voulons jouir d'un spectacle grec, nous sommes obligés d'épouser pour un moment leur système. Il est insensé à la vérité; mais nous devons faire effort pour ne le pas trouver tel" (*Théâtre des Grecs* [Paris, 1730], I, 97).

[5] There is no reference to the religious origins of Greek tragedy in the *Poetics*, a fact which one modern commentator describes as a "surprising defect" in the work. See W. Hamilton Fyfe, *Aristotle's Art of Poetry* (Oxford: Clarendon Press, 1940), pp. xxvii-xxix.

[6] See Adam, p. 15.

[7] Adam states of Chapelain: "Nous avons, de sa main, la preuve qu'il n'entra dans ce débat qu'avec de fortes répugnances et pour obéir à un ordre exprès de Richelieu (*op. cit.*, p. 111). See also p. 268.

[8] D'Aubignac, *La Pratique du théâtre*, ed. P. Martino (Paris: Carbonel, 1927), pp. 16-17. It is clear from these pages that as long as Richelieu was alive D'Aubignac would not have been allowed to drop the project.

[9] D'Aubignac, p. xiii.

[10] "Les règles du théâtre ne sont pas fondées en autorité, mais en raison. Elles ne sont pas établies sur l'exemple, mais sur le Jugement naturel . . . Dans tout ce Discours j'allegue fort rarement les Poëmes des Anciens; et si je les rapporte, ce n'est seulement que pour faire voir l'adresse dont ils se servoient dans la Pratique de ces règles, et non pas pour autoriser mes sentiments" (D'Aubignac, p. 26).

[11] "La raison estant semblable partout à elle-mesme, elle oblige tout le Monde . . . Il n'y a point d'excuse contre la raison . . ." (D'Aubignac, pp.26-27). The limitations of this reason are clear in many parts of the *Pratique* — in the fallacious arguments found in the first two paragraphs of the chapter "Des Actes" (pp. 214-15), for example.

[12] D'Aubignac, pp. 24-27.

[13] They were published in 1660. D'Aubignac claims that Corneille "a confessé plusieurs fois, et tout haut, qu'en repassant sur des Poëmes qu'il avait donnez au Public avec grande approbation, il y a dix ou douze ans, il avait honte de luy-mesme, et pitié de ses Approbateurs" (p. 25).

[14] *Mémoires pour l'histoire des sciences et des beaux-arts*, mars 1716, pp. 359-60 (quoted by Martino, *op. cit.*, p. xxix).

[15] In fact French classical tragedy was in some ways even more rigid than D'Aubignac, whose models were often tragi-comedies, had suggested.

[16] André Dacier, *La Poétique d'Aristote, traduite en français avec des remarques critiques sur tout l'ouvrage* (Paris, 1692; photoreprint Hildesheim: Olms, 1976). The Preface is not paginated.

[17] "Les Philosophes . . . inventèrent donc la Tragedie . . . comme un moyen qui pouvoit corriger la dissolution, où [les hommes] se plongeoient dans leurs fêtes . . . Ils se porteront aux excez les plus criminels, si on ne leur donne des plaisirs, qui soient reglez et sages . . . On traite des malades, et la Tragedie est le seul remede dont ils soient en état de profiter."

[18] Especially père Le Bossu, for whose *Traité du poème épique* of 1675 Dacier expressed excessive praise.

[19] D'Aubignac's *Pratique du théâtre* is for Dacier "moins une explication d'Aristote, qu'une suite et un supplément, dont on connoîtra le bon et le mauvais quand on sera bien instruit des regles anciennes." Corneille's *Discours* are criticized as inadequate and wrong both in the Preface and elsewhere — the notes on purgation (pp. 80-83), for example.

[20] It is clear from the Preface to his translations of Sophocles' *Oedipus tyrannus* and *Electra*, also published in 1692, that he translated these two plays to show French theatre-goers who could not read Greek how French tragedy ought to be written.

15

[21] Dacier's attempt in his notes on the purgation passage to refute Corneille is not successful (pp. 80-83). Fontenelle (*Réflexions sur la Poétique* in *Œuvres* [Paris, 1818], III, 17) and Saint Evremond (*Œuvres meslées* [Paris, 1692], II, 59) followed Corneille in saying that nobody understood what purgation was all about. Dubos (*Réflexions critiques sur la poésie et sur la peinture* [Paris, 1719], I, 262) implies that love can be purged — which Dacier had denied (p. 83). Brumoy does not use the word at all, but brings a discussion of tears into his writings on the subject (*Théâtre des Grecs* [Paris, 1730], I, lv-lvi). And so on.

[22] There is little evidence that the study of Greek authors was anything like as important as the *Ratio studiorum*, Jouvency's *De ratione discendi ac docendi* and Rollin's *Traité des études* might suggest, and considerable evidence to suggest that it was not.

[23] Charles Porée, *Discours sur les spectacles* (Paris, 1733), p. 28. This is a translation by Brumoy of the original discourse, which was in Latin. The language was colorful; French tragedy had, Porée declared, decided to "prostituer la scene aux flambeaux du fils de Vénus" (p. 32).

[24] *Orationes*, II, 411. Quoted by J. De la Servière, *Un Professeur d'Ancien Régime, le P. Charles Porée, S. J.* (Paris: Oudin, 1899), p. 362.

[25] The question of the choice of subject and composition of *Œdipe* is dealt with at greater length in my introduction to the play in the *Œuvres complètes* (Oxford: Voltaire Foundation), vol. 2 (as yet unpublished).

[26] He mocked Dacier's use of Aristotelian jargon at the start of the third of the *Lettres sur Œdipe* (*Œuvres complètes*, ed. L. Moland [Paris: Garnier, 1877], II, 48).

[27] Dacier, *L'Œdipe et l'Electre de Sophocle* (Paris, 1692), pp. 190, 224.

[28] Voltaire, *Correspondance*, ed. T. Besterman, vol. I, letter D26, in *Œuvres complètes* (Genève: Institut et Musée Voltaire, 1968), vol. 85. Further references to the letters are to this edition.

[29] The latest work on "Voltaire et l'antiquité grecque," by Michèle Mat-Hasquin, SVEC, 197 (1981), has a number of references to the *Lettres*, but does not examine them as a whole or put them in the context that was Voltaire's in 1719. Continuing the tradition of viewing the *Lettres* only in the light of Voltaire's later writing on the theatre, the author again makes the traditional incomplete and inadequate interpretation of them.

[30] *Apologie de Sophocle* (Paris, 1719), p. 5.

[31] Published in 1750 under Dumolard's name; in 1757 under Voltaire's. See Voltaire, *Œuvres complètes*, ed. Moland, V, 167, n. 1.

[32] E.g. Best. D3990, D4010.

[33] See Best. D4294, D4828, D6055, D6908, D7988, D8249, D8261, D8669, D9352, D9485, D9579, D9683, D9716, D9736, D9755, etc.

[34] See Best. D9902, D9910, D9933, D10037. It is likely that this success was due at least in part to the popularity of non-theatrical works such as *Candide* and the *Poème sur le désastre de Lisbonne* that he had written recently.

[35] See L. Bertrand, *La Fin du classicisme et le retour à l'antique* (Paris: Hachette, 1897).

16

Machiavelli at the Comédie-Italienne

By its very nature, the *commedia dell'arte* is elusive. How does one describe an art form that, through improvisation, is never exactly the same two times running? And what great literary monuments has it left behind, at once witnesses to the *commedia*'s past glory and clues to its secret essence? On the other hand, can one be satisfied with broad generalizations about the "spirit" of the phenomenon, the "types" it created, with biographies of the celebrated professional actors it called forth, or musings on the graphic representations it so often inspired? Such are the Scylla and Charybdis of the *commedia* historian who must chart a modest course in documentary Seas of Tranquillity — with the hope of finding scraps of illuminating new evidence. To him belong the contemporary journals, the travel diaries, the government archives, the various actors' *spicilèges*, the theatrical dictionaries and essays and, above all, the collections of scenarios.

Among these last, the *Histoire de l'Ancien Théâtre-Italien* of the Brothers Parfaict (Paris: Lambert, 1753) has long enjoyed a privileged position, for it offers the only printed anthology of Italian-language plays improvised by the troupe of the Comédiens Italiens du Roi (c. 1653- 97).

In point of fact, the *Histoire* is quite derivative. As the brothers freely acknowledged, their work depends heavily on an extensive manuscript by the Parisian magistrate Thomas-Simon Gueullette both for the general history of the Ancien Théâtre-Italien and the scenarios.[1] If the so-called scenarios are in the hand of Gueullette, they are not *by* this Italophile, who was also instrumental in acclimating the early eighteenth-century troupe of Luigi Riccoboni to their new life in Paris.[2] Presumably in recognition of all he had done for Lelio and company, on the death of their Trivelin, Pierre-François Biancolelli (1734), Gueullette received an Italian manuscript written by Domenico (or Dominique) Biancolelli (c.1637-1688), Pierre-François's father and highly praised Arlequin of the Ancien Théâtre-Italien. This manuscript, which has long since disappeared, is the original version of the scenarios that Gueullette proceeded to translate into French "en m'amusant," as the magistrate wrote.[3] The scenarios of the *Histoire* are thus doubly removed from the initial text, for, if they are based on Gueullette's translation (known generally as the *Scénario de Dominique*), they were subjected to further stylistic modifications by the Parfaicts.[4]

The *canevas* in the *Histoire* are not only peculiarly derivative; they are also incomplete. Of the some seventy-seven titles in the Gueullette translation, approximately thirty-six were reproduced by the Parfaicts.[5] Most systematically, they eliminated all plays after 1674, which they reserved for a second volume that never materialized. It is one of the post-1674 plays, *Le Voyage de Scaramouche et d'Arlequin aux Indes* (1676), that constitutes the subject of the present article. The ensuing unpublished text follows the Gueullette version. The reader should bear in mind that the first person of this scenario (and all the others) is Dominique-Arlequin speaking of himself.[6]

Le Voyage de Scaramouche et d'Arlequin aux Indes[7]

[Acte Premier]

1. J'arrive et je dis, "Je suis perdu dans ces bois où il y a trois jours que je n'ai mangé. Oh, mes chers boyaux, autrefois labyrinthes délicieux où coulaient les soupes succulentes, où passaient les jambons accompagnés d'un cortège de saucisses et de pigeons qui s'y promenaient à droite et à gauche et erraient dans vos spacieux détours, à présent tristes et abandonnés, on entend vos faibles murmures, qui font *flu flu flu*, causés par un jeûne trop long. Oh, destin cruel, pourquoi pourvoir un aussi petit homme que moi d'un aussi grand appétit? Et puisque je devais avoir une faim aussi violente pourquoi ne m'as-tu pas fait un animal vorace qui trouve à vivre aux dépens des autres? Oh vous, courtois satyres, ayez compassion d'un fameux étranger;[8] *Métamorphoses* d'Ovide, venez à mon secours. Changez ces pierres en pain, cette eau en vin, ces papillons en poulardes afin que mes pauvres boyaux trouvent en vous une nouvelle vigueur et puissent faire votre éloge avec justice. Je ne sais à qui demander mon chemin dans ce bois. Toutes les boutiques sont fermées."

2. Arrive Scaramouche. Nous faisons ensemble une scène de nuit. Il contrefait la voix d'un animal; je dis que c'est apparemment quelque rossignol de ces bois.

3. Cinthio survient. Après quelques lazzis, il me force à demander du secours à l'embouchure d'un antre.

4. Il en sort un monstre qui me renverse de frayeur. Une magicienne paraît qui me relève.

5. Je dis à Cinthio que je viens de l'enfer. Il me demande quelle nouvelle il y a. Je lui réponds, "On vous y attend, Monsieur, avec impatience. Je me suis trouvé au bord d'une rivière où j'ai vu Charon avec une grande barbe lequel était dans sa barque. Je lui ai dit, 'Monseigneur, voudriez-vous bien me passer?' 'As-tu de l'argent?' m'a-t-il demandé. 'Non.' 'Eh bien, reste où tu es.' Moi qui ai vu qu'il ne voulait pas me passer et qu'il se mettait à dormir, comme j'ai toujours été curieux de voir le pays, je me suis avisé d'une fourberie. J'ai battu le fusil que je porte toujours sur moi, j'ai fait du feu, j'ai allumé une chandelle. Je suis entré dans sa barque tout doucement, tout doucement. J'ai mis le feu à sa barbe, il s'est éveillé, s'est courbé dans son bateau pour l'éteindre dans le fleuve. Dans ce moment je l'ai pris par les pieds, je lui ai fait faire la culbute dans l'eau. J'ai pris les rames et à force de voguer j'ai passé de l'autre côté et je me suis trouvé aux portes de l'enfer que j'ai vues toutes ouvertes et un grand chien dessus qui aboyait. Ensuite, je vis dans la rivière un homme qui, lorsqu'il voulait boire, voyait l'eau s'abaisser.[9] Un diable malicieux lui avait mis un morceau de lard sur le nez et, quand il élevait sa bouche pour le manger, ce même diablotin le levait en l'air de façon qu'il mourait de faim et de soif. Un chat malicieux qui aperçut ce lardon se jeta dessus, l'attrapa et se sauva. Le chien, qui vit cette friponnerie, courut après pour en avoir sa part. Moi, voyant la porte sans portier, j'entrai dans l'enfer où je trouvai un apothicaire qui faisait de l'onguent pour la brûlure. Un

18

peu plus loin j'aperçus Pluton avec une paire de lunettes sur le nez qui lisait la gazette. Et, comme il fait chaud en ce pays, deux petits diables lui faisaient de l'air avec des éventails. Proserpine était assise à côté de lui qui travaillait à la layette du petit diablotin dont elle était grosse. Aux pieds du monarque des enfers était un homme qui portait sur une montagne une grosse pierre et, quand il était au haut, il la laissait rouler jusqu'en bas et recommençait cet ouvrage. Voyant la folie de cet homme-là je lui ai donné un coup de ma batte sur les doigts. La pierre lui est échappée, elle est tombée sur le pied de Charon qui y avait un cor. Il a crié comme un beau diable. Alors, il en est venu un demi-cent qui m'ont enlevé et m'ont conduit à Pluton qui a ordonné qu'on me mît bouillir dans un chaudron. Proserpine lui a dit alors, 'Mon mignon, j'ai envie de manger un petit cochon de lait à la broche.' Je m'écrie aussitôt, 'Ah, Diabolique Majesté, n'en faites rien. Proserpine serait bientôt dégoûtée de moi parce que j'ai la gale. Mais, si vous voulez me laisser aller, je vous amènerai dans peu une personne beaucoup plus grasse que moi et dont Votre Majesté sera contente.' Pluton m'a dit, 'Je le veux bien, mais qui m'amèneras-tu?' Je lui ai répondu, 'Je vous amènerai Crogne, moucheur de chandelles à la Comédie.'"[10]

6. Ensuite, nous faisons le lazzi de manger par-derrière. On attache deux chapons sur deux tables derrière notre dos et l'on nous attache les bras ensemble face à face. Comme je ne puis manger, je dis à Scaramouche qu'il s'abaisse. Il le fait; par-dess[u?]s son échine, je mange le chapon.[11] Scaramouche fait ensuite la même chose.

Acte [II]

7. Dans l'acte du Turc, Flautin[12] me dit qu'il me donnera une flûte et à Scaramouche une basse par le moyen desquelles nous obtiendrons la liberté du sultan et que lui Flautin il se servira de sa guitare. Je porte la flûte à ma bouche, Flaminio derrière moi en joue.[13] Je m'imagine que c'est moi qui produis cet air et je m'en réjouis. Scaramouche joue de la basse, un diable qui est derrière lui fait le même lazzi. Flautin me donne un papier. Il me dit de me le mettre à côté de l'oreille et qu'aussitôt je chanterai à merveille. J'ouvre alors la bouche et une musicienne derrière moi chante un air et des paroles. J'en suis si charmé que je me baise moi-même de satisfaction. Nous nous retirons.

8. Le sultan arrive. Scaramouche me dit d'avancer. Je culbute un Turc qui tombe sur le sultan auquel je dis que je suis un virtuose. Il m'ordonne de m'asseoir, je lui ôte son turban et je m'en fais un tabouret. Puis, je souffle dans la flûte; un Turc par-derrière sonne dans un cornet à bouquin. Le sultan en colère ordonne que je sois empalé. Je dis que c'est la chanterelle qui n'est pas d'accord. Scaramouche veut jouer de la basse; derrière lui on sonne une grosse sonnette de mulet. Je dis au sultan qu'où j'excelle, c'est dans le chant. Je mets ce papier derrière mon oreille, j'ouvre la bouche, un des Turcs[14] chante un air ridicule. Le sultan étonné demande, "Quelle chienne de musique est-ce là?" Je me désespère et je dis que je ne puis pas bien chanter si je ne suis accompagné de la basse de Scaramouche. Il en veut jouer, deux diables font un carillon étonnant avec un

cornet à bouquin et une grosse cloche de mulet. Le sultan se couvre les oreilles et s'enfuit avec la sultane en criant, "Qu'on les empale, qu'on les empale!"

9. Je fais mes lazzis de frayeur. Je monte à cheval sur le dragon qui m'emporte et cela finit l'acte.

Acte III

10. Quand le chimiste me donne le livre des secrets et qu'il me dit qu'il y en a un pour rajeunir, je dis que je veux aller à Rome, que l'on m'a dit que le Colisée était bien vieux et que je ferai un grand gain si je puis le rajeunir.

11. Quand Scaramouche arrive, je lui lis la table des secrets. Ensuite, nous exécutons celui du rajeunissement. Scaramouche se met dans l'alambic. On souffle, on fait l'opération, on rompt l'alambic et il en sort un jeune enfant vêtu en Scaramouche qui fait les mouvements et donne les marques d'étonnement de se voir rajeuni. Il sort. Un moment après, paraît Scaramouche. Je m'en étonne et dis, "Il faut qu'il soit de la race des champignons pour croître ainsi en si peu de temps."

12. Quand je suis dans la scène des Turcs, on me demande si j'ai vu une mosquée. Je réponds[15] que j'ai vu une ruche avec toutes ses mouches qui faisaient leur miel.

The "scenario" of *Le Voyage* prompts several remarks. For one thing, the last "scene" should not really be considered one since it consists only of a play on words ("mosca" — "moschea"). It is also out of place and belongs manifestly somewhere in the Turkish elements of Act II. For these reasons, scene 12 must be an improvisation, perhaps added by Dominique some time during the run of the play. Such misplaced, improvised *trouvailles*, quite common in the Gueullette manuscript, give a definite *commedia* flavor to the collection.

Of greater significance are Arlequin's developed speeches and the careful detail of some of his "lazzi" which, together, form a rather clear picture of his character in the play. He is timorous (the *scènes de frayeur*), preoccupied with food (the monologue of scene 1) and always ready for rough and tumble (smacking Sisyphus with his wooden sword, his "batte," knocking over the Turk and sitting on the sultan's turban). If Arlequin has some pretensions to learning, all his erudite references are inevitably twisted, materialized, reduced to something resembling his silly word plays. In short, he presents all the characteristics, delightfully illustrated, of his traditional rôle of "goffo," or "balourd."

In contrast to the thorough delineation of Arlequin, the presentation of the other characters, even the closely allied Scaramouche, is very superficial. There is almost nothing we may say of them, and for good reason: the narrative first person is the only element of the play that interests Dominique. In this respect, *Le Voyage* is typical of the entire collection, for, in the words of the translator Gueullette, "[le] manuscrit [de Dominique] est un recueil qu'il avait fait des scènes qui lui étaient personnelles . . . [et] comme il n'écrivait rien que pour lui-même, qu'il était censé connaître ces pièces à fond et qu'il n'avait qu'à jeter un coup d'œil sur son manuscrit pour être au fait de ses scènes, il n'avait pas jugé à propos d'en faire davantage."[16] Thus, the Gueullette version of Dominique's *Scénario*[17] does not qualify as a full-fledged scenario collection. Yet, this is precisely how the Brothers Parfaict describe their material in the subtitle of the *Histoire*: *Extraits ou canevas des meilleures pièces italiennes qui n'ont jamais été imprimées.* They apparently believed they could transform Dominique's "extraits" into something more "[en suppléant] à la plupart de ses canevas"[18] by filling the gaps with products of their fertile imagination. Let us apply the "Parfaict" method to *Le Voyage*.

There seem to be three main characters: Arlequin, Scaramouche and Cinthio. If the normal relations among them hold, the first two are servants of Cinthio, and all three have inexplicably been cast upon a mysterious alien shore before the play opens (Act I). This land is, in fact, inhabited by Turks who put the servants, at least, in danger of their lives (Act II). Although Act III is too brief to be clear, since the play is a comedy, our heroes must escape to safety in the end, possibly with the help of the "chimiste." This hypothetical scenario is not particularly tidy (what is the rôle of the "magicienne" of Act I and, above all, what does all of this have to do with "les Indes" of the title?), but it is the best possible under the circumstances. The question is, of course, how closely the reconstruction resembles reality. Fortunately, it can be answered in the present case, and this is precisely why I chose the example of *Le Voyage*.

In volume II, folios 129 r to 148 r, of the Gueullette manuscript, the magistrate copied a rare document: the argument in French of *Le Voyage d'Arlequin et de Scaramouche [sic] aux Indes.* The now lost original of the argument was a thirty-two page in-quarto printed in Paris "[qui] se vend à la porte de la salle de la Comédie où l'on prend les billets," as the statement immediately following the title reads. It is impossible to say whether the practice of selling résumés was common at the Comédie-Italienne in the late seventeenth century, but the procedure is not surprising.[19] What better way to overcome the language barrier separating actors and audience before the former began speaking French in the 1680's? In any event, the first paragraph of the argument reveals that *Le Voyage* is based on a work by Machiavelli. One thinks immediately of his plays, *La Mandragola* or *Clizia*, but this perfectly logical assumption is wrong. "Le seul nom de Belphégor," states the initial sentence of the argument, "suffit pour vous faire connaître le sujet de cette comédie dont le fameux Machiavel nous a fourni les idées." It is therefore the Florentine's *Belfagor*[20] that served as inspiration for *Le Voyage*. Since this "favola" is not among Machiavelli's best known works, a brief summary would seem in order.

Belfagor arcidiavolo consists of three main sections. The first takes place in a classical-Christian lower world where Pluto is informed that most, if not all, of the lost souls complain of being "damned" for taking a wife. To examine the question, Pluto convenes a council that finally recommends a devil be sent to earth in human form with the charge of selecting a spouse. After ten years, the infernal agent is to return and make a report on his experiences. For want of a volunteer, Pluto and associates resort to a chance selection process that designates the archdevil Belfagor. The scene now shifts to the second location, Florence, where, under the name of Roderigo di Castiglia, wealthy Spanish merchant, Belfagor carries out his mission by marrying Monna Onesta. The carping and exactions of beautiful, spoiled Onesta soon bring a harried Belfagor-Roderigo to bankruptcy, and this situation leads to the third part of the tale. To escape his creditors, Belfagor leaves Florence precipitously and seeks refuge from hot pursuit in the cottage of the peasant Gianmatteo del Brica. As a reward for the latter's help, Belfagor promises to make him wealthy through trickery. The archdevil will take possession of women and allow them to be exorcised by Gianmatteo. This process is repeated twice to the glory and enrichment of the peasant, but, after the second exorcism, Belfagor rather arbitrarily informs Gianmatteo that the debt is settled. No longer may he count on the cooperation of the diabolical spirit, who then proceeds to Paris, where he enters the body of the king's daughter. So great is Gianmatteo's fame that he is forced unwillingly to the court of the French king, who offers him the alternative of a fortune or the gallows for success or failure. Desperate when Belfagor refuses to quit the king's daughter, Gianmatteo hits upon a brilliant scheme that also succeeds in uniting totally disparate sections two and three. He whispers to the archdevil that he sees Onesta coming for her husband, whereupon, frightened out of his wits, the poor devil flees, choosing "to return to Hell sooner . . . than . . . subject himself again to the matrimonial yoke" ("più tosto tornarsene in inferno . . . che di nuovo . . . sottoporsi al giogo matrimoniale"). As for Gianmatteo, "who proved cleverer than the devil" ("che ne seppe più che il diavolo"), he went home triumphant.

Successively an antiuxorious diatribe and a celebration of human resourcefulness in the face of adversity (unless it is an indictment of human nature more perverse than the worst the devil can do),[21] Machiavelli's "favola" is a charming Renaissance creation, but it bears no resemblance to the reconstruction of *Le Voyage* from the Gueullette scenario. What could the Comédiens Italiens du Roi have meant by the first sentence of their argument, where they spoke of the debt to "Belphégor"? It is time obviously to turn to that document for clarification.[22]

The argument indicates that the play begins with a prologue set in Hades, a circumstance that creates an immediate parallel to the opening of *Belfagor*. The parallel is only partial, however, for the episode of the damned souls' lamentations is grafted onto another event: the anniversary of Proserpine's abduction, when all infernal suffering temporarily ceases. This is, in fact, a joyful day expressed by the musical overture and a celebratory song. The light-hearted atmosphere is suddenly interrupted by news of matrimonial complaints among the shades. (It is well to note here a new sexual equality unknown to Machiavelli. Since *both* husbands *and* wives reciprocally accuse their partners, the diabolical envoy on earth will ostensibly have as his task to discover which of the sexes is truly guilty of damning the other.) Pluto reassures his informant that he has already attended to the matter by placing "tous les esprits des démons infernaux" in an urn. At his command, four dancing monsters carry it on stage and out pops Belphégor, disconsolate at having been chosen for the mission. After some musical chiding of Belphégor (e.g., "Qui ne va jamais sans cornes / A-t-il peur d'être cocu?") and a hymn to young love, the rest of the prologue is devoted once more to the light, anniversary atmosphere in the form of song and dance.

As in Machiavelli's *Belfagor*, section two (in *Le Voyage*, the play, as distinct from the prologue) involves a change from the lower to the terrestrial world. However, rather than Florence, the play chooses for its first scene a desolate mountain region near Rome including "une caverne profonde et affreuse." Into this fearsome place wanders hungry Scaramouche lamenting that he had ever left Rome with his master Cinthio and comrade Arlequin, for they were set upon by robbers, Cinthio killed and the servants put to separate flight. Scaramouche then hides on hearing the voice of an approaching stranger who turns out to be Arlequin. The latter goes through similar expressions of despair (Scene 1 of the Gueullette version) and is joyfully reunited with Scaramouche "après plusieurs plaisanteries" (Scene 2 of Gueullette). It is now Cinthio's turn to arrive unharmed on stage, but, since the servants think him dead, they react in fear until convinced of the contrary (Scene 3).

After Scaramouche has been sent to look for food, Cinthio reveals his purpose in coming to this dangerous spot. His father has arranged his marriage to Diamantine, the Docteur's daughter, whom Cinthio does not know for the simple reason that Diamantine and the Docteur live in "les Indes." (By this term, Cinthio and the title are referring to a vague West Indies, since, in fact, father and daughter reside in Lima, Peru!) In his perplexity, the young fiancé decided to consult the fairy Mélisse, who dwells in the cave to which he now orders Arlequin (Scene 3). The latter falls into disarray when a monster issues forth (Scene 4), but he is obliged to return by his master. This time, Mélisse herself appears (Scene 4), and Arlequin's reaction is to faint away. During his unconsciousness, Mélisse agrees to help Cinthio with his matrimonial problem and, to this effect, she casts a spell "accompagné d'une agréable symphonie" that conjures up Belphégor in human form. She thereupon requires the archdevil to go to Lima and marry Diamantine under the name of Cinthio. After Belphégor has left to do her bidding, Mélisse revives Arlequin (Scene 4), who "fait un récit bouffon de ce qu'il a vu dans l'autre monde" during his swoon (Scene 5).

At this point Scaramouche returns with the promise of food. Mélisse suggests that Cinthio remain with her so that his father will think him in Lima, and, to while away the time, she promises to show him "le monde de la lune, les Iles Fortunées et les Espaces Imaginaires," a trip to be made in her "char tiré par deux esprits en forme de dragons." Because, less adventurous, Arlequin and Scaramouche decline the excursion, the fairy calls upon the "esprit follet" Astarot to serve them in her absence and adds *sotto voce* that he, Astarot, has her permission "de [les] tourmenter par des illusions."[23] *Exeunt* Mélisse and Cinthio and, a bit later, Astarot after assuring his charges that they will be satisfied. For the audience's benefit, as he leaves, Astarot "whispers" "qu'il va les troubler [Arlequin et Scaramouche] par cent visions et qu'ils ne verront que des démons et esprits follets déguisés en toute sorte de forme."

In the first "vision," the goblin Rubican arrives dressed as a native of the "pays de Cocagne," gives a flattering description of his homeland and promises that King Colin-Tampon will grant them citizenship. The stage now becomes the "pays de Cocagne," Colin-Tampon enters in his "char de triomphe" followed by his retinue, he naturalizes our two gulls and orders they be dressed in the national costume. The appropriate ceremonies, which end Act I, are performed to the accompaniment of danced "figures grotesques" and a song honoring Bacchus and wine.

Although the opening of Act II is still set in "le pays de Cocagne," the specific locus has apparently changed, since the stage directions now speak for the first time of a "fontaine enchantée," whose function will become clear somewhat later. Enter Arlequin and Scaramouche totally delighted with their new easy life. Their contentment can only increase when Astarot, he too in local costume, gives each a bottle of wine and sings an Italian song in praise of the fermented grape. Next, Rubican returns to explain the special nature of the fountain: the new citizens have only to name a drink and the fountain will supply it. Reiterated experiments corroborate the assertion, and Rubican leaves, whereupon the fountain goes berserk, producing only fire and water. Astarot responds to their calls for help and then asks for biographical information about his two guests. When the goblin learns they are shoemakers by trade and married, he gives each a magic mirror in which he may see what his wife is doing. A new, pantomime "vision" is thus prepared in which "esprits follets" dance Arlequin and Scaramouche working at their benches, their quarrels with their wives and the consolation the latter find through their "galants."

Arlequin and Scaramouche are saddened by what they have witnessed but are distracted by two Turks who come and dress them in Turkish fashion in a "scène muette."[24] The mirth of the two zanies at their strange attire soon gives way to astonishment upon the arrival of the "Grande Sultane" followed by her court, for she immediately proceeds to make love to them. Caught in the act by the "Grand Turc" and trembling with fear, Arlequin and Scaramouche are condemned to impalement. Once more, Astarot (now garbed as a Turk?) comes to their rescue by promising to teach them music of which the sultan is so fond he will pardon them. There follows a quick series of "lessons" in which Arlequin is made to believe that he is first playing the flute,[25] then singing a song on the pleasures of requited love, and Scaramouche, in turn, that he is performing on the "basse" (Scene 7).[26] The sultan, his wife and their retinue return and listen to an Italian song celebrating the happiness of lovers reunited, after which Astarot introduces his two "très habiles musiciens." The ensuing charivari causes the sultan to reaffirm the death sentence, and he stalks out in a fury with his entourage (Scene 8). Before this imminent danger, Astarot promises to save the zanies by extraordinary means: "deux dragons monstrueux" that will carry them to "les Indes" and Cinthio. Most reluctantly, Arlequin and Scaramouche mount the beasts "[qui] les emportent avec des frayeurs et des cris mortels" (Scene 9). Astarot laughs heartily at all his pranks and leaves. The only actor remaining on stage is the "esprit follet" who had sung the Italian air before the sultan, and he concludes the act by another song, in French this time, stressing the absolute necessity and supreme power of love.

Act III transfers the scene to the world of the moon where "l'on voit dans son centre paraître plusieurs figures différentes et fort divertissantes." It is here Mélisse conducts Cinthio after showing him "les Iles Fortunées et les Espaces Imaginaires," presumably in the time elapsed since their departure in Act I. Now, to keep her promise, it only remains for her to have him see "le monde de la lune," and this she does by making the "figures différentes," accompanied by her explanations, pass before them.[27] Cinthio also asks for news about Belphégor and learns that, after marrying Diamantine, he has known only torment because he loves her and she cannot stand even to have him touch her "par l'aversion qu'elle a pour tous les hommes." In addition, she is constantly finding ways to make him "le plus jaloux de tous les hommes." Mélisse, finally, informs the inquiring Cinthio that his servants will soon join him here, but that first they must retire to the wings to enjoy the rest of her lunar magic show. This continues with words and music now. Endymion appears to speak of his love for Diana and thereafter falls asleep. There follows a pastoral interlude sung by plaintive Silvie, constantly rejected by Endymion, and faithful Tircis who at last wins Silvie's heart when she is rebuffed once again by Endymion.

After this interlude, Astarot and Arlequin arrive on the moon and, while the latter is relating his adventures, Astarot slips away. Finding himself alone, Arlequin experiences fear until he meets a chemist, who suddenly becomes sad. A thousand years before, a magician had taught him the secrets of "la pierre philosophale" and rejuvenation, with the warning that he was one day to pass his science on to Arlequin and then die. The "esprit follet" gives his book to the zany (Scene 10), who tries to console the chemist as the latter exits. Immediately, Scaramouche arrives, tells of *his* adventures and asks Arlequin to make him young upon learning of his comrade's powers.[28]   After the experiment is executed, Arlequin is surprised to see "un esprit follet en jeune Scaramouche" and even more astonished when the impersonator disappears and is replaced by the real Scaramouche (Scene 11). Astarot reenters to tell his two charges that they are to leave for "les Indes" on horseback and that he is giving them a magic ring that has the power to enamor any woman they touch with it. Off go the two excited zanies leaving Astarot who waits for Mélisse and Cinthio and urges them to follow the servants. (Belphégor intends to leave his wife and return to hell "plutôt que de demeurer avec elle.") Mélisse agrees and leaves with Cinthio.

The scene changes for the last time to represent "la mer des Indes avec des rochers et des bocages, et l'on voit quantité de vaisseaux." To this place come Arlequin and Scaramouche totally disoriented. Their bewilderment increases when they meet an "Indien" who speaks to them in an incomprehensible language. Next, they come upon a knight errant and learn they will have to fight another knight for the possession of a rich "fille de haute naissance," unless, of course, they prefer being thrown into a fiery furnace. Willy-nilly, they accept the combat and eventually win, but, when they are about to kiss the beautiful damsel, she suddenly changes into a frightful ghost.

This will be the last "vision" for our "heroes." The next person they meet is the very real Diamantine, whom they touch with their magic ring on learning her father is a wealthy merchant. The magic works and she invites them both passionately into her home. Unfortunately, Belphégor-Cinthio has seen the men enter and remonstrates with his wife, who mocks him roundly. The ensuing scenes create a little *commedia* play not unworthy of Molière's *George Dandin*. When Belphégor complains to the Docteur about his wife's latest escapade with two men, Diamantine counterattacks with a ruse according to which she has just saved the life of a man (Arlequin) his enemy (Scaramouche) was pursuing by hiding the former in her private "cabinet." To give weight to this invention, Scaramouche, sword in hand, leaves Diamantine's house as he threatens the man he knows is still in there and, some time later, Arlequin steps out thanking father and daughter for protecting him in his hour of danger. Thus do Diamantine's two lovers go free while "Belphégor déteste la subtilité des femmes." As a last effort to persuade his father-in-law, he is about to recite the whole list of pranks of which Diamantine has made him butt when the true Cinthio appears with

25

Mélisse. Belphégor can now reveal his veritable identity, point out the real Cinthio, explain to the Docteur how all these things came about and depart for the realm of Pluto, to whom he will report "que les femmes sont plus méchantes que les hommes."

The dénouement continues to unwind rapidly. The Docteur forgives Cinthio's deception when he learns of Diamantine's peculiar aversion to men. He also promises to write a letter of explanation to Cinthio's father and invites the young man to share his roof until the ships (seen in the backdrop) are ready to sail. Arlequin and Scaramouche reenter and are reunited with their master, to whom they begin to tell their adventures. Before returning to her cave, Mélisse interrupts them to reveal that their trials were the effects of her magic. With the departure of the last supernatural being, the humans can witness a ceremony with which *Le Voyage* ends: an annual wrestling match among the Indians to decide and crown the national champion. This ceremony is preceded by a final Indian ballet and a song (in French) whose refrain is, significantly: "Elles [les femmes] font le bien des amants, / Mais des pauvres maris elles font le tourment."

The preceding detailed summary of *Le Voyage* should make abundantly clear how far off the mark our reconstitution of the plot was. Dominique simply did not give enough scenes in his "scenario" to permit a reasonable guess about the events of the play. Indeed, the Gueullette version of *Le Voyage* can only abusively be called a scenario at all; it is, rather, a collection of some (*not* all) scenes, or parts of scenes, performed by Dominique Biancolelli in the play. Since this "scenario" is broadly representative of Dominique's manuscript (as translated by Gueullette), a general caution is in order. The "Parfaict" method of reconstruction having proved inadequate, even misleading, in the present case, should not all the plot summaries of the *Histoire de l'Ancien Théâtre-Italien* be viewed with similar reserve? In short, is not this work by the brothers an unreliable document for studying the *commedia dell'arte* in France in the late seventeenth century?

Whatever limitations the Gueullette version of *Le Voyage* presents as a scenario, the scenes contained therein are not superfluous repetitions of the plot summary presented in the argument. The two documents are extraordinarily complementary. Where the argument offers a rare example of a *complete* "commedia" improvisation in seventeenth-century Paris, the Biancolelli scenes show how Arlequin and company breathed life into the schematic plot outline. This life nowhere contradicts the outline on which Biancolelli cleverly expands in his scenes. It is he who finds the humorous comment, the "motto," and the gesture, the "lazzo," that add sparkle to the situation (e.g., the relation of Arlequin's trip to Hades [Scene 5], using the sultan's turban as a stool [Scene 8]). But Arlequin and his associates never hesitate to take liberties with the sequence of events of a given scene — as in Flautin-Astarot's music lessons to Arlequin and Scaramouche, which do not follow quite the same order in the two versions.[29] The supreme liberty consists in adding a scene not called for in the outline. I am not speaking of Scene 12, which is nothing but a misplaced *bon mot* added late by Arlequin, but rather of Scene 6, where Arlequin and Scaramouche succeed in eating two capons despite their being tied together. This episode may be an extended "lazzo" rather than a true scene, but, whatever its nature, it is not mentioned at all in the argument. It belongs undoubtedly to the "pays de Cocagne" sequence, but only the Comédiens Italiens du Roi knew how or where. Such is the irrepressible vitality of *commedia dell'arte* improvisation reflected in all the plays of the Gueullette manuscript.

If we turn from the Biancolelli "scenario" to the argument, we are confronted by the problem of the relation between *Le Voyage* and Machiavelli's *Belfagor*. At best, it is tenuous. The Florentine's third section, the Gianmatteo episode, has totally disappeared, and the remaining subject (the disastrous marriage of Belfagor-Roderigo and Monna Onesta) has been so diluted in the extraneous affairs of Cinthio and Diamantine as to become unrecognizable. The theme subtending the Roderigo-Onesta episode has, moreover, been seriously warped. What in *Belfagor* was clearly antiuxorious in intent is uncertain in *Le Voyage*. From the prologue on, Machiavelli's unequivocal indictment of women has been replaced by the hypothesis that man may be the guilty party in marriage. Yet this new line of inquiry is never probed in the play, which arbitrarily rejoins Machiavelli in its conclusion "que les femmes sont plus méchantes que les hommes." This ultimate wisdom of Belphégor is unconvincing because his barely witnessed experience is limited to one, rather atypical wife, Diamantine (whereas Belfagor's Monna Onesta is touted as a pearl among women before the marriage). Machiavelli's simple intention is further undermined in *Le Voyage* by still another new motif: the distinction between love and marriage. How many hymns to the beauty, the joys, the irresistibility of love have we heard in the course of the play? Thus, Belphégor's lame condemnation of "les femmes" seems not even to apply to one's "maîtresses," a differentiation made only too clear by the refrain of the last song in *Le Voyage*: "Elles font le bien des amants, / Mais des pauvres maris elles font le tourment." What started out a male jibe at the other sex in Renaissance Italy winds up a "galanterie" in the Paris of Louis XIV.

It cannot be determined whether the new directions of *Le Voyage* are fully deliberate. There is some justification for thinking not, given the presence of other inconsistencies in the play. Why attribute to Diamantine her peculiar aversion to men? If she must have this character, why or how does she make Belphégor jealous — within a seventeenth-century context? Why do Arlequin and Scaramouche touch *her*, of all people, with the magic ring, and what, finally, happens to her sudden passion as the final curtain comes down? These questions are all alien to Machiavelli's "favola." They are as foreign to the original as the general Cinthio-Diamantine plot, the new motifs of man versus woman *qua* source of turmoil in marriage, the sanctity of pure love, and they all have in common their tentative, casual formulation. They could have been worked out better, perhaps, if the inventor(s) of the play had devoted more time to developing these details, but such logical coherence is not the point of *Le Voyage*.

That the purpose of the play is something different is evident from the initial paragraph of the argument immediately following the mention of the debt to Machiavelli and his *Belfagor*: "[Cette comédie] est faite à notre mode, c'est-à-dire, que le plaisant et le risible y règnent partout et que nous nous sommes plus attachés à faire paraître Arlequin et Scaramouche dans leur caractère agréable qu'à conserver une exacte régularité. Nous y avons ajouté des ornements assez diversifiés pour satisfaire les curieux et . . . nous avons quelque sujet d'espérer que les agréments que vous trouverez dans notre *Voyage aux Indes* . . . auront . . .

de[s] charmes pour vous." Light-hearted amusement is a primary objective of *Le Voyage* and to achieve it the two zanies are given free reign. Indeed, Arlequin and Scaramouche, the two "valeurs sûres" of the troupe, are on stage three-quarters of the time, in discrete "saynètes" (the "visions") designed to stress the elemental emotions they so well incarnate: rough petulance, fear, thirst, hunger, obscenity, simple-minded compassion, and bumbling successfulness. But there is something else in the play too, what the introductory paragraph calls "ornements" and "agréments." These terms refer, undoubtedly, in part to the multiplicity of tones to be found in *Le Voyage*: exoticism, magic, courtly adventure, mythology and slapstick. They refer even more to the *total spectacle* granted to the audience. In addition to the acting, the spectators are treated to the "agréments" of instrumental music, song,[30] ballet, machines and scene changes, often before their marveling eyes. Except for performances at the Royal Court and for the emerging Opéra, rarely had seventeenth-century Paris witnessed so elaborate a music-hall revue.[31]

It would be interesting to learn, finally, how the "extravaganza" of *Le Voyage* was received, but, to date, I have discovered no journalistic reference to it. This silence is not surprising. The *Mercure galant* was not published in 1676, and the *Gazette* never would have deigned to discuss so unpolitical an event. Subsequently, no one evoked *Le Voyage* (but, in a similar vein, to what extent do the *Ziegfeld Follies* and the *George White Scandals* still serve as memorable literary references today?). We can only assume (and hope) that our play met an honorable success. Yet, in a curious way, it may not have been "sans lendemain." Six years later, in 1682, La Fontaine published a collection entitled *Le Quinquina et autres ouvrages en vers* which included one of his last "contes": its title, *Belphégor*. Was he not among the spectators of *Le Voyage* some time in 1676, did he not see a copy of the argument and discover thereby Machiavelli's "favola," which he was to adapt more artfully and much more faithfully? After all, *Belfagor* is not one of Machiavelli's most renowned works and La Fontaine apparently did not read Italian well enought to browse at will in its literature.[32] If *Le Voyage* played the role of intermediary between Machiavelli and La Fontaine, this is sufficient glory for our modest work.[33]

Philip Koch
University of Pittsburgh

Notes

[1] The Parfaicts make their frank acknowledgment on pp. [v]-x of the "Préface" to their *Histoire*. The two volumes of the Gueullette MS. are housed in the Bibliothèque de l'Opéra under the call number Rés. 625 (1-2).

[2] For Gueullette's role in the occasionally painful adjustment to the new environment, see J.-E. Gueullette, ed., *Notes et souvenirs sur le Théâtre-Italien au XVIIIe siècle* (Paris: Droz, 1938). In the *Notes*, J.-E. Gueullette has culled from his forebear's MS those passages dealing with Riccoboni's troupe.

[3] In his "Avis au lecteur" which immediately precedes his Dominique translation (Rés. 625 [1], fol. 29 r). The Parfaicts reproduced the "Avis," with minor stylistic changes, in their "Préface," pp. viii-ix, note a.

[4] For the disconcerting, even dangerous liberties the Parfaicts took with their source, see my article "L'*Histoire de l'Ancien Théâtre-Italien*: La Part des frères Parfaict," *SVEC*, 199 (1981), 25-46.

[5] The number of plays in the *Histoire* is approximate because, although there are thirty-eight entries in the table of contents, it is doubtful whether two separate *Suites du Festin de Pierre* should be considered as independent of *Le Festin de Pierre*. Similar reasons to hesitate make it difficult to reach a definitive count for the Gueullette MS.

[6] The transcription of *Le Voyage* comes from an edition I am preparing of the entire Gueullette translation of the *Scénario*. Although the text is completely faithful to the original (Gueullette MS., II, fols. 42 v -47 r), spelling and punctuation have been modernized, and conjectural readings have been bracketed. In the present case, I am also numbering the scenes to facilitate the subsequent analysis.

[7] The French title is accompanied by another in Italian, presumably the original one (*Il viaggio di Scaramuccia e [di] Arlecchino [nelle] Indie*), and followed by an incomplete list of "Acteurs" drawn up, as was his custom, by Gueullette: "Arlequin, Cinthio, Scaramouche, Flautin, Le Sultan, Une Magicienne."

[8] Behind "fameux étranger" there is undoubtedly an Italian play on words involving fame ("fama") and hunger ("fame"), but the exact nature of the *calembour* cannot be determined.

[9] The watchdog is, of course, Cerberus, the tormented man Tantalus and the "homme qui portait sur une montagne une grosse pierre," mentioned somewhat later, Sisyphus.

[10] Crogne was, in fact, a candle snuffer at the Comédie-Italienne who occasionally performed the bit parts of a "gagiste" in the troupe's plays.

[11] This sentence in the Gueullette MS. reads: "Il le fait par dessous son échigne je mange le chapon." At the end of the scene, the magistrate added the note: "Je ne comprends pas cette façon de les lier et de pouvoir manger." It is this difficulty of interpretation that prompted my internal punctuation and the change from "par dessous" to "par-dessus," which together make the "lazzo" perfectly comprehensible.

[12] The name Flautin elicits the following note by Gueullette: "Nota: C'est la première fois que Dominique en parle. Il avait pourtant joué dans *le Berger de Lemnos*." Flautin was the stage name of the zany Giovanni Gherardi, father of Evariste Gherardi who compiled the six-volume edition of French plays performed at the Ancien Théâtre-Italien (Paris: Cusson et Witte, 1700). *Le Berger de Lemnos*, the play immediately preceding *Le Voyage* in the Gueullette MS., was performed in 1674 and 1675.

[13] Even if Flaminio is not a misreading of Flautin, they seem, nevertheless, to be the same actor. See below, note 25.

[14] Gueullette annotates the word "Turcs": "qui passent tous pour des diables."

[15] At this point, Gueullette adds the note: "en faisant allusion à *moschea* qui signifie aussi une ruche." Although Gueullette is right in thinking this "scene" turns on an Italian word play, the specific observation is wrong. "Moschea" means only mosque, and Arlequin is "naively" confusing it with "mosca," "mouche," i.e., "mouche à miel" or "abeille." The confusion might also be with "moscaio" (rarely, "moscaia") swarm of flies.

[16] "Avis au lecteur." See above, n. 3. *Le Voyage* is also typical in length of the other Dominique "scenarios." Since some situations are described in much greater detail, there tend to be fewer scenes than in the average play, however.

[17] I use the expression "the Gueullette version of Dominique's *Scénario*" advisedly, because the language used is not the only difference between them. As Gueullette observes in his "Avis," he has also allowed himself the right "d'en retrancher ce qui était totalement inutile." *Le Voyage* could have suffered such deliberate excisions. In the left-hand margin of his translation, the magistrate placed a consecutive series of numbers referring, in all likelihood, to the corresponding folios of the Dominique MS. According to this foliation, our play begins on 131 and ends on 132. The next play, *Arlequin cochon par amour*, starts on folio 134. Did Gueullette suppress a whole folio of *Le Voyage*, or part of one, or was the intervening sheet totally blank?

[18] "Préface," p. xi.

[19] There exists only one other similar résumé in the Gueullette MS. — for *Le Collier de perles* (1672). It is reproduced, almost complete, in the Parfaicts' *Histoire* as the principal text (pp. 388-405), while Dominique's "scenario" is relegated to the notes.

[20] This brief work bears three titles: the simple designation *Favola* in the autograph, *Novella del diavolo che prese moglie* and *Belfagor arcidiavolo*, the last two added by sixteenth-century editors. The date of composition is uncertain too, but critics tend to place it somewhere between 1516 and 1524 (or 1523). It is curious to note that in the French résumé the name of this character is almost invariably spelled Belfégor, a middle ground, as it were, between Italian and French.

[21] The latter is the thesis of Luigi Russo in his *Machiavelli*, 2nd ed. (Bari: Laterza, 1969), pp. 158-59.

[22] All quotations of the argument will be taken from the Gueullette transcription, with the customary modernization of spelling (e.g., Belfégor > Belphégor) and punctuation. No folio references will follow the quotes.

[23] Astarotte is a famous mischievous devil of Luigi Pulci's *Morgante*. As we shall see (note 25), this role was played by Flautin.

[24] The term surely refers to another pantomime or ballet. Is it not reasonable to assume as well that the arrival of the Turks entails again a "changement de scène à vue"?

[25] The role of Astarot in the "music lessons" proves not only that this "esprit follet" and Flautin are one but also that Flautin-Astarot must be identified with the Flaminio of the Gueullette MS. (Scene 7). The latter *rapprochement* becomes apparent from the description of the flute lesson in the argument: "[Astarot] donne la flûte à Arlequin. Comme il veut la porter à sa bouche, Astarot derrière lui fait la flûte." At this point, Gueullette adds the note: "C'était Flautin qui jouait ce rôle et qui contrefaisait avec le gosier toute sorte d'instrument." Indeed, this particular imitative talent explains Giovanni Gherardi's stage name, "flautino" being a small flute.

[26] The order of instruction is not precisely the same as in Scene 7 of the Gueullette MS., where Scaramouche "practices" his instrument before Arlequin "sings."

[27] Presumably, this sequence involves, once more, a pantomime or ballet in which the "figures" relate to lunar mythology. The subsequent Endymion episode adds weight to the hypothesis.

[28] Born in 1608, Tiberio Fiorilli, alias Scaramouche, was in reality 68 at the time of *Le Voyage*. Thus, as in the reference to Crogne, the "gagiste"-candle snuffer (Gueullette version, Scene 5), we see the deliberate effort of the Italiens to make reality and fiction coincide in order to heighten comic pleasure.

[29] See above, n. 26.

[30] The informative first paragraph of the argument concludes with the observation that "la symphonie et les airs qui se chantent" are the work of "l'admirable génie de M. Oudot." The musician-composer Claude Oudot (? -1696) wrote both sacred and profane works. That many of his creations did not reach posterity suggests the limited stature of the composer.

[31] In *L'Esprit de la commedia dell'arte dans le théâtre français* (Paris: Librairie Théâtrale, 1950), pp. 321-22, Gustave Attinger describes these music-hall qualities, especially exoticism, astonishing machines, elaborate stage settings and emphasis on the zany, as innovations of the "théâtre de la foire" in the early eighteenth century. In fact, as the present examination shows, such elements are already present and fully developed some twenty-five to thirty years earlier. Most of the plays in the Gueullette MS. are not representative of this new trend, however.

[32] "Il n'est pas sûr que La Fontaine lût couramment l'italien," writes Pierre Clarac in *La Fontaine*, 2nd ed. (Paris: Hatier, 1959), p. 33.

[33] There are two striking similarities between *Le Voyage* and *Belphégor*. Both make the arch-devil's assignment to discover whether it is husband *or* wife who has primary responsibility for marital discord, and both distinguish between love and marriage. In La Fontaine, the latter distinction is expressed in the following way:

> C'est le cœur seul qui peut rendre tranquille:
> Le cœur fait tout, le reste est inutile.
> Qu'ainsi ne soit, voyons d'autres états;
> Chez les amis, tout s'excuse, tout passe;
> Chez les amants, tout plaît, tout est parfait;
> Chez les époux, tout ennuie et tout lasse.
> Le devoir nuit: chacun est ainsi fait.

Neither idea, it will be remembered, is found in *Belfagor*, but to pursue this question further would entail a new article.

French Theatre from 1700 to 1750:
The "Other" Repertory

"Otherness" implies perceived difference, an awareness of that which lies beyond the realm of the familiar. The rapid growth of knowledge that characterized the French Enlightenment brought about a revolutionary expansion of this realm which suddenly had to accommodate a multitude of hitherto uncharted geographical, anthropological, scientific and philosophical discoveries. The assimilation of these fresh findings into the corpus of the already-known was not achieved without struggle; at stake each time a new fact, category or theory was advanced was what Jean Duvignaud has called "l'ordre sécurisant des choses."[1] Whatever threatened to disrupt an order viewed as reassuring was summarily dismissed, frequently by means of the derogatory epithet "l'autre."

It is primarily since the middle of the present century that a concerted effort has been made to expand the limits of what is meant by the term "eighteenth-century French theatre." Before the appearance of studies such as Gustave Attinger's *Esprit de la Commedia dell'Arte dans le théâtre français*,[2] excursions beyond the long-established frontiers of neo-classical dramaturgy were seemingly uncharacteristic both of the period in question and, indeed, of the criticism written about it. Pierre Larthomas quite rightly summarizes the inaccurate impression to be gained by most accounts of the theatre between 1700 and 1800: "On pourrait donc être tenté de penser que le théâtre est à cette époque un genre littéraire peu vivant, qu'entre la tragédie classique et le drame romantique il subit une éclipse et n'intéresse plus personne."[3] Of course, recognition *had* been given in isolated studies to some highly important developments which occurred after the middle of the eighteenth century. These included the popularity of sentimental comedy, the rapid growth of *théâtres de boulevard*, the move toward stage naturalism implied by the adoption of realistic costumes and by the banning of spectators from the stage, and, finally, the publication of Diderot's project for theatre reform.[4] However, by placing too much stress on the resistance which these new developments finally overcame, theatre historians prior to Attinger generally exaggerated the image of unyielding orthodoxy which continues even now to plague our perception of early eighteenth-century French drama.

Elements of the reforms of the 1750's, and of the spirit that fueled them, are to be found throughout the period 1700 to 1750; they come to a large extent from what will be called here the "Other Repertory."[5] Not surprisingly, because it ran counter to an entrenched neo-classical dramaturgy with attendant imperatives of high purpose, taste, refinement and moral propriety, the Other Repertory was regularly decried in terms similar to those of Grimm's 1753 plea for greater loyalty to the Comédie-Française: "Il ne reste plus, ce semble, qu'un pas à faire vers la barbarie, à un peuple qui déserte ce spectacle pour courir en foule aux farces plates et indécentes des histrions italiens et de l'opéra-comique."[6] It is this kind of verbal exorcism, practiced by defenders of conventional theatre in the eighteenth century, that has hindered full recognition of the Other Repertory. In this context, otherness implies not only awareness (however grudging) of the unfamiliar, but also a clear reluctance to accept what is different. In Jean

Duvignaud's words: "Que le théâtre soit, en cet impérieux XVIIIe siècle, un genre privilégié, tout l'atteste . . . Tout ce qui n'entre pas dans ce cadre soigneusement défini est rejeté vers la barbarie et les ténèbres extérieures."[7]

The lack of recognition which Grimm's lines suggest is not synonymous with lack of influence. The scope and importance of the role played by the Other Repertory in reshaping French drama have simply yet to be accurately measured. Viewed in isolation, individual attempts to move away from consecrated theatrical forms and practices may appear relatively insignificant. However, when viewed collectively, they may be said to constitute an identifiable trend of theatrical innovation prior to 1750. It is neither my intention — nor possible here — to summarize the history of non-official French theatre in the first half of the eighteenth century. Scholars such as Oscar Brockett and Jacques Scherer have already done so.[8] What I propose to do is to describe some of the prominent features of the Other Repertory in an attempt to isolate elements of a non-classical dramaturgy already in place before the middle of the century. In addition, I will suggest that the confident partiality of the critical Establishment from which Grimm (and many of his successors) derived his (their) aesthetic values explains in part the fact that this field of study has so long suffered from neglect.

It is a well-known fact that French theatre between 1700 and 1750 evolved within a context of considerable institutionalization. Functioning under the impetus of a veritable drive to regulate, groups such as the Opéra and the Comédie-Française adopted institutional means as a way of surviving in the State apparatus of which they were a part. These methods were acceptance of the constraints of censorship, legal enforcement of monopolies in the face of competition, reliance on government subsidies administered by the Gentilshommes de la Chambre du Roi, and regular participation in command performances before the court at Fontainebleau and Versailles. At the same time, not enough attention has been paid to the fact that throughout the period being considered here the "institutions" of French theatre were — to use Brockett's terminology — "undermined" regularly. Grimm's denunciation of "un peuple qui déserte ce spectacle [the Comédie-Française]" is understandable in the light of Henri Lagrave's confirmation that support for the Other Repertory came to a considerable extent from the very public upon which official theatre relied most for its backing: "En effet, depuis le début du siècle, soit par désœuvrement, soit pour pimenter ses plaisirs, l'aristocratie, qui de tout temps aime à "s'encanailler," envahit les enclos de la Foire et les loges des bateleurs."[9] Their behavior confirms that, official disapproval notwithstanding,[10] there existed another theatre world beyond the limits of institutionalized spectacle in early eighteenth-century France.

The general contours of this other world, still largely unexplored, may be summarily characterized as follows: plays and/or related theatre activities (i) which encompass or imply criticism of the conventions of neo-classical drama; (ii) which reflect a desire for change by highlighting novelty on the level of minor detail, or which are clearly innovative in their overall thrust; (iii) which deny literary values; and (iv) which resist compartmentalization in existing typologies.

Much early theatre criticism in France took the form of parody. The unprecedented popularity of theatrical parody which spanned the entire eighteenth century[11] had already attained significant proportions during its first decade. Virtually every major production at the Opéra and the Comédie-Française became the butt of jokes or mere chiding on non-official stages, frequently within the space of a few days. Given the fact that many of the same spectators frequented both types of theatre, we must assume that theatre-goers of the day almost simultaneously applauded familiar productions and took pleasure in being made more aware of their conventionality. One way this was accomplished was through the establishment of a dimension of self-consciousness in the theatre. Roger Lewinter has suggested in a study of Diderot's *Fils naturel* that the aim of classical writers was to create an impression of apparent artlessness;[12] an artlessness also lauded by Voltaire in this comment on Corneille's style: "Il y a toujours de l'art, et l'art s'y montre rarement à découvert."[13] The effect of parody, on the other hand, is precisely to uncover the hidden workings of a text or genre, thereby creating an attitude of critical detachment which belies the classical goal of beholder involvement.

It is not entirely coincidental that the popularity of parodies had as one of its counterparts the insipidness of theatre criticism in journals. The widely-read *Mercure de France*, in spite of the fact that it established a separate heading for drama reviews in 1721, pursued a policy of studied neutrality throughout the period which interests us here.[14] The critical function was accordingly relegated to parody, as well as to the innumerable one-act prologues which the Italians and the Fair actors frequently used as curtain-raisers.[15] The result in both cases was the same; parodies and prologues of the Other Repertory contributed to the establishment of a distancing effect necessary for the eventual reform of French theatre.

The first signs of this reform were countless minor breaks in the still-familiar patterns of neo-classical drama. These generally occurred under the banner of *nouveauté*:

> La nouveauté rend la Foire féconde:
> Dans ces lieux chacun abonde,
> Malgré les chaleurs de l'Eté.
> Quel charme, quels attraits attirent tant de monde?
> La nouveauté.[16]

Accordingly, events in Lesage's *Foire de Guibray* (1714) were described as "fort nouvelles,"[17] a celebration in his *Ceinture de Vénus* (1715) as "plus nouvelle,"[18] and the absence of novelty in Fuzelier's *Arlequin au Parnasse* (1732) as potentially damaging: "nous n'avions point de Nouveautés pour reparoître à Paris."[19] Although such modifications were slight, some, nevertheless, represented more distinct departures from what was considered usual. Examples include the scene — conventionally unconventional in itself — in D'Orneval's *Arlequin traitant* (1716) where an actor emerges from the audience to join in the action on stage (II, 1), and the one in Lesage's *Retour d'Arlequin à la Foire* (1712) where the actors leave the stage to finish their sequence in the audience (Scene 4).[20]

Novel twists in endings also abound in the Other Repertory. Self-consciously signaled by the title of Marivaux's *Dénouement imprévu* (1724),[21] reversals of the expected likewise mark Lesage and Fuzelier's *Tableau du mariage* (1716),

34

where the traditional marriage rites associated with comic dénouements are replaced by a non-marriage instead, and Fuzelier's *Rupture du Carnaval et de la Folie* (1719), where, instead of restoring order, the play retains disorder by allowing Folly to triumph. What is particularly striking in the above-mentioned instances of transgression of theatrical codes is the use of familiar conventions (the separation of *scène* and *salle*, comic dénouements linked to marriage rites) in an unfamiliar way. Such novelties, although not at all radical, point the way to more substantial formal deviations in the theatre.[22]

What helped motivate the desire for novelty? Any answer to this question would have to include a rejection of exclusiveness and repetitiveness. The vigorous attempts of the French Players to enforce their monopoly on dramatic performances between 1697 (the year the Italians were banned because of *La Fausse Prude*) and 1708 (the year the Opéra first sold rights to stage sung dramatic performances to what became the Opéra-Comique) were symptomatic of the forces trying to maintain order — *their* order — in French theatre. In the face of such attempts at repression, repeated sporadically until after 1750, it is not surprising that the Other Repertory should emerge as a strong counter-force to dramaturgical orthodoxy.

A second explanation of the popularity of the Other Repertory may have been the repetitiveness of official theatre which Jacques Truchet's *Tragédie classique en France* describes thus: "Retour . . . de types, de situations. Retour aussi d'expressions, d'hémistiches, de vers entiers . . . Tout le théâtre du XVIIIe siècle est rempli d'emprunts de ce genre, notamment d'hémistiches fameux reparaissant soudain dans de nouveaux contextes."[23] This frequent practice of quotation and modification suggests that the whole area of early eighteenth-century French theatre studies should be subjected to analysis from the perspective of intertextuality. To be complete, any such approach would have to include the Other Repertory.

The precise point at which re-writing ceases to be imitative, and becomes creative continues to elude theorists of *écriture*. A similar dilemma confronts theatre historians who seek to fix the borderline between uninspired repetition and "true" innovation. When (or where?) does the type of minor twist associated with novelty take on the proportions of a totally new dramatic form? Claude Abastado has described parody as a genre that confirms at one and the same time the apotheosis and imminent downfall of the object of its mockery.[24] Therefore, while the *Forains* were feasting on the successes of the Opéra, confirming them as such, and the Italians on those of the Comédie-Française, other criticisms of the official repertory were being formulated that would lead to the envisaging of new genres to replace those currently fashionable. Michel Linant diagnosed as follows public boredom in 1733 with neo-classical drama: "Je suis persuadé qu'on est las au théâtre françois de la dureté des tirans et de la fierté des princesses, des vers guindez et des chapeaux de plumes, qu'il ne s'agit pas tant de faire paroitre des rois que d'exprimer des passions."[25] In response to this perceived need, Linant undertook — although never completed — a three-act *tragédie bourgeoise*, announced fully eight years before Paul Landois' innovative *tragédie bourgeoise* of 1741, *Sylvie*. The latter was not only completed, but achieved official recognition of a sort through staging at the Comédie-Française and acknowledgment by Diderot as the prototype of his *genre sérieux*.[26]

Two other works, famous in the annals of non-official theatre for their peculiarity, go far beyond the limits of traditional theatre between 1700 and 1750. Louis Fuzelier's second play, *Le Ravissement d'Hélène, le siège et l'embrasement de Troye* (1705), has been cited by several critics, including V. B. Grannis and V. Barberet, as being, in the words of the latter,[27] "d'une incontestable originalité." At the same time, their attempts to account for the work reveal the inappropriateness of the critical concepts at their disposal. Barberet was unable to decide if it was an unsuccessful parody, or the product of inexperience. Grannis described it, and plays like it, from the perspective of classical dramaturgy: "the unities of time and place were not observed and very daring scenes were inserted."[28] Both failed to realize that *Le Ravissement d'Hélène* was staged by marionettes[29] and that, therefore, their criteria did not apply. At the same time, their attempts to incorporate Fuzelier's work into the sphere of traditional theatre lead one to speculate about the role of "wooden actors" in the process of theatrical evolution. Piron's *Arlequin-Deucalion* (1722) and Lesage, D'Orneval and Fuzelier's contributions to the Marionnettes Etrangères de la Foire (the same year) attest to the fact that interplay between the two types of spectacle was frequent.

Jean du Mas d'Aigueberre's *Trois Spectacles* (1729) illustrates a response to the inflexibility of the classical rule governing separate genres. D'Aigueberre combines them. Comprising a one-act tragedy (*Polixène*), a one-act comedy (*L'Avare amoureux*), and a one-act heroic pastoral (*Pan et Doris*), d'Aigueberre's text (or texts)[30] was originally conceived for the entertainment of the Duchesse du Maine and her court at Sceaux. From the point of view of this study, the reduction of a tragedy to a single act, purported in the play's prologue to contain all that is quintessential to the genre, is the most noteworthy of the three acts. Also significant, although on a different level, is the fact that from Sceaux, *Les Trois Spectacles* traveled to the stage of the Comédie-Française, thereby crossing the boundary separating the Other Repertory from the official repertory, and from there its first act re-crossed the same boundary by appearing at the Comédie-Italienne re-written in the form of a parody.[31]

Neo-classical tragedy and molièresque high comedy were as much literary forms as they were scripts for live dramatic performances. Accordingly, authors such as Voltaire frequently staked their reputation as artists on the poetic qualities of their texts. The Other Repertory differs from official theatre by virtue of its rejection of the "literariness" of such texts. A notable manifestation of this would be the move toward use of prose in serious drama. It is a well-known fact that Houdar de la Motte's attacks on verse drama preceded Diderot's by more than thirty years. What is important in the context of this paper is the fact that La Motte's theoretical stance led also to concrete attempts at writing prose tragedy. La Motte himself prosified the first scene of Racine's *Mithridate*, after having implied that the prose version of his *Œdipe* was in fact superior to the versified version staged by the French Players in 1726. In 1970, it was discovered that a fellow "Modern," Marivaux, had also tried his hand at prose tragedy with the first act of an incomplete *Mahomet Second*.[32]

Recourse to, or preoccupation with, gesture rather than word in French theatre represented a more extreme move away from the notion of drama as literature. The highlighting of non-verbal dramatic action was apparent as early as the first decade of the eighteenth century, and continued throughout the period being considered here. By 1708, the *Forains* had turned to *pièces à la muette*. Under the aegis of the Duchesse du Maine, patroness of the "Grandes Nuits de Sceaux," an experiment was attempted in 1714 whereby two dancers from the Paris Opera portrayed a scene from Corneille's *Horace* in pantomime. Adolphe Jullien considered the performance a significant advance in the development of dramatic dancing: "elle marque le premier essor du ballet d'action qui devait être bientôt importé à l'Académie de musique et qui offrait un large horizon à l'art chorégraphique."[33] Theoreticians were also to dwell on the problem; l'abbé Du Bos, in his *Réflexions critiques* (1716), studied at great length the "lost" tradition of pantomime that had constituted such an integral part of the theatrical heritage of Greece and Rome. Although, characteristically for his century, he placed little stress on the survival of this tradition in popular theatre, the *Forains*, for their part, were not unaware of the link. The prologue of Fuzelier's *Arlequin Enée* (1711) credits them with just such a *retour aux sources*: "... Notre siècle qui ressemble si bien à celui d'Auguste, n'a pas manqué d'adopter les Pantomimes."[34]

Since the eighteenth century, it has been customary to treat the Opéra, the Comédie-Française, the Comédie-Italienne and the Opéra-Comique[35] as four distinct types of theatre, each with its own repertory. In reality, there were constant incursions by partisans of one theatre into areas claimed by one or another of their rivals. Indeed, resistance to compartmentalization through movement across boundaries is another major characteristic of the Other Repertory.

Specific instances of what might be called the "mobility factor" are several and varied. They include the introduction of atypical fare into the repertory of a given company of actors, the physical relocation of a company in a building or geographical zone associated with another company, and the regular moving about of personnel from one theatre to another. As early as 1702, we find the French Players staging Dancourt's *Opérateur Barry*, a one-act *pièce foraine* which attempted to combat their principal competitors with the latters' own weapons. The writer-actor Marc-Antoine Legrand also encouraged the French Players to incorporate such lighter fare into their more serious traditional repertory, particularly during the annual fall performances of his tragedy-oriented colleagues before the court at Fontainebleau or Versailles. In 1725, the lesser actors of the Comédie-Française so appealed to the public's taste for novelty by staging Legrand's *Française italienne* that they too were summoned to perform before the court.[36] The *Forains*, always quick to point out such deviations in the course normally followed by their adversaries, leapt at opportunities to ridicule them for giving in to the public's demand for novelty.

The Comédie-Française was not the only acting company to venture into unfamiliar territory. Both the Italians and the actors of the Opéra-Comique undertook frequent tours outside their habitual locations. During the seasons 1721-22 and 1722-23, the Italians left their theatre in the Hôtel de Bourgogne to occupy the spacious Pellegrin *loge*[37] at the St. Lawrence Fair. For their part, the *Forains*, frequent guests of the Regent on the stage of the Théâtre du Palais Royal (then site of the Opéra), returned regularly to that location after his death for the end-of-season week preceding Palm Sunday. In terms of figurative moves, it should be noted that the Opéra-Comique did not venture into the French Players' realm of tragedy. They did, however, compete with the Opéra, although somewhat later, through the development of its "comic" counterpart. If we are to believe Carolet's *Amour désœuvré* (1734), the Italians sought to compete with the Comédie-Française by staging tragedies: "Chez nous [the Italian Players] la Tragédie est en règne à présent."[38]

The mobility factor on the part of performers and authors is a further facet of the movement between theatres. The *Mercure* of March 1740 describes how artistic personnel from the Opéra and the Comédie-Italienne worked together with the French Players in command performances of Gaultier's *Bazile et Quitterie* (March 6, 1740) and Legrand's *Roy de Cocagne* (March 23, 1740):

> Nous dirons ici un mot des Intermedes de Chants & de Danses, qui ont été executés par les principaux Acteurs & Danseurs de l'Opéra, dans les Piéces de *Basile & Quitterie*, & du *Roy de Cocagne*. Le premier Divertissement fut executé par les Sieurs Dupré, du Moulin, Javilliers, Hamoche [formerly an actor with the Opéra-Comique] et du May, & par les Dlles Sallé, Mariette, le Duc, Frémicourt & Barbarina. La Dlle Antier & le Sieur Jelyot chanterent chacun deux Ariettes, avec beaucoup d'aplaudissement. La Dlle Barbarina dansa, pour terminer le Divertissement, en Pantomime avec le Sr. Riccoboni, Comédien Italien, un Pas de Deux en Paysans, qui fit un extrême plaisir à toute la Cour.[39]

Authors such as Lesage regularly wrote for both the official and the Other Repertory. It is indicative of our neglect of the problem that the writer who best embodies this eclectic tendency has been the subject of so little research. Louis Fuzelier was the librettist for Rameau's *Indes galantes*, author or co-author of some 237 dramatic scripts, many of them unpublished,[40] and — according to Henri Lagrave — the only author to contribute to all Paris theatres of his day.[41] Approaches to theatre history based on a rigid compartmentalization of repertories account for Fuzelier by labeling him "minor" and "unimportant."

However numerous, the elements of what has been called here a trend of theatrical innovation before 1750 would still appear disparate were it not for the coalescing of many of them in the theatre of Marivaux. Stigmatized from the very beginning for its *singularité*, this corpus of some thirty-six plays did not itself complete the journey from otherness to recognition until the present century. Contemporaries of Marivaux, including Voltaire and Desfontaines, later critics like Grimm, and the nineteenth-century editor, Duviquet, who felt obliged to rewrite many of his scripts, were disconcerted by his originality. Lucette Desvignes-Parent, in *Marivaux et L'Angleterre*,[42] attributes it to the influence of English literature. Marivaux's uniqueness should also be viewed in the context of the Other Repertory.

Few theatres stress self-consciousness more than Marivaux's. Commencing with *Le Père prudent et équitable* (1712), progressing through *La Fausse Suivante* (1724), *Le Triomphe de l'amour* (1732) and *Les Fausses Confidences* (1737), and culminating in an explicit play-within-a-play structure in *Les Acteurs de bonne foi* (1757), Marivaudian plays remind the spectator that what he/she is viewing is a contrived illusion. While more subtle, their effect is nonetheless similar to that of parody. In his use of novelty, Marivaux was more open: the staging of shrinking Europeans in *L'Ile de la raison* (1727) and the development of sentimental comedy as early as *L'Ecole des mères* (1732) are two examples of his inventiveness. Whereas the language spoken by Marivaux's characters is now seen as one of the playwright's greatest literary achievements, he was criticized in his lifetime as a poor writer of dialogue.[43] These characteristics, his close association with the Comédie-Italienne, and even the mobility resulting from his incursions into the repertory of the Comédie-Française, make Marivaux a writer for the Other Repertory.

It is apparent from the instances of unconventional and/or innovative activity cited above that impetus to expand the scope of official theatre cannot be attributed to one specific group, nor to a specific type of individual. Supporters of all theatres — actors, writers, patrons, theoreticians — shared on occasion a concern for reform although, admittedly, they did not consciously form a single movement with precise goals. Indeed, one is struck by the paradoxical loyalty which some of them displayed toward the values they occasionally (or elsewhere) subverted. In considering Voltaire as an early proponent of Diderot's theatre reforms, John Pappas underlines the "master's" ambiguous attitude toward *drame bourgeois*; although ideologically opposed to it, Voltaire was drawn at the same time by its potential for success.[44] This contradictory behavior was typical also of theatre-goers who simultaneously applauded official theatre and the Other Repertory.

The relationship between official theatre and the Other Repertory is equally ambiguous; the latter needed the former as a point of reference while at the same time implying rejection of what it stood for. It is ironical that the monopoly of the Comédie-Française should have been in great part responsible for the eventual loss of the French Players' exclusive rights to stage plays in Paris. Jules Bonnassies has explained the evolution of *Foire* theatre as a series of often ingenious attempts to differentiate itself from the official repertory, because of the French Players' dogged insistence that their monopoly be enforced. In response to constant legal pressure, the *Forains* evolved forms and subjects that were consciously different from those of classical drama.[45] The inflexibility of supporters of official theatre thus made them the unwitting instigators of the otherness of their rivals.

This otherness has been maintained by historians of the theatre who view the Other Repertory negatively, as *anti*-classical drama.[46] They consider its contribution to the reshaping of official theatre to have been made solely through subversion and opposition, coloring thereby the clash between two repertories with ideological hues. H. C. Lancaster concludes *Sunset* with just such a political simile: "One may liken them [the "regulars" in the Comédie-Française and the actors of the Théâtre-Italien, "on the side of irregularity"] to the right and left wings of French politics . . ."[47] John Lough acknowledges that "the Théâtres de la Foire wore down the resistance of the Comédie-Française," but emphatically denies them a more positive role: "Despite their popularity it cannot be maintained that these little theatres contributed anything of importance to the drama of the century."[48]

The eventual incorporation of the Other Repertory into a wider view of early eighteenth-century French drama requires the solution of major problems of accessibility. Whereas the records of the Comédie-Française are relatively complete, archives of the so-called "minor" theatres are rare and/or unedited. A reappraisal of the criteria to be applied to this corpus is also required. These include (i) the concept of theatre as primarily a well-written text; (ii) the relevance of neo-classical dramaturgy; (iii) the tendency to overly compartmentalize Paris theatres and their repertories; (iv) the notion that only serious or "high" art was important; and (v) the belief in the overwhelming prevalence of neo-classical drama during the period studied.

In one sense, the solutions and reappraisals envisaged threaten the otherness of non-official theatre, since increased familiarity with the unknown — witness Marivaux's emergence from oblivion — can result in absorption into an enlarged and redefined official repertory. In another sense, however, the Other Repertory entails more than simple critical perception. Its difference is an inescapable fact, as the examples presented above have shown. Neo-classical theatre of the type advocated in France between 1700 and 1750 was unquestionably convention-ridden, particularly when viewed from the perspective of the twentieth century. We have seen how, already in the eighteenth century, the Other Repertory called these conventions into question through self-conscious imitation, ridicule and varying degrees of experimentation. Nevertheless, those who accepted the conventional premises of what has been called here official theatre were able to appreciate it as "real." Indeed, they were *obliged* to do so, for this type of theatre derives from the mimetic tradition in art, and seeks to maximize beholder identification with compelling imitations of "reality." The classical doctrine of *vraisemblance* and Diderot's seemingly contradictory call for greater stage realism are therefore two historically-limited manifestations of the same view of art-as-mirror. The Other Repertory between 1700 and 1750 did not share a similar need for the external referent, "reality." In fact, it denied the extra-referential thrust of official theatre, preferring self-referentiality (i.e., to theatre) instead. If anything, it discouraged spectator identification by shifting emphasis to the very process of simulation that links theatre to the activity of play. This non-serious nature of Other Repertory productions initially angered defenders of the official order who moved to discourage such apparently gratuitous acts. Only since the rediscovery of Marivaux's theatre in the twentieth century, with a concomitant birth of interest in self-conscious art, has it been possible to begin the mapping-out of the Other Repertory.

David Trott
Erindale College
University of Toronto

Notes

[1] *Le Jeu du jeu* (Paris: Editions Balland, 1980), p. 11.

[2] Paris: Librairie Théâtrale, 1950.

[3] *Le Théâtre en France au XVIIIe siècle* (Paris: P.U.F., 1980), p. 6.

[4] These developments were attested, respectively, by Madame de Graffigny's *Cénie* in 1750, the weakening of the French Players' monopoly after 1752, Madame Favart's choice of costume in *Bastien et Bastienne* (1753), the 1757 ban on stage spectators at the Comédie-Française, and the publication of *Entretiens sur le "Fils naturel,"* also in 1757.

[5] For the purposes of this study, a working distinction will be made between "Official Theatre" (those theatrical texts or productions which upheld the reigning values of eighteenth-century French drama and which gained thereby, or deserved, official consecration through staging at the Comédie-Française or the Opéra) and the "Other Repertory" (tentatively, those non-official works staged at the Comédie-Française, at the Comédie-Italienne, at the various theatres of the Paris fairs, and in private theatres, in addition to all known attempts at innovative playwriting). The Other Repertory includes certain plays by Dancourt, Fuzelier and Legrand, the nearly 100 plays published in *Le Théâtre de la Foire, ou l'Opéra-comique*, the many more that exist in manuscript form, the repertory of Riccoboni's Italian Players, including the 31 collected *Parodies du Nouveau Théâtre Italien*, spectacles premiered at Sceaux, the early *parades*, to give only a partial list.

[6] *Correspondance littéraire*, juillet 1753.

[7] *Le Théâtre, et après* (Paris: Casterman, 1971), pp. 11-12.

[8] Oscar G. Brockett, "The Fair Theatres of Paris in the Eighteenth Century: The Undermining of the Classical Ideal," in *Classical Drama and its Influences: Essays Presented to H. D. F. Kitto*, ed. M. Anderson (London: Methuen, 1965), pp. 249-70; Jacques Scherer, *Théâtre et anti-Théâtre au XVIIIe siècle* (Oxford: Clarendon Press, 1975).

[9] Henri Lagrave, *Le Théâtre et le public à Paris de 1715 à 1750* (Paris: Klinksieck, 1972), p. 256.

[10] There is an obvious parallel to be drawn between the denied perception of popular culture in 18th-century France and that of non-official theatre: "La culture populaire en France sous l'Ancien Régime: c'est à notre sens un niveau culturel méconnu, oublié, que les historiens, éblouis par les réussites de la culture savante, et victimes des silences, des lacunes de l'information immédiatement accessible, ont négligé d'étudier" (Robert Mandrou, *De la Culture populaire aux XVIIe and XVIIIe siècles* [Paris: Stock, 1975], pp. 13-14).

[11] Valeria Belt Grannis's *Dramatic Parody in Eighteenth Century France* (New York: Publications of the Institute of French Studies, 1931) refers to a projected bibliography of parodies by G. L. Roosbroeck containing between seven and eight hundred titles.

[12] Diderot, *Œuvres complètes*, ed. R. Lewinter (Paris: Le Club Français du Livre, 1970), vol. III, Introduction to *Le Fils naturel*, p. 25.

[13] Voltaire, *The Complete Works* (Banbury: Voltaire Foundation, 1975), vol. 54, "Commentaires sur Corneille," ed. David Williams, p. 109.

[14] "Quant au Mercure, il se propose d'observer une exacte neutralité. Il ne s'ingerera point d'être auxiliaire pour l'un des deux partis. L'impartialité doit être le premier attribut de son caractere" (*Mercure*, Novembre 1744, Préface, p. viii).

[15] Plays entitled "Prologue" appear in Fair annals in 1716, 1721, 1722, 1726, 1739, to mention only a few.

[16] Marc-Antoine Legrand, *La Foire Saint-Laurent* (1709), Sc. 24, in *Œuvres de Le Grand* (Paris: Libraires Associés, 1770), vol. I.

[17] Sc. 5 in *Le Théâtre de la Foire, ou l'Opéra-comique* (Paris: E. Ganeau, 1721-37), vol. I.

[18] II, 8, in *Le Théâtre de la Foire*, vol. I.

[19] Sc. 1 in *Parodies du Nouveau Théâtre italien* (Paris: Briasson, 1731), vol. I.

[20] Henri Lagrave describes similar instances of actor-spectator interchange as "une sorte de déviation de la 'participation' dramatique," and ascribes them to the carnival spirit: "L'allégresse de ce public, surexcité par l'atmosphère de fête qui entoure la représentation . . . le pousse à s'insérer dans le spectacle, à participer à la comédie" (*Le Théâtre et le public*, p. 217).

[21] Staged at the Comédie-Française. The heroine ends up falling in love with the suitor she had originally rejected by virtue of his being chosen by her father.

[22] Many comedies of the day refer to "unthinkable" changes while at the same time implementing some of them. For example, in Legrand's play, *La Nouveauté* (1727), Mercure scoffs at a provincial's assumption that he is speaking of a one-act tragedy by Molière: "En voilà bien d'un autre! une Tragédie de Molière, en un Acte & intitulée la Nouveauté encore! Oh! pour le coup c'est ce qu'on n'a jamais vu, & qu'on ne verra peut-être jamais" (Sc. 5, in *Œuvres de Le Grand*, vol. III).

[23] (Paris: P.U.F., 1975), pp. 13-14.

[24] "Situation de la parodie," *Cahiers du 20e siècle*, No. 6 (1976), 9.

[25] Voltaire, *The Complete Works* (Toronto: University of Toronto Press, 1969), vol. 86, "Correspondance," ed. T. Besterman, D674, Michel Linant to Pierre Le Cormier de Cideville, p. 419.

[26] See Diderot, *Œuvres esthétiques*, ed. P. Vernière (Paris: Garnier, 1968), p. 118 and p. 190 *et seq.* Luigi Riccoboni's *Réflexions historiques et critiques sur les différens théâtres de l'Europe* (1738) also refers to the emergence of a genre blending elements of tragedy and comedy.

[27] *Lesage et le Théâtre de la Foire* (Nancy: Imprimerie Sorduillet, 1887), p. 227.

[28] Grannis, *Dramatic Parody*, p. 29.

[29] "En 1705, Fuzelier fit jouer à la foire Saint-Germain son second ouvrage, *Le Ravissement d'Hélène, ou le Siège et l'embrasement de Troie*, grande pièce en trois actes (je transcris l'affiche), qui sera representée avec tous ses agrémens au jeu des Victoires, par les marionnettes du sieur Alexandre Bertrand . . ." (Charles Magnin, *Histoire des Marionnettes en Europe* [Paris: Michel Lévy, 1852], p. 153).

[30] ". . . Tantôt, comme à l'Opéra-Comique, le spectacle est constitué par trois pièces artificiellement groupées pour former un ambigu-comique" (Henri Lagrave, *Le Théâtre et le public*, p. 355). Lagrave includes *Les Trois Spectacles* in this category.

[31] A. Joannidès *(La Comédie-Française de 1680 à 1900* [Paris: Plon-Nourrit, 1901]) indicates that *Les Trois Spectacles* opened on July 6, 1729, at the Comédie-Française and went through 20 performances. Clarence Brenner (*A Bibliographical List of Plays in the French Language, 1700-1789* [Berkeley, 1947], p. 25), attributes a one-act parody of *Polixène*, entitled *Colinette*, to d'Aigueberre. *Colinette* was staged at the Comédie-Italienne on September 4, 1729.

[32] Henri Lagrave, *"Mahomet Second*: Une Tragédie en prose inachevée de Marivaux," *RHLF* (1970), 574-84.

[33] *La Comédie à la cour: les théâtres de société royale pendant le siècle dernier* (Paris: Firmin-Didot, 1885), p. 85.

[34] *Arlequin Enée, ou la Prise de Troyes* (Paris, 1711), "Avertissement."

[35] Although the title "Opéra-Comique" was limited to a single company during a given fair, competitors frequently brought the total number of public theatres in Paris to many more than four.

[36] Much of the popularity of *La Française italienne* came from imitations of Pantalon and Arlequin by the French Players, Legrand's own daughter playing Arlequin. See Mary Scott Burnet, *Marc-Antoine Legrand* (1938; rpt. Genève: Slatkine, 1977), p. 131.

[37] Lagrave, *Le Théâtre et le public*, pp. 98-99.

[38] Sc. 6, in *Théâtre de la Foire*, vol. IX.

[39] *Mercure*, Mars 1740, p. 569.

[40] See my "Louis Fuzelier et le théâtre: vers un état présent," *RHLF* (1983), 604-17.

[41] *Le Théâtre et le public*, p. 612, note 63.

[42] Paris: Klincksieck, 1970.

[43] Hence, the defense of his style in the preface to *Les Serments Indiscrets* (1732): ". . . Mon dessein était qu'il plût comme naturel, et c'est peut-être parce qu'il l'est effectivement qu'on le croit singulier, et que, regardé comme tel, on me reproche d'en user toujours" (Marivaux, *Théâtre complet*, ed. F. Deloffre [Paris: Garnier, 1968], I, 967).

[44] "Sur le plan théorique il reste fidèle à ses principes classiques. Sur le plan pratique, il tient à être applaudi et modifiera ses principes selon le goût de son public" (John Pappas, "Voltaire et le drame bourgeois," *Diderot Studies*, 20 [1981], p. 228).

[45] Jules Bonnassies, *Les Spectacles forains et la Comédie-Française* (Paris: Dentu, 1875), p. 64.

[46] J. Scherer speaks of "*anti*-théâtre." See note 8 above.

[47] *Sunset: A History of Parisian Drama in the Last Years of Louis XIV, 1701-1715* (Baltimore: John Hopkins Press, 1945), p. 335.

[48] *Paris Theatre Audiences in the Seventeenth and Eighteenth Centuries* (London: Oxford University Press, 1957), p. 166.

A Tapestry of Sensual Metaphors:
The Vocabulary of Lesage's Theatre

While the structure of Lesage's theatre is linear — at best a "ricochet of *fourberies*"[1] and at worst a string of cameo sketches, a *théâtre à tiroirs*,[2] the vocabulary employed is like a rich tapestry in which coarse cotton is interwoven with precious silks lending metaphoric depth to the composition. Many critics have praised the dramatic qualities of Lesage's novels. Few have sought to discover the same mastery in his theatre, especially that written for the *foires*.[3] Yet the dramatist's creations for the *théâtre forain* had to recompense the sketchy backdrops washed by the rain with verbal descriptions.[4] The structural flatness and brevity of scenes had to be offset by a rich vocabulary and witty dialogue.

While Paul Chaponnière praised the vocabulary of the *théâtre forain* as lively, frank, the language of the people (literary only by satirical reference), we would postulate that the tapestry woven by Lesage is much more than the language *of* the people. It employs a language which spoke *to* the people by virtue of its colorful metaphors. Chaponnière states that metaphors were replaced by common objects. "Les personnages osent alors parler le langage de leur profession, de leur classe, sans souci d'employer des mots académiques et nobles, à moins que l'auteur n'imite, pour le railler, le jargon des salons; ils s'intéressent aux détails de table et de maison qui accompagnent nécessairement la vie pratique."[5] We maintain that the common objects became metaphors in their own right and that they are put into relief by their proximity to the very literary metaphors (based on mythology, fable literature, and salon vocabulary) the absence of which Chaponnière greeted as a return to the *mot cru*, to Molière and to Rabelais. Thus we find the *crudité* dressed in a fairly sophisticated sauce. The *cru* is rendered piquant by the *cuit* of linguistic refinement.[6]

To illustrate this point, we will pull one of the most recurrent threads of the tapestry, the food metaphor. The plays which feature gods and goddesses frequenting taverns to joke with the barman and *petits-maîtres* waiting at the Elysée gates invite a close inspection of the verbal menu.[7] Furthermore, if Gil Blas, like his picaresque predecessors, is an *affamé* whose travels in society are a culinary adventure, Arlequin, his theatrical counterpart, is no less conscious of his stomach and is more often seduced by a sausage than a smile.[8]

Léo Claretie's description of Lesage's characters in novels can be applied to those in the theatre as well: "Si les personnages de Lesage accusent une vie si intense, c'est en partie grâce à la vivacité du style, c'est aussi peut-être parce que Lesage les nourrit bien. Il fait dans ses développements une grosse part à la gastronomie; ses personnages ont le teint fleuri, la bouche fendue; on nous les montre à table, on nous communique leurs menus; ils prennent une réalité expressive et pleine de santé, comme si tous ces gens venaient nous dire, la bouche pleine: 'Je mange, donc je suis!'"[9]

The metaphoric and metonymic uses of food in both the theatre and the *théâtre forain* serve four basic purposes. They are employed to create realism, satire, contrast and humor. Four equations can be made in relation to these purposes. In creating realism, Lesage employs culinary images as a substitute for life. In satire they represent money, in contrast they evoke sexual gratification and in humor they represent the verbal version of the visual buffoonery of the pie in the face. Many plays in the *théâtre de la foire* portray a fantasy world. Mythology and oriental tales provide the inspiration for the plot and setting. Yet this fantasy world is inhabited by real people. The fact that Arlequin and Pierrot, transported by a bird or flying fish into Merlin's enchanted *monde renversé*, begin their exploration of this land by consuming "un bon saucisson de Bologne, une pinte de vin mesure de St. Denis, un dindon tout cuit, des macarons, du biscuit, du laitage [pour se rafraîchir les poumons], du fromage, et quelques petits ratons,"[10] underlines their humanness. Despite the fairytale surroundings, the spectator or the reader remains on *terra firma* thanks to the well articulated menu. On the stage the heroes' appetites are universal and easily portrayed aspects of their mortality.

The ingestion of food is equated to living, while the absence of nourishment brings about death. When Arlequin disguises himself as a *Calender*, who is, he explains, a "gueux philosophe" not a "philosophe gueux," it is as a "préservatif contre la faim" (VI, 147). The organism cannot survive without replenishing its supply of calories. Arlequin recognizes that "j'ai grand besoin de remonter ma pendule" (V, 271). Of the enchanted lands of Friston, Léandre says: "Rien dans cette retraite aimable / D'ailleurs n'empoisonne ton sort: / Vins exquis, et chère admirable." Arlequin prosaically replies: "Oh! sans cela je serais mort!" (II, 329). Food is a necessity in his eyes. Even death is envisioned in gastronomical terms. The chief *Calender* swears his allegiance to Arlequin, stating that if he were ever guilty of treachery, "Il me faudrait écorcher, / Me tenailler, me hâcher/ Me mettre . . . / En capilotade, / Puis en marmelade" (VI, 204). Death is threatened by an oral route: "Je leur ferais manger jusqu'à leurs flèches et leurs carquois" (VI, 361). Death may be risked by over-consumption. In *Arlequin, Roi de Serendib*, the doctor chides Arlequin: "Quoi, Seigneur, vous mangez encore? / C'est trop exposer votre vie: / . . . / Ces plats sentent l'apoplexie" (I, 29). In *La Tontine* the doctor and his accomplice, an apothecary, create a special diet for the young medical student, who yearns for a sausage and some wine which are forbidden to him. He retorts: "Trop salé, trop doux, trop cuit, trop cru; que diable voulez-vous donc que je mange?" He is offered "du fromage mou" and some "tisane hépatique," to which he replies: "Je suis mort, je suis enterré."[11] He tries to win the complicity of Lisette and some forbidden food: "Si tu voulais me donner une bouteille de vin, je te devrais la vie" (TF, I, 376). The verbal link between alimentation and life is firmly established.

A number of plays feature characters such as the *Comédie Française*, the *Opéra* and the *Théâtre de la Foire*. These illustrious and abstract personages are humanized by their eternal ailments, for which alimentary cures are inevitably prescribed. In the *Querelle des Théâtres*, the *Théâtre de la Foire* says to the *Comédie Française*: "Il me semble que vous preniez plaisir à vous laisser mourir de faim" (III, 45). The life of the theatre is dependent on its authors who nourish it. A conversation between Frontin and Arlequin gives voice to this sentiment in *Les Désespérés*:

Arlequin.	On peut dire que nous [les Comédiens Italiens] vivons de critique et de parodies.
Frontin.	C'est vivre de viandes bien creuses.
Arlequin.	Et cependant, quelque mauvaise que soit cette nourriture, croiriez-vous bien que les Comédiens Français en veulent avoir leur part? (IX, 124)

Similarly, in *Les Funérailles de la Foire*, M. Craquet, the doctor, diagnoses the ills of the *Théâtre Forain*: "Ce sont des viandes délicates qui vous ont perdue" (III, 386). In *Les Spectacles Malades*, Dame Alizon, the doctor's assistant, puts the *Comédie Italienne* on a diet: "Abstenez-vous sur toutes choses de mets trop solides; ils vous gâteraient l'estomac, que vous avez très délicat." The *Comédie Italienne* promises to follow the cure: "Je vivrai donc, ma Chère, / Au défaut de cela, / De viande fort légère, / D'abattis d'Opéra [de parodies]" (VII, 232). Thus we see a metonymical system at work within the framework of the original metaphor. Food is life and life for the theatre is a successful play.

Consuming food is a ritual of life. The accoutrements of eating take on sacred functions. The air sung in *Arlequin, roi de Serendib*, describes a table as the altar on which one must solemnly swear one's love: "Sur ces couverts, sur cette nappe blanche, / Sur cet autel redoutable aux poulets / ... / Je fais serment d'être à vous à jamais" (I, 28). Arlequin's love is bottle-shaped. The *nœud* of almost all the plays is a *contretemps*, a problem which stands in the way of a happy resolution of the plot (usually the marriage of the young lovers). It is significant that the joyous conclusion is accompanied by a meal and a ballet (in that order). Arlequin sums up the relative importance of feast and festival: "Il faut songer à nos provisions de noces, tant pour la panse, que pour la danse" (IV, 169). Marriage signifies the continuance of life — as Pierrot elegantly expresses it when he requests Elmazie's hand in marriage in *La Princesse de Chine*: "Et vous, belle Elmazie, ne voulez-vous pas aussi me donner des successeurs?" (VII, 207). The union of flesh and blood are symbolized by the consumption of bread and wine. Arlequin arrives on the island of the ogres and his perils are summed up by the fact that he is almost eaten twice. The first time he is rescued from wild animals by the ogres. The second time he is rescued from the ogres' cooking pot by Scaramouche. Their victory is celebrated with a meal. Arlequin begins the play with a declaration that he is very hungry. He is thwarted in each of his attempts to satisfy his appetite, and until the obstacles and dangers to his own life are removed, he cannot indulge his Epicurean penchants. Made king, in *Arlequin, Roi de Serendib*, his first official act is to order a meal. Any cause for celebration is a reason to eat and drink. Arlequin, captured by a group of robbers, participates in their banquet and, since he is their victim, nearly meets his death when they stuff him in the wine cask he helped empty and leave him to satisfy the appetites of a hungry wolf. Food is life and the characters enjoy it in a Rabelaisian manner. However, unlike giants, these immodest men are victims of their own appetites. In the comic vision, they fear death but only suffer discomfort from a surfeit or deficit of comestibles.

Culinary metaphors and metonyms add to the realism of the plays by making the characters human and easily identifiable: "il aime le jeu, le vin, les femmes; c'est un homme universel . . ." (TF, II, 109). The foods are also named.

Entire menus are repeated and quantified. In *Turcaret*, for example, 80 bottles of champagne are ordered for the dinner guests and 100 bottles of Suresnes for the orchestra. This measure of Turcaret's wealth, a characteristically ostentatious display, adds to the immediacy of the event and enriches the portrayal of master and valet, both concerned with wealth (the first with what he can obtain with it, the second with obtaining it).

In a satirical context, we must note that the society painted in Lesage's theatre is one divided into two classes: the eaters and the eaten: "Nous plumons une coquette, la coquette mange un homme d'affaires . . ." (TF, I, 235). Food is money and vice versa. People eat their inheritances and revenues. They are themselves consumed by their passion for wealth. Money is a measure of the kind of food one can consume, thus of one's social status. The consumers are social climbers: "Voyez un peu ce misérable valet qui veut manger à la table des maîtres" (TF, I, 68). When Clitandre says to his servant, whose tricks have saved the day: "Ah! mon cher Arlequin, que je t'ai d'obligation! Je me souviendrai toute ma vie de ce que tu as fait pour moi," Arlequin coldly replies: "Je dirai cela à mon boulanger" (IV, 499). Clitandre understands and awards Arlequin the desired money. The value of money is closely related to its food-purchasing power. Again, in *Les Trois Commères*, when the three lady friends find a diamond, they declare, immediately translating its value into edible products: "Que de fricassées de poulets!" (IX, 429). The quality of people is measured by the food they consume. A gambler has trout one day and the next day nothing, which is indeed little compared with "la marmite des chanoines!" (V, 29). A M. de Plaidanville is obviously "friand de procédure" (V, 379). Husbands are of two varieties: "Le vieux mari nous laisse son bien en mourant, et l'autre ne meurt souvent qu'après avoir mangé le nôtre" (TF, I, 402). These starving, brutal characters are also willing to eat each other to obtain their ends. They are portrayed as animals: "Les loups ne s'entremangent pas" (VI, 296). They have animal traits: "dans quelles pattes êtes-vous tombé?" (VI, 323). If the aggressors are wolves, their victims are fattened pigs: "L'argent roule chez les coquettes philosophes, qui s'occupent sérieusement à des sciences solides, comme à l'anatomie, en disséquant pièce à pièce un cochon de Finance" (VI, 413). This is a violent and venomous world in which one must be able to distinguish correctly the species with which one is dealing: "C'est un moineau franc dans la peau d'un hibou" (VI, 201). Food equals money which buys aliments, the quality and luxury of which define one's status in society. The consumers of the chain are aggressive animals, and their victims, "un pourceau qu'on engraisse" (VIII, 111), for example, do not evoke our pity. This is the world of comedy and the victims are deserving of their punishments. When the Turcarets are imprisoned or beaten (usually with a sausage) at their own game, we are not to be upset but rather to follow the Marquis' advice: "Ah, ah, ma foi, Chevalier, tu me fais rire, ta consternation me divertit, allons souper chez le traiteur, et passer la nuit à boire" (TF, III, 370).

Food as marker of contrast distinguishes between two classes and two types: the noble and the servant, and the romantic lover and the Pantagruelian lover of life. The first loses his appetite when he becomes consumed by his love. The second rarely manages to utter a word, so replete is his mouth with the bounties of the table. The first says: "L'amour me fait . . ." The second echoes: "La faim me fait . . ." (I, 267). The romantic lover sees the object of his desire as a poetic

47

beauty: "belle tulipe du parterre de mon cœur" (V, 312). The Gallic lover identifies his love as a dainty morsel, an object fit to satisfy the second of his pressing appetites. The first cries: "J'ai vu cent beautés charmantes sans m'en laisser enflammer." The second chimes in: "Cent dindons appétissants m'ont prié de les aimer" (III, 110). The first is consumed by his flame. The second seeks to consume the object of his desire. To move the latter, Cupid must soak his arrow in wine (V, 97). This juxtaposition of divergent reactions based on class and taste, which is traditional in the theatre and can be seen as well in Marivaux or Molière, for example, is a dynamic source of humor.

This contrast is not limited to the masculine gender. For example, in *Le Corsaire de Salé*, Isabelle, the broken-hearted mistress, drinks some poison as she doubts she will ever see her lover again. Her servant, Inès, in the same situation, wants to copy her. Isabelle tries futilely to dissuade her by saying that she must live to tell the tragic tale. When Don Juan, the lost lover, arrives on stage to inquire: "quel chagrin vous dévore?," it is discovered that the supposed poison was only some "eau de Barbade." Inès sighs happily at this news and admits: "Je ne suis donc plus fâchée d'en avoir avalé un bon verre" (VII, 281). Her penchant for spirits is nearly as strong as that of an Arlequin.

The coarse lover, in viewing his love as an object of consumption — "un amant bien affamé / Veut avoir de la pâture" (VII, 38) — employs the only arms he knows to win his love: "Je vous regarde comme une place qui va bientôt manquer de vivres. Je veux vous assiéger par mes entretiens spirituels; par mes vives insistances, et si je ne vous puis prendre d'assaut, je vous aurai par famine" (V, 156). However, he is paid in like money. The women understand his appetites: "un amant est un chien gourmand" (V, 398). They know that "Quand l'amour est trop bien nourri, / Le Fripon se dégoûte: / Pour le voir toujours vif et sain, / Il faut qu'il meure un peu de faim" (VII, 38). And even their parents know the value of their daughters on the monetary market. Fathers refuse to marry their daughters "de peur de faire brèche à [leur] magot" (VI, 80). Females are also seen as animals (*minets, poulettes, tigresses, moutons, dragons, vipères*, depending on their malleability) which need to be ensnared: "elle mord à la grappe" (V, 202). Again, there are the consumers and the objects of consumption. However, in this context, the victims are only supposed victims. Their weapons are as effective as those of their aggressors and at the conclusion it is difficult to decide who is the victor of this equally-matched combat.

Lesage also employs a metonymical subsystem in which food is the recipient of the attentions and caresses ordinarily bestowed on a person of the opposite sex. For example, Ramire, Don Félix's valet in *Don Félix de Mendoce*, notices that their room has been rifled: "On a même donné très indiscrètement quelques baisers amoureux à une bouteille que j'avais dans la ruelle de mon lit" (TF, I, 205).

Contrast works on two levels: that of the consumer (two types of lovers) and that of the object of consumption (the edible woman and the disguised bird of prey). The counterpoint creates humor while satirizing social and literary customs. Quite often the appetizing woman is a *précieuse* with an armor-plated tongue or an innocent protected by a servant whose bag of tricks matches that of both the pursuer and his valet. The reversal of the object of the hunt and the hunter as well as the substitution of the valet for his master offer broad perspectives for social satire.

Culinary terminology is another source of humor. Characters' names are appropriately chosen: Pinte-Broc (a Swiss drunkard), Mme Tartelin (pastry cook), Beurrefort (her shop boy), Tire-Bouchon (waiter in a tavern), Farinette (baker), M. Gourmandin (canon), M. Gloutonneau (a poet who eats and thinks a lot), etc. Humor is derived from culinary non sequiturs. In *Le Jeune Vieillard*, Adis speaks: "Mais ce qui me charme davantage c'est l'amitié qu'il a pour moi." Arlequin, with his one-track mind, replies appropriately: "On fait ici grand'chère apparemment" (V, 143). Humor emanates from plays on words. In both *L'Ile des Amazones* and *La Forêt de Dodone*, there is an extended play on words based on the mispronunciation of *marier (mariner, marinade)*. In *Arlequin, roi des Ogres ou les bottes de sept lieues*, the cannibals present the unsuspecting Arlequin with a young girl. The ensuing conversation is droll:

Pierrot (cuisinier). Hé bien, Seigneur, voulez-vous qu'on l'habille tout à l'heure?
Arlequin. Hé, n'est-elle pas habillée, Benêt? Elle est à manger.
Pierrot. A quelle sauce souhaitez-vous que je vous la mette?
Arlequin. Belle demande?
Pierrot. Vous la servirai-je à la croque-au-sel? L'aimeriez-vous mieux au bleu, au basilic, à la broche?
Arlequin. Tais-toi, impertinent. Je t'apprendrai à rire avec ton Maître. (IV, 151-52)

Comedy is derived from nonsense in cases such as the following:

Don Garcie. Tu as bu, je pense, tu es ivre.
Galindo. J'ai bu, il est vrai, j'ai bu, mais je ne suis pas ivre; tout homme qui est ivre a bu, cela est sans contredit, mais tout homme qui a bu n'est pas ivre . . . Tous les coups que je buvais, étaient autant de coups de poignard . . . Je suis entré si vivement dans vos chagrins, que je me suis bourré d'une cinquantaine de coups pour le moins. (TF, I, 113)

The example combines a pun with a ridiculous dissertation pronounced with great levity by a drunkard just as the play, *Le Traître puni*, reaches its climax. The little speech, like Shakespeare's clowns, provides relief from the dramatic tension, while postponing the dénouement and heightening the suspense.

Culinary proverbs or recast maxims extend the leitmotif of gastronomic concerns. We find, for example: "Il n'y a si petit pot qui ne trouve son couvercle" (IV, 475); "Fille, dit-on, est plus trompeuse qu'un melon" (IV, 60); "L'appétit vient en mangeant [des femmes]" (VII, 174); "La faim fait sortir les loups des bois" (III, 451); "Le vin est tiré, il faut le boire" (TF, I, 320); "L'honneur est une prune qu'on ne saurait toucher sans ôter la fleur" (TF, I, 334); "Buvons un coup; un verre de vin porte conseil" (III, 320); "La soupe choit souvent entre la bouche et l'écuelle" (VIII, 350). Some simply recall the omnipresence of gustatory concerns, while others create humor by substituting an unexpected element in the familiar formula. This shock parallels that created by the intermingling of these expressions with formulas of a more noble tone. The image of the woman who is more unfaithful than a melon is presented in juxtaposition with the substantiated metaphor of virtue, a mirror which becomes tarnished by desire. The linguistic contrast reflects that in class (the noble is more abstract and refined) and in type of lover (the Rabelaisian lover is still so concerned with his stomach that he is not entirely logical). In the expression "la nuit porte conseil," night is replaced by "un verre," which suits the concern of the speaker and creates comedy by the unexpected. A similar shock in tone is created by the juxtaposition of noble (generosity) and exaggeratedly ignoble sentiments and activities (intoxication). Scaramouche tries to end an argument with Arlequin: "Ami, laissons là Colombine; / Allons en rivaux généreux / Vider chacun une chopine." Arlequin replies: "J'en boirai quatre, si tu veux" (II, 56).

Humor is furthermore indicated by the non-metaphoric rendering of a metaphor as in "C'est un puits d'érudition. / Un puits d'eau toute clair" (V, 419).

Food is dressed in metaphoric garb worthy of the salon of a *précieuse* in *Les Trois Commères*, where beets are called "rougets de Phlegeton," and is contrasted with those "little, round, black things" which are dubbed "huîtres du Styx" (IX, 510-11). While the same technique is employed (ennobling the baser elements), the extended linguistic play is consistent with the surroundings. In hell, where Pierrot believes himself to be, he learns: "on ne boit pas ici à la santé," and concludes joyously: "On peut donc boire et manger tant qu'on veut sans appréhender de crever" (IX, 511).

The ailing theatres are served medicines, composed of plays and operas which were presented with success: "de la Rhubarbe d'Amadis," "du Chiendent de Tarsis," "de l'Elixir de Proserpine," "trois onces de Colonie," etc. Here again, abstractions are rendered concrete and the familiar is presented in a humorously pseudo-noble tone.

Cannibalism lends itself to a comic use of metonyms. Nations and professions figure on the satirical menu. Dutch are too soft, Spanish smell of garlic and scallions. *Petits-maîtres* are nothing but skin and bones and prosecutors are so tough that after twenty-four hours of cooking they remain inedible. Actresses are reassured of their safety: "Ne craignez rien, mes Déesses, les ogres n'en veulent qu'à la chair fraîche" (IV, 171). Not only does the menu selected by the character reflect his propensities (see above), but the characters take on the characteristics of that which they consume. A formidable giant "n'a pas un sabre à la main pour des prunes," and will cut off heads cleanly like a turnip (IX, 72). The humor derives from the fear expressed in an uneducated manner by Colas, the shepherd, and from the rhyme which equates the vegetable world with humanity. The colloquial expression "des prunes" ("for nothing") is highlighted by the context, which restores to it some of its original color.

The abundant gastronomic terms operating as metaphors and primary metonyms in Lesage's theatre create a complex system in which life, women and money are consumed with hearty appetite. While creating very lively characters, Lesage succeeds in satirizing their manner of living. Gluttony and consumption are diseases of the human race, maladies rendered grotesque by the objects digested. Mankind is human because man is a consumer. The very act of eating, however, illustrates his inhumanity. Man is a cannibal when he ingests his brothers. On the one hand, he dissipates his animal nature by satisfying his carnal desires. On the other, he becomes ill by projecting these desires on inappropriate objects. Lesage cannot hope to curb these appetites. However, with the comic use of the food metaphors, he may succeed in purging his spectators of their desire to imitate the actors. Much of the humor, indeed the very success of the emetic, depends on the juxtaposition of coarse and refined vocabulary. The image presented by the magnifying side of the lens is given significance by the presence of another standard. The peasant's dialect and pragmatic view become comic only when contrasted with the noble's pure speech and romantic concept. The tension created by the servant who sees his master's ethereal love as an appetite for ripened fruit, by the master who fails to see the truth in utterances of a valet whose face is eternally besmeared with cream, by the woman who sees the man as a hungry wolf, by the man who sees the woman as a bird of prey, and by the errors in interpretation (those seeing the harpy as a goddess of love and the rapacious financier as a great philanthropist), gives rise to a rich mode of expression, a tapestry of sensual metaphors.

Roseann Runte
Université Sainte-Anne

Notes

1 In *Turcaret*, Frontin says: "cela fait un ricochet de fourberies le plus plaisant du monde." Eugène Lintilhac calls *Le Traître puni* "un ricochet de méprises tragiques" (*Lesage* [Paris: Hachette, 1893], p. 29).

2 Paul Chaponnière, "Les Comédiens de mœurs du Théâtre de la Foire," *Revue d'histoire littéraire de la France*, 20 (1913), 833.

3 Charles Lenient (*La Comédie en France au XVIIIe siècle* [Paris: Hachette, 1888], p. 130) says: "L'étude des mœurs, des caractères, la vivacité du dialogue s'ajoutent à l'agrément du récit. Comment donc tous ces avantages l'abandonneraient-ils sur le théâtre?" Maurice Albert (*Les Théâtres de la Foire (1660-1787)* [Paris: Hachette, 1900], p. 73) does seem to invite a comparison: "Ce malicieux et pénétrant observateur voulut que son théâtre nouveau fût une sorte de second *Gil Blas*, un *Gil Blas* dramatique et populaire . . ." Charles Dédéyan (*Lesage et Gil Blas* [Paris: S.E.D.E.S., 1965], I, 161-63) notes the dramatic qualities of Lesage's novels but not the opposite. A rather more typical view is that of F. C. Green (*Minuet* [London: Dent, 1935], p. 150): "In one comedy, his only memorable one, he almost leads one to regret that he was a great novelist."

4 Chaponnière, p. 833.

5 Chaponnière, p. 843.

6 N.-M. Bernardin, *La Comédie italienne en France et les théâtres de la foire et du boulevard (1570-1791)* (Paris: Editions de la Revue Bleue, 1902), p. 107: "La plaisanterie est beaucoup plus délicate dans les parodies de Lesage, qui remplace souvent les gros mots et les équivoques grossières par des traits d'une gaieté fine et légère." See also Bernardin, pp. 107, ll3; Lintilhac, pp. 129-30; and Constant Mic, *La Commedia dell'arte ou le théâtre des comédiens italiens des XVIe, XVIIe et XVIIIe siècles* (Paris: Schriffrin, 1927), pp. 88-139.

7 Bernardin, p. 29 *et seq.*

8 Bernardin, p. 127: "Arlequin est gourmand; c'est son péché mignon." Paul de Saint-Victor (*Hommes et Dieux* [Paris: Michel Lévy, 1867], p. 364) says of the characters in *Gil Blas*: "La largeur de leurs consciences n'est égalée que par la capacité de leurs estomacs." Roger Laufer, *Lesage ou le métier de romancier* (Paris: Gallimard, 1971), p. 249: "L'habillement occupe avec la nourriture et l'argent une place exceptionnelle dans l'univers lesagien." D'Origny (*Annales du Théâtre italien depuis son origine jusqu'à ce jour* [Paris: Veuve Duchesne, 1788], I, 4) says, like Bernardin, of Arlequin: "Il est naturellement gourmand, poltron et balourd." See also Roseann Runte, "Gil Blas and Roderick Random: Food for Thought," *French Review*, 50, No. 5 (April, 1977), 698-705.

9 *Lesage* (Paris: Lecène, 1894), p. 223.

10 Alain-René Lesage, *Le Théâtre de la foire ou l'opéra comique* (Paris: Etienne Ganeau, 1721), III, 206-09. All future references will appear in the text. Spelling has been modernized when appropriate.

11 Lesage, *Recueil des pièces mises au Théâtre français* (Paris: Jacques Barois fils, 1739), I, 373. Subsequent references to plays in this volume appear in the text and are distinguished as follows: TF, volume, page.

52

Rococo Style in European Theatre

By comparison with poetry and the novel, drama has largely been neglected by specialists of the rococo. This is both curious and regrettable. Regrettable, because the superficiality of the thesis that Voltaire was the *Rokokomensch* "par excellence" is nowhere more clearly demonstrated than in the domain of the theatre, where Voltaire, in spite of a few technical innovations, clearly reveals himself to be devoted to empty imitations of seventeenth-century Classicism. Curious, because the central figure in French literary rococo is Marivaux, chiefly known for his theatre.

In the present essay, previous contributions to the concept of rococo theatre will first be reviewed and then the distinguishing features of this theatre will be established by a discussion of such aspects as generic preferences, the treatment of the theme of love, the dynamics of rococo psychology, and the stylistic model. The concept of rococo used here is drawn from French furnishing and interior decoration of the Louis Quinze style.[1]

I

Previous Assessments

Some theatre has been assimilated aesthetically to rococo painting.[2] The Goncourt brothers, presumably thinking of the adolescent combination of passion and innocence, called Fragonard the Chérubin of erotic painting.[3] Larroumet, in the first large-scale work devoted to Marivaux, compared him to Watteau because of his combination of charm and saucy gaiety with a love idealized by a tasteful moderation and an emphasis on the courting stage.[4] Deschamps stesses in Watteau and Marivaux the aristocratic and pastoral aspects, the view of nature as an artificial theatrical setting, the passion for pleasure, entertainment and luxury, the subtlety and superficiality of emotions and their gay and witty expression, the refusal to admit of unhappiness and death.[5] Lintilhac compares the theatre of Favart to the works of Vanloo, Boucher, Lancret and Larmessan, emphasizing its prettiness, its affectation of naivety, its naughtiness, its pastoral and mythological settings.[6] He stresses Marivaux's fantasy and idealization.[7] Neubert refers approvingly to Larroumet's likening of Marivaux to Watteau.[8] Brandes says of Goethe's *Die Laune des Verliebten*: "Das Kleine Stück hätte sich ganz dazu geeignet, von Boucher illustriert zu werden, der freilich schon das Jahr zuvor gestorben war."[9] Schürr compares Marivaux's idealization and vague longing to that of Watteau.[10] Maurice Donnay writes rather vaguely of Marivaux: "Comme Watteau, il est une expression de son époque";[11] Trahard, however, just as vaguely, finds the comparison rather artificial.[12] Jamieson remarks more precisely: "Marivaux cultivates his scanty plot of ground as intensively as his contemporaries Pater, Lancret and Watteau in another medium."[13] Xavier de Courville speaks of the "correspondances réelles entre l'art de Marivaux et celui de Watteau,"[14] and of "toutes les affinités qu'un dieu favorable a véritablement établies entre un tel peintre et un tel écrivain, par le trait d'union de cette scène extraordinaire,"[15] a reference, of course, to the Théâtre-Italien. Pierre Reboul declares: "On a pu parler d'un 'style Watteau' — je ne sais quelle rêverie un peu triste dans le plaisir. On trouve cela dans un Lélio ou au détour d'une conversation."[16] Arnold Hauser writes: "Marivaux has often been compared with Watteau, and the similarity of their witty and piquant style certainly suggests the comparison."[17] George Poulet agrees with the comparison, but on the basis of Reboul's criterion, not that of Hauser: "L'œuvre marivaudienne a, au fond, un accent douloureux. L'on n'a pas tort de la comparer à celle de Watteau . . ."[18]

Hatzfeld relates that in *L'Embarquement pour Cythère* "Watteau has actually painted the finale of Florent Carton Dancourt's comedy *Les Trois Cousines*.[19] Ortensia Ruggiero stresses a similarity between Marivaux and Watteau based on a common emphasis on the dawn of love, treated in a delicate, refined and idealized manner and leading inevitably to a happy ending.[20] Meyers writes: "As in the plays of Marivaux, that arbiter of the fine art of courting, Watteau depicted a theatre-influenced, highly artificial concept of love in which conversation plays a leading role."[21] Chérel says of Marivaux: "Son caractère rappelle volontiers le caractère de Watteau, à l'œuvre galante de qui l'on a si souvent comparé son œuvre."[22] Leroy equates Watteau with Dancourt ("charmant tableau de mœurs"), Boucher with Marivaux (portrayal of a gay and tender love), and Fragonard with Beaumarchais (the gay and charming love of adolescence).[23]

Jean-Louis Bory makes a seemingly pointless historicist protest based on chronology: "Il respire le même air que Watteau, oui (Oh! l'inévitable *Finette*, l'inévitable *Indifférent*, l'inévitable *Embarquement pour Cythère*, à quoi l'on travaille toujours à réduire Marivaux!), mais le même air aussi que l'abbé Prévost et Lesage."[24] Emile Henriot likewise makes the dubious claim that Prévost shared with Watteau and Marivaux, his contemporaries, the same combination of charming grace and almost bitter melancholy.[25]

In connection with Chérubin, Boissy and Folacci invoke not Fragonard, as do the Goncourt, but Watteau, stressing tenderness, perversity, sophistication, amorality.[26] Simches declares: "Marivaux *est* vraiment 'la fantaisie XVIIIe.' Il représente l'esprit de son temps dans le théâtre comme Watteau dans la peinture."[27] Minguet writes of Marivaux: "Le parallèle est banal entre lui et Watteau; il n'en est pas moins fondé, éclairant."[28]

In a recent manual directed by Thoraval, we find Marivaux compared to Watteau on the basis of easy elegance of psychology and morals, deliciously unstable equilibrium of feelings, exquisite subtlety and delicacy of expression.[29]

The melancholy or nostalgia attributed to Marivaux and Watteau by Schürr, Reboul, Poulet, Henriot is a fragile, flimsy link. Does it stem from a Régence nostalgia for the grandeur of the Sun King's reign? Perhaps. But it has also been suggested, by Zayed, that it is above all a figment of our own imaginative sensibility — "surtout le regret des générations modernes, et des Goncourt en particulier, pour une époque toute de joie, de charme et de beauté, à jamais disparue."[30] According to Minguet, the reason for this impression is that "notre pensée de rêve ne peut pas ne pas ressentir comme doucement amère l'union de l'amour et du fugitif."[31] And, in any case, even if there is something "painful," "nostalgic," "melancholic" about Watteau and Marivaux, it is not this that makes them rococo. Neither Boucher nor Fragonard is particularly nostalgic — nor Couperin, for that matter, nor Crébillon *fils*; and even the Voltaire of *L'Epître des Vous et des Tu* is not "painfully" so.

Lionel Gossman links Marivaux to Watteau through sexual non-differentiation[32] and the ambiguity of sentimental eroticism.[33] Van Voris finds throughout all of Congreve's comedies a feminine cadence analogous to Hogarth's "line of beauty."[34]

What we may note at this point is the extraordinary predominance of comparisons between rococo artists and Marivaux. Goethe, Dancourt, Favart and Congreve are also mentioned, but Marivaux is referred to ten or twenty times as often. (Beaumarchais is also thought of in this connection, but exclusively because of one character: the youthful Chérubin.) The critical consensus therefore clearly suggests that rococo style in European theatre is best exemplified in the plays of Marivaux.

The term and concept of rococo style have been applied to the theatre directly but not with any frequency. Lintilhac applies it to Favart's *Les Trois Sultanes* because of its sweetness and elegance.[35] Fritz Neubert bases himself largely on Marivaux to describe the rococo as gay and flirty, human and anti-heroic, cheerfully unheedful of deep sorrows, freedom-loving, seeing life as a gay and sophisticated entertainment.[36] Schürr also takes the rococo to be best exemplified in Marivaux, whose theatre uses a language at once precious and familiar — the language of the salons.[37] Kindermann, like Brandes, proposes Goethe's *Die Laune des Verliebten* as his candidate,[38] but it is Lessing's *Minna von Barnhelm* — "ein Spielwerk der Mode" — that is characterized as rococo by Hiller in 1933.[39] Momigliano says of Goldoni that "pur restaurando nel teatro il senso del reale rimane uno dei più caratteristici poeti del rococò."[40] For Hatzfeld, Marivaux is rococo but this is a trait he has in common with virtually every artist of the eighteenth century.[41] Jamieson says of Marivaux's "intensive cultivation of his scanty plot of ground": "This method seems generally characteristic of the rococo art of the Regency period."[42] Cysarz, like Hiller, sees *Minna von Barnhelm* as rococo.[43] Hauser emphasizes the role of the notions of beauty and taste in rococo writers like Marivaux.[44] Fischer associates Marivaux with the rococo because of his affiliations with the aristocratic gallantry and hedonism of the neo-*précieux* salons.[45] Walter Binni accepts Marivaux as rococo.[46]

The Fleissners write of Goethe's *Die Laune des Verliebten*: "'The Lover's Caprice' is a pastoral play of the Rococo period, written in the somewhat trivial fashion of the dramatic idyll of those days."[47] Minguet finds in Marivaux the rococo traits of femininity, virtuosity, intricacy, subtlety, ambiguity, wit, gallantry, preciosity.[48] Jean Fabre has described Marivaux as rococo.[49] Mandel writes: "Marivaux is rococo in his transparence and mobility (a mobility without violence); in the come-and-go of moods, actions, decisions, which we can take as the literary equivalents of curls and garlands; in his sanity, his gaiety, his unbelievable happiness, his light roses and blues which only a darker rose and blue can threaten; in his unfaltering grace."[50] Hatzfeld, likewise, applying to theatre his criteria of wit, eroticism and elegance, finds them in the plays of Marivaux, Beaumarchais and Goldoni.[51]

Of these various critical assessments, perhaps the most difficult to accept is the categorization as rococo of Lessing's play *Minna von Barnhelm*. This thesis of Hiller's and Cysarz's appears to be founded on criteria such as *Empfindsamkeit* and *Optimismus*, which are irrelevant to the rococo and lead one rather to conclude that these critics have confused rococo with Enlightenment. Indeed, as with *Le Mariage de Figaro*,[52] so with Hiller's study of *Minna*, the characterization as rococo is totally dependent on a single secondary character: in *Minna*, it is that of a stereotyped *petit-maître*. This is, of course, a central social symbol for the rococo,[53] as is the coquette,[54] but, as with the Beaumarchais play, that is not enough to make of the whole work an example of rococo style. Just as in the English novel rococo is best represented not by *Tristram Shandy* (nor even by *Joseph Andrews* with its portrait of the fop Beau Didapper) but by Congreve's *Incognita*, so in German theatre it is best represented not by *Minna von Barnhelm* but by *Die Laune des Verliebten*.

The remaining critical suggestions (Congreve, Favart, Dancourt, Goldoni, the young Goethe) are all reasonably plausible. Again, as with the comparisons with rococo painting, there is a remarkable predominance of references to the theatre of Marivaux as archetypally rococo. Our discussion of rococo theatre will therefore concentrate on Marivaux, while giving ancillary consideration also to representative playwrights in English, Italian and German rococo.

II

From Classical Tragedy and Farce
to Tragi-Comedy and Comedy of Manners

In seventeenth-century England and France, the waning of the baroque aesthetic that preceded the rococo is accompanied by the elimination of the dimension of the sacred, that is, of transcendence, and a movement away from true tragedy. This is already visible in English Restoration tragedy, which tends towards ludic technical ingenuity, tragi-comedy and happy endings, catastrophe being reserved for the villains while the virtuous find their reward, at least in a promised hereafter.[55] In France, the tradition of great tragic writing illustrated by Corneille and Racine dies away before the dawn of the eighteenth century, a victim of the passage from the sacred to the profane and the rococo thrust towards a new euphemization. If the French had to wait until the end of the seventeenth century to see the beginnings of the replacement of baroque Classicism by proto-rococo tendencies, the English on the contrary had experienced an even more marked liberation as early as 1660. However, because the restored Stuart court was impregnated with French culture, Restoration theatre was as French as it was English: it expressed all the French sauciness and gaiety (later evident in the Régence) then being carefully suppressed at Versailles in an effort to promulgate an image of responsibility and greatness.

Just as the rationalistic idealism of the late eighteenth century was present but repressed in the ludic scepticism of the earlier, rococo period, so the preceding baroque era contained (in Racine, for example, in whom Cornelian heroism is replaced by a more human psychology) the seeds of reductive immanence which were to germinate and flower in the early eighteenth century. Thus the Cartesian rationalism, idealism and transcendentalism of baroque Classicism are replaced by the empiricism, scepticism and immanence of the rococo.

Our view of the sequence of culture-periods postulates not a series of mutually exclusive currents but on the contrary an alternation of dominance between two antithetical but in a sense mutually dependent tendencies, both of which are always present in either dominant or subordinate — that is, temporarily latent — form. At any given moment, both antagonistic mechanisms are present, the one dominating all areas of mental activity and determining the images and symbols through which they are expressed, the other constituting an opposition in dialectical relationship with the first.[56] This coexistence of overt or expressed tendencies with covert or repressed ones is exemplified in Restoration and rococo society and literature: what the Restoration expresses in such tragedy as it does produce is the sentiment and idealism excluded from the comedy as from the real life of the period with their materialism and corrosive cynicism. The purely compensatory function of these expressions of emotion is indicated by their exaggeration and general unreality.[57]

In cultural history, mythical projection of needs and ideals tends to be followed by literal imitation and execution. The playful but unreal and fantastic utopianism which English and French rococo toyed with as a safety-valve was to bear strange fruit in the latter part of the eighteenth century, giving on the one hand the totally Arcadian eroticism[58] of Wieland's *Komische Erzählungen* (the manners orientation disappears completely as it does in Goethe's rococo pastoral *Die Laune des Verliebten*) and on the other the idealistic programs of the ideologists of the French Revolution. A similar rhythm may be detected in the periodic emergence and disappearance of tragedy as a genre. Tragedy meets death strongly and squarely and refuses to euphemize it; it expresses the will to face and even exaggerate the tragedy of the human condition so as to oppose it rebelliously and reject it without compromise. Tragic pleasure is the pleasure of seeing man facing death with courage. This pleasure is foreign to the rococo. The taste for tragedy requires an acceptance of death and of the role of suffering; the rococo refuses to accept or even contemplate death and suffering, and herein lies its own unconscious tragedy or perhaps pathos — in its total loss of nerve. The flooding but oblique sunshine of beauty which beams down on all these rococo miniatures casts correspondingly long shadows, whose penumbra is the transience of the joy and beauty of life (reflected in the "melancholy" or "nostalgia" of the world of Watteau) and whose umbra is the ultimate fact of death.

If there is such a thing as valid rococo "tragedy" in French literature, it may well be found, paradoxically enough, in the theatre of Marivaux, with its studies of the difficulties of communication, of the difference between the real and the ideal, of the pain of illusion, and its endings which at first glance may appear happy but are really fraught with ambiguity.[59]

The pre-rococo period was distinguished in both France and England by fine comic theatre — Restoration comedy in England, and in France the plays of Molière. This was in the main a robust theatre of hearty laughter, especially in France. Molière's strength was always in farce, through the whole spectrum of his theatre, from the sheer buffoonery of *Les Fourberies de Scapin* to the social problem of *Le Misanthrope* (which inspired Wycherley's *The Plain Dealer*). Even when a serious moral or ethical subject is chosen, as in *Tartuffe*, the treatment, which is to say the art, is farcical.[60] The world of Etherege and Congreve, already verging on "proto-rococo," was motivated primarily by the struggle between the parvenus, who must pretend to virtue (and are ridiculous) and the socially elect, who need not pretend because their virtue is "innate, hereditary and self-defined"[61] — being of the saved, they can and do ignore morality with impunity. While both the social climber and the well-born fop (male or female) are types of False Wit, the latter type is merely an exaggeration of quite familiar and acceptable traits and is therefore treated with an amused affection. Restoration comedy moves precariously between sentiment and vulgarity to satirize the follies and vices of the day. Those plays, like *The Country Wife* and *The Man of Mode*, which epitomized the values of English Restoration comedy owed much of their success to a combination of stylistic elegance and moral inelegance, or at least ambiguity — to the deliciously disturbing, even perverse, spectacle of a shiny, superficial, brittle veneer of fastidious manners and exquisite nonchalance, clothing, if scarcely disguising, depths of vulgar materialism, corrosive cynicism and ruthless egotism. Restoration comedy of manners, from Etherege's *The Comical Revenge* (1664) to Congreve's *The Way of the World* (1700),[62] is characterized by unimportance of plot, freedom of dialogue, grace of wit, an atmosphere of emancipation and refined cynicism, and the avoidance of any deep emotion, while crude realism was also gradually eliminated. To these aspects, often noted by critics and historians,[63] a comparatist, with his mind on the later rococo theatre of France, Italy and Germany, will add that the English works are distinguished by a rich embroidery of the trivial and ephemeral ornaments of everyday life in a luxury-loving society.

After the passage in 1688 from the licentious Stuart court to that, more decorous, of William and Mary, courtiers frequented the theatre less and audiences were soon dominated by bourgeois patrons looking for light and reasonably innocent entertainment. Consequently, Restoration comedy underwent a gradual refinement, and by the year 1700 (date of *The Way of the World*) had lost enough of its coarseness to be aligned with the rococo aesthetic — although French rococo will be distinctly more refined, less coarse and less cynical. In spite of these differences, the resemblance between the English and French modes of rococo comedy has been sufficiently demonstrated by the exhaustive investigations of Lucette Desvignes.[64]

The central aim of the rococo comic playwright appears to be to provoke not a laugh but a smile. He is the heir not of Aristophanes, as was Molière, but of Menander. Rococo theatre, as exemplified in the plays of Marivaux, reflects a very different society from that of Molière: it excludes both the tears of tragedy and the laughter of farce, both deep moral concern and biting caricature. Exquisitely well-mannered, its discretion preserves it from emotional display and sentimentality.

III

Woman as Central Myth: The Courting Syndrome

Changing social conditions enabled the rapidly-growing importance of woman in society to flower in that considerable refinement of both manners and taste that marks the Régence and later the Louis Quinze period. Just as the minuet mimes love, so love in turn, at this period, approximates to a minuet, becomes a decorative society game, indefinitely repeated, the noncommittal ornament of the drawing-room, and the ex-*courtisan*, now *homme du monde*, turns his attention from public to private life, to amorous idylls, between flirting and sighs, treading the primrose path of dalliance: "... the sanctum of the house is the boudoir, its idol is woman, and its mood is caprice."[65] Montesquieu writes in 1721: "Celui qui est à la cour, à Paris, dans les provinces, qui voit agir des ministres, des magistrats, s'il ne connaît les femmes qui les gouvernent, est comme un homme qui voit bien une machine qui joue, mais qui n'en connaît point les ressorts."[66] During the first part of the century, which is our concern, the type of woman who is influential is what the Goncourts call the *caillette*:

[La caillette] représente son temps et le particularise en ce qu'il a de plus propre et de plus délicat . . . [Elle] représente en elle le dédain du monde qui l'entoure pour le sérieux de la vie, le sourire dont il couvre tout . . . sa manie d'être toujours à voltiger sur ce qu'il dit . . . Son idéal en toutes choses est fait de petitesse, de brièveté, d'agrément . . . [Elle est] emportée dans [un] tourbillon au bout duquel elle trouve cette folle et coquette ivresse des grâces du XVIIIe siècle: le *papillotage*, — un mot trouvé par le temps pour peindre le plus précieux de son amabilité et le plus fin de son génie féminin.[67]

Woman is its ideal but also its plaything: this is the oft-neglected paradox of rococo femininity and feminization. The *précieuses* emphasized courting rather than consummation and thus threw into jeopardy the deepening interpersonal relationship whose cultivation normally takes consummation as its threshold. This postponement of consummation led to deviations such as excessive verbalization (as in the *précieux* and in Marivaux's theatre, where words are everything) and voyeurism (often satisfied by plastic or even merely verbal substitutes). Of the three stages of love — courtship (cerebral), consummation (sensual) and cultivation (emotional) — the *précieuses* de-emphasized the second and attempted to maintain the third by over-emphasizing the first. In the process, however, the third withered away, leaving only the first, so that when the second stage was restored and emphasized in the rococo, there was nothing to follow it except repetition of the now two-stage pattern.[68]

Marivaux's theatre is devoted to Woman and he deals with her lovingly, with a finesse and subtlety that woman alone, perhaps, can fully appreciate. He does not only study her in various characters and situations, such as her stages of consent to love; sometimes he waxes lyrical and exalts her charms, as in the following passage from *La Surprise de l'amour*:

Arlequin.	En vérité, c'est pourtant un joli petit animal que cette femme, un joli petit chat, c'est dommage qu'il ait tant de griffes.[69]
Lélio.	Tu as raison, c'est dommage; car enfin, est-il dans l'univers de figure plus charmante? Que de grâces, et que de variété dans ces grâces!
Arlequin.	C'est une créature à manger.
Lélio.	Voyez ces ajustements, jupes étroites, jupes en lanterne, coiffure en clocher, coiffure sur le nez, capuchon sur la tête, et toutes les modes les plus extravagantes: mettez-les sur une femme, dès qu'elles auront touché sa figure enchanteresse, c'est l'Amour et les Grâces qui l'ont habillée, c'est de l'esprit qui lui vient jusques au bout des doigts. Cela n'est-il pas bien singulier?
Arlequin.	Oh, cela est vrai; il n'y a mardi! pas de livre qui ait tant d'esprit qu'une femme, quand elle est en corset et en petites pantoufles.
Lélio.	Quel aimable désordre d'idées dans la tête! que de vivacité! quelles expressions! que de naïveté! L'homme a le bon sens en partage, mais ma foi l'esprit n'appartient qu'à la femme. A l'égard de son cœur, ah! si les plaisirs qu'il nous donne étaient durables, ce serait un séjour délicieux que la terre. Nous autres hommes, la plupart, nous sommes jolis en amour: nous nous répandons en petits sentiments doucereux; nous avons la marotte d'être délicats, parce que cela donne un air plus tendre; nous faisons l'amour réglément, tout comme on fait une charge; nous nous faisons des méthodes de tendresse; nous allons chez une femme, pourquoi? Pour l'aimer, parce que c'est le devoir de notre emploi. Quelle pitoyable façon de faire! Une femme ne veut être ni tendre ni délicate, ni fâchée ni bien aise; elle est tout cela sans le savoir, et cela est charmant. Regardez-la quand elle aime, et qu'elle ne veut pas le dire, morbleu, nos tendresses les plus babillardes approchent-elles de l'amour qui passe à travers son silence?
Arlequin.	Ah! Monsieur, je m'en souviens, Margot avait si bonne grâce à faire comme cela la nigaude!
Lélio.	Sans l'aiguillon de l'amour et du plaisir, notre cœur à nous autres est un vrai paralytique: nous restons là comme des eaux dormantes, qui attendent qu'on les remue pour remuer. Le cœur d'une femme se donne sa secousse à lui-même; il part sur un mot qu'on dit, sur un mot qu'on ne dit pas, sur une contenance. Elle a beau vous avoir dit qu'elle aime; le répète-t-elle, vous l'apprenez toujours, vous ne le saviez pas encore: ici par une impatience, par une froideur, par une imprudence, par une distraction, en baissant les yeux, en les relevant, en sortant de sa place, en y restant; enfin c'est de la jalousie, du calme, de l'inquiétude, de la joie, du babil et du silence de toutes couleurs. Et le moyen de ne pas s'enivrer du plaisir que cela donne? Le moyen de se voir adorer sans que la tête vous tourne? (I, 2)[70]

This passage reveals the artificiality of rococo society. Acting the game of love is taken so far that Woman, by virtue of her natural gift for play-acting, seems much more natural than Man — that is not really, however, because she is less contrived, but because Man, being less contrived by nature, seems more false when he does try to act a part.

As in rococo poetry (for example, a poem such as Voltaire's *Epître des Vous et des Tu*), two faces of rococo woman may also be discovered in the theatre of Marivaux, possibly the most important single body of rococo literary works. The Silvia of *Arlequin poli par l'amour* and *La Double Inconstance* and the Angélique of *L'Ecole des mères* and *L'Epreuve* are "jeunes filles" of varying "naïveté," whereas the Comtesse of *La Surprise de l'amour*, *Le Legs*, *L'Heureux Stratagème*, the Marquise of *La Seconde Surprise de l'amour* and *Les Sincères*, and the Araminte of *Les Fausses Confidences* are mature and indeed sophisticated women, women of subtlety, elegance and refinement, at times even rather coquettish and contrived. The Silvia of *Le Jeu de l'amour et du hasard* is somewhere between the two. When love strikes, the heroine often passes from one type to the other — from being well-armed and subtle, she is disarmed and bewildered, becomes unsure and hesitant: the *femme du monde* begins to resemble the *jeune fille*.

Apart from this small number of different types, however, the rococo woman strikes one by her lack of variety: like the expressionless face that characterizes her portraits, her psychology hardly seems to alter from play to play — only the situations change, and even they vary relatively little. On the other hand, the psychology of these basic and restricted characters is presented with great subtlety and in great detail. This attention to and delight in detail is again typical of all the rococo arts. The subtle and sympathetic exploration essential to Marivaux's style relates both to the psychological analysis central to Classicism and even more to the obsessive subtlety and passion for dwelling on delicate nuances that was so characteristic of the *Précieux*.

The stages of consentment to love, portrayed by Watteau as a series in his *promenades sentimentales* and *fêtes champêtres* and as a tableau in *L'Embarquement pour Cythère*, are presented by Marivaux in *Le Jeu de l'amour at du hasard*, *La Surprise de l'amour*, *La Seconde Surprise de l'amour* and *Les Fausses Confidences*. This is appropriate to the rococo figures of a Watteau, which have the supple slenderness of adolescence, the time of love's first awakening: it is also appropriate to the coquettish, sophisticated woman, who is determined to be wooed before she is won.

We find this sentiment eloquently expressed by Mrs. Millamant, the heroine of Congreve's *The Way of the World*: "I'll fly and be follow'd to the last moment, tho' I am upon the very Verge of Matrimony, I expect you shou'd solicit me as much as if I were wavering at the grate of a Monastery, with one foot over the threshold. I'll be solicited to the very last . . ." (IV, 1, lines 160-64).

Love, jealousy and *amour-propre* are the central themes of Congreve's *The Way of the World* (1700), Marivaux's *Le Jeu de l'amour et du hasard* (1736), Goldoni's *Il Ventaglio* (1763)[71] and Goethe's *Die Laune des Verliebten* (1766). The miniaturizing so typical of the rococo is well represented in the central importance given to a fan by Goldoni, to a flower, a dance and a kiss by the young Goethe,[72] but there are more interesting links between these writers, especially

61

Congreve and Marivaux. The view of beauty is one example. Thus Congreve has this passage of dialogue: "*Fairall*: You do her wrong; for to give her her Due, she has Wit. *Mirabell*: She has Beauty enough to make any Man think so . . ." (*The Way of the World*, I, 1, lines 151-53). And Marivaux: "Nous autres jolies femmes (car j'ai été de ce nombre), personne n'a plus d'esprit que nous quand nous en avons un peu; les hommes ne savent plus alors la valeur de ce que nous disons: en nous écoutant parler, ils nous regardent, et ce que nous disons profite de ce qu'ils voient" (*La Vie de Marianne*, p. 82).

It is true, of course, that themes may be shared but treated differently. We should be surprised to find in Marivaux a declaration as cynical as the following from Congreve: "A Wit shou'd no more be sincere, than a Woman constant; one argues a decay of Parts, as t'other of Beauty" (*The Way of the World*, I, 1, lines 319-21) — and we do not. However, in *L'Heureux Stratagème*, the Comtesse does defend infidelity in a manner which recalls the frequency of this theme not only in other Marivaux plays (*La Double Inconstance*, *Le Dénouement imprévu*, and so on) but also among the baroque poets of the seventeenth century and especially rococo poets like Chaulieu (*Apologie de l'inconstance*). The Classical Princesse de Clèves had feared this baroque tendency (embodied in Nemours) — the suffering it caused was "le plus grand de tous les maux"; the unfaithful lover was condemned by the Classical Molière in Don Juan; and we may take it that the flighty mistress is condemned likewise by Marivaux in *L'Heureux Stratagème*. But coquetry (and therefore inconstancy) is, in Marivaux's opinion, as inevitable as it is deplorable: it is he who declares that "une femme qui n'est plus coquette, c'est une femme qui a cessé d'être."[73] To admit that such a trait constitutes an essential aspect of Woman goes a long way toward removing the possibility of blaming her for it. Marivaux also writes: "Notre vanité et notre coquetterie, voilà les plus grandes sources de nos passions, voilà d'où les hommes tirent le plus souvent tout ce qu'ils valent. Qui nous ôterait les faiblesses de notre cœur ne leur laisserait guère de qualités estimables" (*Les Serments indiscrets*, V, 2).

Coquetry takes a form in Congreve that will reappear in Marivaux. In *The Way of the World*, Lady Wishfort reflects: "I'll receive him in my little dressing room, there's a Couch — Yes, yes, I'll give the first Impression on a Couch — I won't lie neither but loll and lean upon one Elbow; with one Foot a little dangling off, jogging in a thoughtful way" (IV, 1, lines 22-26). This is how Jacob sees Mme de Ferval in *Le Paysan Parvenu*: "Je la trouvai qui lisait, couchée sur un sopha, la tête appuyée sur une main, et dans un déshabillé très propre, mais assez négligemment arrangé. Figurez-vous une jupe qui n'est pas tout à fait rabattue jusqu'aux pieds, qui même laisse voir un peu de la plus belle jambe du monde; et c'est une grande beauté qu'une belle jambe dans une femme! De ces deux pieds mignons, il y en avait un dont la mule était tombée, et qui, dans cette espèce de nudité, avait fort bonne grâce" (p. 708).

It is fairly clear that similar thematic preoccupations, typical of the rococo spirit, prevail in the world of Congreve and in that of Marivaux.[74]

IV

Loving and Lying: The Role of Disguise

The detailed description of the obstacles to love, in the form of social status, *amour-propre*, misunderstandings, and tests set by hero or heroine, shows the characteristic rococo attitude: that the game of love, the wooing, is as important as love itself, if not more so.

The rococo predilection for surprise (found in architecture and interior decoration, often allied with displays of ingenuity, even virtuosity, or sometimes mere playfulness and apparent spontaneity) are found in the *surprises de l'amour* characteristic of Marivaux's theatre, and also in the naïve astonishment of such figures as the Arlequin of *La Double Inconstance*.

Surprise is often associated with disguise, another central feature of the style.[75] Marivaux himself in real life masked his poverty with the disguise of beautiful clothes — a physical and social mask. This indicates the importance he attached to appearances and his consciousness of the frequent divorce between appearance and reality. In such plays as *Le Jeu de l'amour et du hasard* and *Les Fausses Confidences*, rococo comedy and playfulness are introduced by the disguises, and by the burlesque love-scenes between the servants, often (but not always) a parody of the main love-scenes.

The use of double plots and disguises is parallel with rococo *trompe-l'œil*, illusions, mirrors — the unexpected, the surprises, the play, the game. We find truth disguised as in the pictorial "gallery of beauty" — "images full of the splendor of costumes which disguise the human individual and hide his soul beneath a decorative pattern,"[76] and yet, it is the ornament that is the essential, not what is ornamented: only when the lie of the disguise (disguised identity, disguised feelings, disguised language) is adopted, is the veritable truth seen, just as the glory of rococo portraiture lies in the silken robes, lace and powdered wig, and that of rococo furniture in the magnificence of the veneer, the lacquer, the gilding (the outlawing of the latter in 1759 coincided with the ending of the rococo), as that of Watteau's models lay in their being dressed up as Italian Comedians.

On the surface it may appear that one of the important elements of what Jean Rousset calls the "structure du double registre" depends on the unmasking ability of the "personnages spectateurs."[77] We have indeed said that when the lie of disguise is adopted the truth is seen. But what is this truth which is seen when disguise is adopted? It is not the truth obtained by penetration of the disguise (as implied by Rousset) but the truth that the disguise itself is the operative and ineradicable reality. The criteria for Dorante's judgment of Silvia in *Le Jeu de l'amour et du hasard* are distorted both by the subconscious permanence of the mask (Silvia being remarkable only if judged by servant standards) and also by contrast with Lisette, who falsely represents upper-class ladies. We may indeed generalize this view of truth, even suggesting that such "truth," if it does really exist as a separate entity, cannot be reached. Furthermore, a close reading of *Les*

Fausses Confidences shows that in Marivaux love is presented as of such a nature as inevitably to attract and stimulate deceit and self-deceit.

   The psychology of this theatre is not the relatively static psychology of crisis, as in the Classical theatre, but the dynamic psychology of development. The result is a dilution of the concept of fixed psychological identity, and a demonstration of the metamorphoses through which a character passes. All these traits — the scepticism as to the possibility of sincerity, the accessibility of truth and the reality of fixed psychological identity, together with the emphasis on deceit, self-deceit and comforting illusions — are of such a sophisticated nature and are portrayed in such a subtle manner as to lend strong support to the view of this theatre as rococo.

   The servants' failure to disguise their language convincingly (i.e., succeed in speaking as their masters do — for they do try) has a comic effect. The masters' failure to disguise their language to resemble that of the servants (they do not even try — except, of course, for the obligatory *tutoiement,* and this is adopted only reluctantly by the ladies) has no comic effect but an important, in fact essential, *dramatic* effect (of a psychological and social nature). The difference may lie in the fact that in their everyday life the masters are much more carefully masked than the servants.

   As we see from the passage quoted earlier from *La Surprise de l'amour*, the servants element provides a feet-on-the-ground version to counterbalance the otherwise possibly embarrassing, non-rococo lyricism (the rococo eliminated lyricism as it did all spontaneous expression of emotion) of Lélio's effusions. The author disclaims responsibility for such ridiculous naivety by provoking laughter at it. This is another illustration of the double thrust of the rococo, evident in the combination of subtle psychological exploration (*réflexions ennuyeuses*) and realistic lower-class dialogue (*détails ignobles*) in *La Vie de Marianne*, as in the combination of exquisitely decorated interior and relatively very sober exterior in rococo church architecture (Wies, Vierzehnheiligen).

   The theme of class-distinctions is another link between Congreve and Marivaux, and both dramatize this theme by cross-class role-playing in such plays as *Le Jeu de l'amour et du hasard*, where the servants Arlequin and Lisette change places with Dorante and Silvia, and *The Way of the World*, where Waitwell masquerades as Sir Rowland. But where Congreve merely disguises one member of the servant couple, Marivaux disguises both of them and also both of the upper-class lovers.[78]

   Marivaux's attitude to class-distinctions is actually very enlightened for his time, as we know from several of his plays, and finds an echo in *Il Ventaglio:*

Conte.	. . . un cavaliere, come son io, non arbitra e non dispone del cuor di una donna.
Coronato.	Finalmente è una contadina.
Conte.	Che importa questo? La donna à sempre donna; distinguo i gradi, le condizioni, ma in massima rispetto il sesso. (I, 5)

Goldoni was early described as the Italian Marivaux by critics such as Rabany[79] and Kennard[80] on the basis of his varied portraits and subtle analysis and because of his desire to develop a mode of realism that combines truth of observation with decency of expression. (*Il Ventaglio* was actually written and first produced in

France, under the title *L'Eventail*.) Consequently, it is not surprising to find him categorized as rococo by Momigliano and Hatzfeld, and his play *Il Ventaglio* may well stand as the Italian contribution to a style represented in other countries by *The Way of the World*, *Le Jeu de l'amour et du hasard* and *Die Laune des Verliebten*.

V

"Une Conversation sous un lustre"

The traditional view of Marivaux was that his theatre was *merely* "une conversation sous un lustre." This cliché was exploded by Roger Planchon,[81] who tried to show that it was *not* that. Our view is rather that it *is*, but not *merely*, "une conversation sous un lustre." It is the very serious *dialectique de l'intersubjectivité* which constitutes any human encounter, struggling with the limitations of language, while at the same time it is defined in part by the social and material circumstances of the eighteenth century (symbolized metonymically by the *lustre*) with the demands it places on subtlety and brilliance while at the same time it prescribes a studied negligence (the brilliance must appear improvised) suitable for a *conversation mondaine*.

Marivaux writes in defense of the style he adopts:

... C'est le ton de la conversation en général que j'ai tâché de prendre: ce ton-là a plu extrêmement et plaît encore dans les autres pièces, comme singulier, je crois; mais mon dessein était qu'il plût comme naturel, et c'est peut-être parce qu'il l'est effectivement qu'on le croit singulier, et que, regardé comme tel, on me reproche d'en user toujours.

On est accoutumé au style des auteurs, car ils en ont un qui leur est particulier: on n'écrit presque jamais comme on parle; la composition donne un autre tour à l'esprit; c'est partout un goût d'idées pensées et réfléchies dont on ne sent point l'uniformité, parce qu'on l'a reçu et qu'on y est fait: mais si par hasard vous quittez ce style, et que vous portiez le langage des hommes dans un ouvrage, et surtout dans une comédie, il est sûr que vous serez d'abord remarqué; et si vous plaisez, vous plaisez beaucoup, d'autant plus que vous paraissez nouveau: mais revenez-y souvent, ce langage des hommes ne vous réussira plus, car on ne l'a pas remarqué comme tel, mais simplement le vôtre, et on croira que vous vous répétez.

Je ne dis pas que ceci me soit arrivé: il est vrai que j'ai tâché de saisir le langage des conversations, et la tournure des idées familières et variées qui y viennent, mais je ne me flatte pas d'y être parvenu; j'ajouterai seulement, là-dessus, qu'entre gens d'esprit les conversations dans le monde sont plus vives qu'on ne pense, et que tout ce qu'un auteur pourrait faire pour les imiter n'approchera jamais du feu et de la naïveté fine et subtile qu'ils y mettent.[82]

Classical resistance to this language and rejection of this defense of it may be seen in critics like La Harpe, who defines "marivaudage" in the following terms: "Le mélange le plus bizarre de métaphysique subtile et de locutions triviales, de sentiments alambiqués et de dictons populaires; jamais on n'a mis autant d'apprêt à vouloir paraître simple, jamais on n'a retourné des pensées communes, de tant de manières plus affectées les unes que les autres; et ce qu'il y a de pis, ce langage hétéroclite est celui de tous les personnages sans distinction."[83]

It is remarkable that, in spite of this polarization, the manuals continue to perpetuate the myth of a purely, or at least a predominantly, Classical eighteenth century: "Le goût classique n'est pas détruit mais prolongé; Marivaux fait suite à Molière, Montesquieu et Voltaire parlent toujours la langue parfaite de La Fontaine et de Racine."[84] Nothing could be more superficial and misleading than such a statement, for Marivaux is not another Molière,[85] nor is the style of the chief writers of the eighteenth century that of the giants of the seventeenth. The delicate tracery of Marivaux's language is on the contrary quite distinctive and may well be considered rococo. It is the language of the rococo Parisian salon.

All the new developments in French society at the end of the Sun King's reign reflected a new ideal which replaced the formal reception by the intimate tête-à-tête, boredom and monotonous routine (typified by the court forms of Versailles) by whim, fancy, fantasy, the court by the salon. Above all, the age of the rococo is the age of the salon.[86] The salon was initiated as early as the mid-seventeenth century in France by the *précieuse* Madame de Rambouillet, and its ultimate roots are Italian. The important salons in the rococo period are those of the Duchesse du Maine (1699-1753: Chaulieu, La Fare, La Motte, Fontenelle, the young Voltaire), the Marquise de Lambert, *néo-précieuse* (1710-1733: Montesquieu, the Abbé de St. Pierre, Marivaux, Fontenelle, La Motte), and Madame de Tencin (1726-1749: the same guests as Mme de Lambert, plus Duclos, Helvétius, Marmontel). In general we may say of the salons that their founders are women, their aim is refinement, their manner is free and informal, light, nonchalant and urbane, and their occupation is primarily that high art of sophisticated conversation in which a studied negligence gives an appearance of effortless grace.[87]

The ludic qualities of rococo society and culture are well illustrated by the importance given to conversation in that society and the character of that conversation. As for the relationship between the salon and the individual, the latter is merely tolerated by the former. The rococo salon is not a place for *serious* conversation: masculine gravity and earnest discussion of profound human problems were considered pedantic and pretentious — and therefore ridiculous: "Tous les genres sont bons, hors le genre ennuyeux." The art of conversation was the art of embroidering upon a theme — a conception which put the emphasis on witty and graceful repartee. The change in the 1750's to serious conversation, political in subject and revolutionary in tone, marks the point at which the precarious balance of rococo society and culture is destroyed by the impact of such writers as Voltaire, Rousseau and Diderot.

This flourishing cult of conversation and dialogue also found expression in amateur theatre, a passion which embraced Watteau,[88] Voltaire,[89] the King himself,[90] the Marquise de Pompadour: "La cour n'est occupée que de plaisirs . . . On ne songe qu'à des comédies de cabinet, où la marquise de Pompadour déploie ses talents et ses grâces pour le théâtre," wrote d'Argenson in his *Journal* on January 7, 1748. The Prince de Ligne remarked: "Plus de dix de nos femmes du grand monde jouent et chantent mieux que ce que j'ai vu de mieux sur tous les théâtres."[91] Such amateur and aristocratic theatricals must also be given a part, however modest, in the spectrum of rococo modes of theatre.

Salon conversation was the stylistic model for French rococo, but what of that of England? London conversationalists were not *salonniers*, but they did have a particular kind of place to meet, and one which was central to the dissemination of such perfect vehicles of English rococo as *The Spectator*. This was the coffeehouse and its cousins, and they were a much more widespread and typical feature of London social life than of that of Paris. It is of course true that the early eighteenth century saw a wealth of locations in both London and Paris for the public consumption of coffee, tea and chocolate.[92] The Grecian is said to have been founded as early as 1652 for the dispensing of coffee; others included Will's, Child's, the Saint James', Squire's, Searle's, Jonathan's and Garroway's (the latter in 1657 brought the price of tea down to a level widely accessible), White's Chocolate House and The Cocoa-Tree. Their names appear in *The Tatler*,[93] *The Spectator* and elsewhere, and they catered to wits and politicians (Will's), authors, booksellers, physicians and clergymen (Child's), Whig statesmen, guardsmen and men of fashion (Saint James'), lawyers and Greek scholars (the Grecian), Tories (The Cocoa-Tree), merchants (Jonathan's and Garroway's).[94] In Paris, the most famous were the Procope (founded 1689), the Gradot and the Laurent. Just as Dryden had presided at Will's, so Duclos, Fontenelle and Diderot were to be seen at the Procope, La Motte and Maupertuis at the Gradot, Crébillon and J.-B. Rousseau at the Laurent. They were centres for informal social encounters and for the dissemination of information of all kinds, and hotbeds of excited literary and eventually political discussion, circulating banned writings and so on.[95] A crucial difference for English and French fashionable conversation resided in the much more dominant role of the coffeehouse in London (there were already some one thousand of them by 1707, whereas Paris could boast only three hundred even in 1715)[96] and, in the English capital, lack of influential salons providing the refining influence of the reigning — and always heeded — *maîtresse de salon*. Nothing could be more repugnant to the anti-pedantry prejudice of the French salon than the great English journals' catering to the specific interests of particular groups. Such particularism is related to that manners strain that is so strong in English Restoration comedy and so weak in the comedy of manners — almost purely psychological — of Marivaux. It is striking that a play like Congreve's *The Way of the World* has actually its first act set in a chocolate-house and that references to the consumption of chocolate and coffee recur in the play: "To the Dominion of the *Tea-Table*, I submit — But with *proviso*, that you exceed not in your province; but restrain yourself to Native and Simple *Tea-Table* drinks, as *Tea, Chocolate* and *Coffee*. As likewise to Genuine and Authoriz'd *Tea-Table* talk, such as mending of Fashions, spoiling Reputations, railing at absent Friends, and so forth" (IV, 1, lines 263-69). This interest in depicting the minutiae of habits skips France but is significant in Italy: the very first words of Goldoni's *Il Ventaglio* are "Che vi pare di questo caffè?" and the use of fans is reminiscent of the

English Restoration. Congreve evokes not only fans but masks, wigs *(perukes)* powdered hair, gambling at cards, fortune-hunting.

An extreme case of the intrusion of ugliness into the beautiful world of the rococo is provided in the following passage of Congreve:

> Out of my house, out of my house, thou *Viper*, thou *Serpent* . . . that I took from Washing of old Gause and Weaving of dead Hair, with a bleak blew Nose, over a Chafeing-dish of starv'd Embers and dining behind a Traverse Rag, in a shop no bigger than a Bird-cage — go, go, starve again, do, do. *(The Way of the World*, V, 1, lines 1-8.)

This is extreme even in Congreve. Needless to say, Marivaux excludes such elements completely from his theatre; but it is worth noting that he finds a place for *éléments ignobles* in his *novels* — witness the slanging-match between the laundrywoman and the coachman in *La Vie de Marianne*. The explanation is simply that the double thrust of the rococo is fully represented in such novels and in the plays of Congreve, whereas in the plays of Marivaux only one of the two elements — that of compensatory beauty and euphemization — is allowed to appear.

VI

Conclusion: An International Style with National Variations

The analysis of Marivaux, both textual and contextual, provides us with the best understanding of rococo style in the theatre, but to this we may reasonably add national variations in the style represented by Congreve, Goldoni and the young Goethe. Just as in rococo furniture we are struck by French subtlety and finesse (Cressent, Caffiéri, Schmitz, Slodtz, Oeben, Riesener), English vigor and elegance (Chippendale), Venetian opulence (Piffetti), and German fantasy (Bauer, Köhler, the Spindler brothers), so in rococo theatre we see national variations. In comparison with the delicate, sentimental idealism of Marivaux, Congreve's realism is coarse and cynical, whereas Goldoni is light and whimsical and Goethe's juvenile play is full of adolescent charm and pastoral simplicity.

Of course, even lesser works also participated in the style. They were often conscious of — and apparently self-conscious about — their inferiority, at least when compared with Classical models, and sometimes proclaimed a poor opinion of themselves and of all the non-Classical works being produced in Europe in the rococo period, as witness the following *Epilogue* to *The Tender Husband* from the pen of Richard Steele:

Britons, who constant War, with factious Rage,
For Liberty against each other wage,
From Foreign Insult save this *English* Stage.
No more th'*Italian* squaling Tribe admit,
In Tongues unknown; 'tis Popery in Wit.
The Songs (their selves confess) from *Rome* they bring;
And 'tis High-Mass, for ought you know, they Sing.
Husbands take Care, the Danger may come nigher,
The Women say their Eunuch is a Friar.
But is it not a serious Ill to see
Europe's great Arbiters so mean can be;
Passive, with an affected Joy to sit,
Suspend their native Taste of Manly Wit;
Neglect their Comic Humour, Tragic Rage,
For known Defects of Nature, and of Age.
Arise for shame, ye Conqu'ring *Britons* rise,
Such unadorn'd Effeminacy despise;
Admire (if you will doat on Foreign Wit)
Not what *Italians* Sing, but *Romans* Writ:
So shall less Works, such as to-Night's slight Play,
At your Command, with Justice die away:
'Till then forgive your Writers, that can't bear
You should such very *Tramontanes* appear,
The Nations, which contemn you, to revere.
Let *Anna*'s Soil be known for all its Charms;
As Fam'd for Lib'ral Sciences, as Arms:
Let those Derision meet, who would Advance
Manners, or Speech, from *Italy* or *France*;
Let them learn You, who wou'd your Favour find,
And English *be the Language of Mankind.*[97]

Contention is evident here between the rococo playwrights of England, Italy and France. However, it is such "less Works"[98] — comedies of manners "such as to-Night's slight Play" — which, coming after the great tragedies and comedies of Shakespeare, Corneille, Racine and Molière, make up the repertoire of European rococo theatre and its most representative exponents, Congreve, Marivaux, Goldoni and the young Goethe.

Patrick Brady
Rice University

Notes

[1] On rococo style in the plastic arts and poetry, see P. Brady, *Rococo Style versus Enlightenment Novel* (Geneva: Slatkine, 1981). On rococo style in the novel, see both the above-mentioned volume and *Structuralist Perspectives in Criticism of Fiction: Essays on* Manon Lescaut *and* La Vie de Marianne (Bern: Lang, 1978).

[2] Besides the comparisons with rococo painting, a few similar comments have been made linking eighteenth-century playwrights with contemporary composers. Thus Girdlestone writes of the "psychological delicacy" of the fifth-act scene with Castor and Telaira in Rameau's *Castor et Pollux*: "Such a scene is the eighteenth-century equivalent of *Pelléas et Mélisande* and the musical counterpart of certain scenes in the plays of Rameau's contemporary, Marivaux, and of later French playwrights like Musset and Giraudoux" (C. Girdlestone, *Jean-Philippe Rameau: His Life and Work* [London: Cassell, 1957], p. 225).

[3] J. Thuillier, *Fragonard* (Geneva: Skira, 1967), p. 137.

[4] G. Larroumet, *Marivaux, sa vie et ses œuvres* (Paris: Hachette, 1882), pp. 174-76.

[5] G. Deschamps, *Marivaux* (Paris: Hachette, 1897), pp. 5-6, 94-95.

[6] E. Lintilhac, *Histoire générale du théâtre en France* (Paris: Flammarion, 1909), IV, 360.

[7] Lintilhac, pp. 328-29 and p. 329, note 1.

[8] F. Neubert, "Französische Rokoko-Probleme," in *Hauptfragen der Romanistik: Festschrift für Ph. Aug. Becker* (Heidelberg, 1922), p. 278.

[9] G. Brandes, *Goethe* (Berlin: Erich Reiss, 1922), p. 32.

[10] F. Schürr, *Barock, Klassizismus und Rokoko in der französischen Literatur* (Leipzig: Teubner, 1928), pp. 38-39.

[11] M. Donnay, "Marivaux ou l'amour au XVIIIe siècle," *Revue des Vivants* (juin 1929), p. 867.

[12] P. Trahard, *Les Maîtres de la sensibilité française au XVIIIe siècle (1715-1789)* (Paris: Boivin, 1931-33), I, 45-46.

[13] R. Jamieson, *Marivaux: A Study in Sensibility* (New York: Columbia U.P., 1941), p. 90.

[14] X. de Courville, *Un Apôtre de l'art du théâtre au XVIIIe siècle: Luigi Riccoboni dit Lélio* (Paris: Droz, 1945), II, 175.

[15] Courville, p. 199. See also p. 191.

[16] P. Reboul, "Aspects dramatiques et romanesques du génie de Marivaux," *L'Information Littéraire* (nov.-dec. 1949), p. 176.

[17] A. Hauser, *The Social History of Art* (New York: Knopf, 1951), II, 527-28.

[18] G. Poulet, *Etudes sur le temps humain*, vol. II: *La Distance intérieure* (Paris: Plon, 1952), p. 3.

[19] H. Hatzfeld, *Literature Through Art* (New York: Oxford U.P., 1952), p. 108.

[20] O. Ruggiero, *Marivaux e il suo teatro* (Milano: Bocca, 1953), pp. xvii-xix.

[21] B. S. Meyers, *Art and Civilization* (New York: McGraw-Hill, 1957), p. 543.

[22] A. Chérel, *De Télémaque à Candide* (Paris: Del Duca, 1958), p. 98.

[23] A. Leroy, *La Civilisation française au XVIIIe siècle, 1700-1789* (Paris: Ventadour, 1958), pp. 218-19.

[24] J.-L. Bory, "La dramatisation d'un style," *Cahiers Renaud-Barrault*, No. 28 (janvier 1960), p. 21.

[25] E. Henriot, *Courrier littéraire: XVIIIe siècle* (Paris: Albin Michel, 1961), p. 73. On the important differences between Marivaux and Prévost, see our *Structuralist Perspectives*.

[26] G. Boissy and D. Folacci, *Les plus beaux poèmes d'amour* (Rio de Janeiro: Americ-Edit, n.d.), p. 115.

[27] S. O. Simches, *Le Romantisme et le goût esthétique du XVIIIe siècle* (Paris: P.U.F., 1964), p. 123.

[28] J.-P. Minguet, *Esthétique du rococo* (Paris: Vrin, 1966), p. 247.

[29] J. Thoraval *et al.*, *Les Grandes Etapes de la civilisation française* (Paris: Bordas, 1967), pp. 248-49.

[30] G. Zayed, *La Formation littéraire de Verlaine* (Genève: Droz, 1962), p. 324 and note 4.

[31] Minguet, *Esthétique*, p. 225.

[32] L. Gossman, "Literature and Society in the Early Enlightenment: The Case of Marivaux," *Modern Language Notes*, 82, No. 3 (May 1967), 328 and note 26.

[33] Gossman, p. 331 and note 27.

[34] W. H. Van Voris, *The Cultivated Stance: The Designs of Congreve's Plays* (Chester Springs, Pa.: Dufour, 1967), p. 164.

[35] Lintilhac, pp. 360-6l.

[36] Neubert, pp. 277-78.

[37] Schürr, p. 33.

[38] H. Kindermann, *Der Rokoko-Goethe* (Leipzig: Reclam, 1932), pp. 35-38.

[39] J. E. Hiller, "Lessing und Corneille: Rokoko und Barock," *Romanische Forschungen*, 47 (1933), 159-76.

[40] A. Momigliano, *Storia della letteratura italiana*, 8th ed. (Milano, 1959), p. 328.

[41] H. Hatzfeld, "Rokoko als literarischer Epochenstil in Frankreich," *Studies in Philology*, 35, (1938), 540.

[42] Jamieson, p. 90.

[43] H. Cysarz, "Literarisches Rokoko," in *Welträtsel im Wort: Studien zur Europäischen Dichtung und Philosophie* (Wien: Berglandverlag, 1948), pp. 125-67.

[44] Hauser, II, 31.

[45] J. L. Fischer, "L'Assise sociale des comédies de Marivaux," *Pragensia*, 1 (1959), 13.

[46] W. Binni, "Il rococò letterario," in *Manierismo, Barocco, Rococò* (Rome: Accademia Nazionale dei Lincei, 1962), p. 232.

[47] E. M. and O. S. Fleissner, *Der junge Goethe* (Boston: Houghton Mifflin, 1963), p. 74.

[48] Minguet, pp. 248-50.

[49] C. Pichois, "Littérature comparée et histoire littéraire: le cas de la France," in *Actes du IVe Congrès de l'Association Internationale de Littérature Comparée*, ed. F. Jost (Paris: Mouton, 1966), I, 361.

[50] O. Mandel, ed., *Seven Comedies by Marivaux* (Ithaca: Cornell U. P., 1968), pp. 14-15.

[51] Hatzfeld, pp. 82-97, 198-208.

[52] The only critic to find anything rococo in Beaumarchais beyond Chérubin is Hatzfeld (*op.cit.*, pp. 106-115).

[53] It inspired such plays as Farquhar's *The Beau's Stratagem*, Mary Pix's *The Beau Defeated or the Lucky Younger Brother* and Marivaux's *Le Petit-maître corrigé*.

[54] See Voisenon's *La Coquette fixée* and Dufresny's *La Coquette de village*. The latter contains a mini-theory of coquetry (I, 3; the text may be conveniently consulted in *Théâtre du XVIIIe siècle*, ed. J. Truchet [Paris: Gallimard, 1972], I, 291), as does Marivaux's novel *La Vie de Marianne*. See Marivaux, *Romans, contes et nouvelles*, ed. M. Arland (Paris: Gallimard, 1949), pp. 121-22. Subsequent quotations from *La Vie de Marianne* and *Le Paysan parvenu* are taken from this edition.

[55] C. Hoy, "The Effect of the Restoration on Drama," *Tennessee Studies in Literature*, 6, (1961), 87-89.

[56] Cf. G. Durand, *Les Structures anthropologiques de l'imaginaire*, 3rd ed. (Paris: Bordas, 1969), p. 450 and note 2.

[57] Hoy, pp. 88-89.

[58] Congreve's *The Judgment of Paris* was followed a half-century later by Wieland's *Das Urteil des Paris*. In the interval, Watteau painted the same subject, so typical of the rococo.

[59] V. P. Brady, *Love in the Theatre of Marivaux* (Geneva: Droz, 1970), pp. 259-64.

[60] T. S. Eliot, "Marivaux," in *Arts and Letters*, 2, No. 2 (Spring 1919), 82.

[61] A. Schiller, "*The School for Scandal*: The Restoration Unrestored," *PMLA*, 71, Part 1 (1956), 695.

[62] P. Seward, "Was the English Restoration Theatre significantly influenced by Spanish Drama?" *Revue de Littérature comparée*, 66, No. 1 (janvier-mars 1972), 123-24.

[63] E.g. A. Nicoll, *A History of Restoration Drama: 1660-1700*, 2nd ed. (Cambridge: Cambridge U.P., 1928), p. 185.

[64] L. Desvignes-Parent, *Marivaux et l'Angleterre* (Paris: Klincksieck, 1970).

[65] P. H. Lang, *Music in Western Civilization* (New York: Norton, 1941), p. 532. See also J. Bertaut, *La Vie littéraire en France au XVIIIe siècle* (Paris: Tallandier, 1954), p. 18 *et seq.*

[66] *Lettres persanes*, Letter CIX, in *Œuvres complètes*, ed. R. Caillois (Paris: Gallimard, 1973), I, 293.

[67] E. and J. Goncourt, *La Femme au XVIIIe siècle* (1862) (Paris: Charpentier, 1890), pp. 407-409.

[68] In countries spared the *précieux* influence that affected Marivaux, things are rather different. Thus in Goethe's rococo playlet *Die Laune des Verliebten*, it is the sensual (pleasure) and the emotional (love) that survive; indeed, the whole play is devoted to promoting the idea that these two can be mutually independent: "O zürne du mit ihr! sie machte sich so schön; / Ich war dem Mund so nah und konnt nicht widerstehn. / Doch kennst du mein Herz, mir kannst du das erlauben, / So eine kleine Lust wird dir mein Herz nicht rauben" (Sc. 9; in *Goethe's Werke*, IV, ed. W. Kayser, 10th ed. [München: Beck, 1981]). Indeed, even in Marivaux, the battle between two conceptions of love — the spiritual and the physical — evoked in the domain of poetry by such writers as Voisenon (*Discours sur la nécessité d'aimer*) and Yalden (*Advice to a Lover*) is to be found at centre stage in such plays as *L'Amour et la Vérité* and *La Réunion des amours*.

[69] Cf. "You're a Woman — One to whom Heav'n gave Beauty, when it grafted Roses on a Briar. You see the reflection of Heav'n in a Pond, and he that leaps at you is sunk" (Congreve, *Love for Love*, IV, 1, lines 634-37). For the theatre of Congreve, our references are to *The Complete Plays of William Congreve*, ed. H. Davis (Chicago: University of Chicago Press, 1967).

[70] For Marivaux's theatre, we refer throughout to Marivaux, *Théâtre complet*, ed. F. Deloffre (Paris: Garnier, 1968).

[71] *"Candida*: Ero agitata da due passioni contrarie. La vendetta mi voleva far vostra, e l'amore mi ridona ad Evaristo" (III, 16). Our quotations from *Il Ventaglio* are taken from *Commedie di Carlo Goldoni*, ed. N. Mangini (Torino: Unione Tipografico-Editrice Torinese, 1971), vol. III.

[72] The caprice (Laune) referred to in the title is the kiss given to Egle by Eridon (Sc. 8). Cf. the miniaturizing treatment of Milton's entrance of Delilah by Congreve in *The Way of the World* (II, 1, lines 323-25) in Mirabell's description of the arrival of Millamant. As for the fan, it inspired long poems by Pignotti (*Il Ventaglio*) and John Gay (*The Fan*).

[73] *Lettres sur les habitants de Paris*, in *Journaux et œuvres diverses* (Paris: Garnier, 1969), p. 28.

[74] For other plausible influences on Marivaux (*Le Triomphe de l'amour*, *L'Héritier de village*, *Les Fausses Confidences* and *Le Père prudent et équitable*, drawing respectively on Crowne's *Sir Courtly Nice* (1684), Burnaby's *The Modish Husband* (1702), Farquhar's *The Beau's Stratagem* (1707) and Taverner's *The Maid the Mistress* (1708), see Desvignes-Parent, *Marivaux et l'Angleterre*.

[75] "Uncertainty and Expectation are the Joys of Life . . . the Pleasure of a Masquerade is done when we come to shew Faces" (Congreve, *Love for Love*, IV, 1, lines 786-90).

[76] Catalogue of exhibition on *The Age of Rococo* (Munich: Herman Rinn, 1958), p. 34.

[77] *Forme et signification: Essais sur les structures littéraires de Corneille à Claudel* (Paris: Corti, 1962), pp. 45-64.

[78] Disguise is eliminated in *Il Ventaglio*, but there are still the pairs of lovers, one middle-class (Evaristo and Candida), one lower-class (Crespino and Giannina), *cittadini* (e.g., Candida) and *contadini* (e.g., Giannina). Even this is lost in the pastoral world of *Die Laune des Verliebten*, where both couples (Eridon and Amine, Lamon and Egle) are equal.

[79] C. Rabany, *Carlo Goldoni: Le Théâtre et la vie en Italie au XVIIIe siècle* (Paris: Berger-Levrault, 1896), p. 3.

[80] J. S. Kennard, *Goldoni and the Venice of His Time* (New York: Macmillan, 1920), p. 398, note 2.

[81] See V. P. Brady, "Producing and Interpreting Marivaux," *Australian Journal of French Studies*, 4, No. 1 (1967), 52-61.

[82] "Avertissement" to *Les Serments indiscrets*, in *Théâtre complet*, I, 967.

[83] Quoted in Ruggiero, pp. 197-98.

[84] Thoraval, p. 192.

[85] See V. P. Brady, *Love in the Theatre of Marivaux*.

[86] G. de Reynold, *Synthèse du XVIIe siècle* (Paris: Editions du Conquistador, 1962), p. 298. On the salon, see among others L. Battifol *et al.*, *The Great Literary Salons: XVII and XVIII Centuries*, trans. M. Robinson (London: Butterworth, 1930); C. B. Tinker, *The Salon and English Letters* (New York: Gordian Press, 1967).

[87] See G. Duby and R. Mandrou, *Histoire de la civilisation française* (Paris: A. Colin, 1958), II, 113.

[88] Cf. the oft-noted influence of the commedia dell'arte in Watteau.

[89] "La mimomanie est répandue dans toute la société: chaque hôtel a ses tréteaux, permanents ou improvisés; il y en a au Temple, chez le prince de Conti; Voltaire en fait installer à Ferney" (Minguet, p. 247).

[90] Louis XV took part in several plays in 1747. See P. Lacroix, *France in the Eighteenth Century* (New York: Ungar, 1963), p. 414 (original French ed. 1875).

[91] This passage and the preceding one are quoted by Minguet, p. 247.

[92] See J. M. Doggett, "A Strange Sort of Liquor Called Coffee," *Forum*, 3, No. 7 (Summer 1961), 43-46.

[93] E.g.: "All Accounts of Gallantry, Pleasure, and Entertainment shall be under the Article of White's Chocolate-house; Poetry, under that of Will's Coffee-house; Learning, under the title of the Grecian; Foreign and Domestic news you will have from Saint James' Coffee-house" (*The Tatler*, No. 1).

[94] Bond (quoting Miège) in notes to *The Spectator* (Oxford: Clarendon, 1965), I, 4 (1 March 1711).

[95] See H. Westerfrölke, *Englische Kaffeehäuser als Sammelpunkte der literarischen Welt im Zeitalter von Dryden und Addison* (Jena: Frommann, 1924).

[96] *The Spectator*, I, 3.

[97] *The Plays of Richard Steele*, ed. S. Kenny (Oxford: Clarendon Press, 1971), p. 273.

[98] French plays that may possibly be considered rococo include: Fontenelle: *Psyché* (1678), *Bellérophon* (1679), *La Comète* (1681), *Thétis et Pelée* (1689), *Enée et Lavinie* (1690), *Idalie* (1720), *Henriette* (1740); Fatouville: *Arlequin Empereur dans la lune* (1684), *Le Banqueroutier* (1689); Dancourt: *Le Chevalier à la mode* (1687), *La Parisienne* (1691); Dufresny: *L'Esprit de contradiction* (1700), *La Coquette de village* (1702); Coypel: *La Princesse d'Elide* (1718); Autreau: *L'Amante romanesque* (1718), *Le Naufrage au port à l'anglais* (1718), *Les Amants ignorants* (1720), and a few other plays by authors like Favart (*La Chercheuse d'esprit*, *Le Coq de village*) and Voisenon (*La Coquette fixée*). English plays include: James Miller: *Harlequin-Horace* (1731), *The Man of Taste* (1735); James Bramston: *The Man of Taste* (1733); Paul Whitehead: *Manners* (1739).

Le Discours de la séduction dans le théâtre de Marivaux

"Toutes les comédies de Marivaux se ressemblent . . . Chacun ici cherche sa vérité, se trouve."[1] Sans doute; mais à trop privilégier cette quête de l'authenticité qui semble avoir été l'obsession du dramaturge moraliste, ne risque-t-on pas de manquer l'essentiel? de négliger ce qui aujourd'hui fait la modernité de Marivaux et qui consiste dans la mise en scène d'un discours qui cherche moins à *faire savoir* qu'à *faire désirer*, moins à dire la vérité qui de toutes façons finira par éclater qu'à *faire jouir*: discours de séduction extrêmement subtil chargé de restituer le malaise que chacun éprouve à ce moment de l'histoire vis-à-vis de soi, de l'autre et du monde, et qui, se prenant soi-même pour fin, conteste d'abord le réel pour en devenir le producteur: discours tout à la fois humoristique et érotique qui combine le plaisir du jeu et le plaisir de jouir, et qui sait d'instinct que tous les signes sont réversibles: apparence et profondeur, naturel et coquetterie, masque et visage, indifférence et intérêt, haine et amour, sincérité et hypocrisie, vérité et mensonge, pouvoir et faiblesse.

Certes, en jouant de ces retournements, le discours marivaudien conduit le personnage à sa vérité en même temps qu'il finit par dépouiller la réalité de ses faux-semblants; mais il a surtout pour effet, en faisant jouer entre eux des signes linguistiques pris à leur propre piège et qui agissent comme des leurres sur les protagonistes, de susciter et d'aiguiser en eux un désir et un plaisir de parler; de parler de ce désir et de ce plaisir qui provoquent à leur insu des glissements de parole et des dérapages de sens, subvertissant les rapports d'opposition par des rapports de séduction. Ce sont quelques-uns des aspects et des fonctions de ce discours séducteur de structure spéculaire, tout à la fois jeu et destin, que nous voudrions analyser.

Ce discours marivaudien, nous le voyons naître d'une double méfiance: à l'égard du réel et à l'égard d'une rhétorique littéraire traditionnelle.
La réalité crue et triviale, Marivaux ne l'ignore pas. Voici Jacob, le héros du *Paysan parvenu* à table face à deux fausses dévotes:

Jamais elles n'avaient d'appétit; du moins on ne voyait point celui qu'elles avaient; il escamotait les morceaux . . .
On voyait ces dames se servir négligemment de leurs fourchettes, à peine avaient-elles la force d'ouvrir la bouche; elles jetaient des regards indifférents sur ce bon vivre: Je n'ai point de goût aujourd'hui. Ni moi non plus. Je trouve tout fade. Et moi tout trop salé.
Ces discours-là me jetaient de la poudre aux yeux, de manière que je croyais voir les créatures les plus dégoûtées du monde, et cependant le résultat de tout cela était que les plats se trouvaient si considérablement diminués quand on desservait, que je ne savais les premiers jours comment ajuster tout cela.
Mais je vis à la fin de quoi j'avais été les premiers jours dupe. C'était ces airs de dégoût, que marquaient nos maîtresses, et qui m'avaient caché la sourde activité de leurs dents.[2]

Cette réalité, si soigneusement occultée aux yeux de Jacob par la coquetterie des deux vieilles filles, c'est celle d'un féroce désir de vivre qui renvoie l'individu à l'espèce et qui s'incarne aussi bien dans la mastication que dans l'appétit sexuel, agressif, dévorateur. Réalité toujours scandaleuse, car elle manifeste sous les goûts et les raffinements appris la permanence d'instincts brutaux, sous l'ordre civil et mondain ostensiblement affiché un ordre sauvage jamais dompté, sous le langage choisi, euphémisant ou oblique de l'être civilisé, le grondement naturel de l'animal refoulé: lever les masques sur cette réalité désormais appréhendée dans sa véracité, dissiper les apparences trompeuses pour faire apparaître ce qui semble se donner comme la vérité première et définitive de l'être, son véritable sens, serait tentant. "Mais que gagnerai-je à cela?" se demande le narrateur du *Voyageur dans le Nouveau Monde*. "En me faisant connaître les hommes, vous allez me dégoûter d'eux . . . Je sais bien en gros que les hommes sont faux; que dans chaque homme il y en a deux, pour ainsi dire: l'un qui se montre, et l'autre qui se cache . . . mais ne dérangeons point l'ordre des choses, n'anticipons point sur les spectacles. Si de même que nos corps sont habillés, nos âmes à présent le sont aussi à leur manière, le temps du dépouillement des âmes arrivera, comme le temps du dépouillement de nos corps arrive quand nous mourons."[3] Psychologue et moraliste, Marivaux est lucide sur les hommes et le monde, mais l'homme de théâtre qu'il est avant toutes choses sait que la levée des incertitudes, des ambiguïtés et des secrets réduit le monde à n'être plus qu'un système objectif de rapports et de fonctions, le renvoie à une radicale et insupportable obscénité. D'autre part, comment se fier à ses sensations, les exprimer en un langage qui ne mente pas, quand le temps nous en apporte sans cesse de nouvelles? Croyant parler de soi, ne parle-t-on pas toujours d'un autre? Mieux, la peur de se tromper sur soi, sur l'autre, sur le monde ne pousse-t-elle pas à l'erreur, comme il advient à ces sincères de profession, la marquise et Ergaste, dont les propos "sincères" sont la pire des faussetés? Ne finissent-ils pas par être dupes de leur volonté de ne pas l'être? "Gardez vos découvertes,"[4] enchaîne le narrateur: peu intéressé, voire dégoûté par ces révélations somme toute prévisibles et dépourvues de romanesque sur la nature humaine, dans l'incertitude d'atteindre et de cerner une vérité complexe et fuyante, Marivaux pense qu'il n'est ni possible, ni souhaitable "d'arracher définitivement les masques, de revenir à un état . . . de sincérité et d'innocence"[5] absolues.

C'est aussi contre un certain langage littéraire synonyme de conventions et d'artifices que s'exerce la méfiance de Marivaux. Quel crédit en effet accorder à une passion qui s'enveloppe de toutes les emphases et de toutes les impostures galantes,[6] qui se dit à travers les mots de *Cyrus* ou de *Cléopâtre*,[7] qui apparaît "formée de tout ce qu'on peut imaginer en sentiments, langueurs, soupirs, transports, délicatesses, douce impatience, et le tout ensemble; pleurs de joie au moindre regard favorable, torrents de larmes au moindre coup d'œil un peu froid"?[8] Hortense, dégrisée, n'est plus prête à se laisser prendre au spectacle d'un amour qui se donne comme la représentation bien littéraire de ce qu'il n'est pas. Certes, "le désir est un fait biologique"[9] que les personnages de Marivaux, à l'instar des pèlerins de Watteau, ne songent à nier, mais il y a en eux une peur d'aimer,[10] d'éprouver cette passion dans laquelle se sont "embarquées" les grandes héroïnes de Racine pour leur malheur, et qui, pour reprendre les propos de Lélio dans la première *Surprise*, ravit aux hommes leur raison, leur liberté, leur repos, les ravit à eux-mêmes et fait d'eux "des pauvres fous, des hommes troublés, ivres de douleur ou de joie" (I, 2). En même temps qu'ils refusent cette tragédie de la passion qui les ferait "tomber dans ces malheureuses situations si pleines de troubles, d'inquiétudes, de chagrins" (III, 2) qui effraient tant la comtesse, ils refusent aussi d'être dupes de clichés linguistiques à la mode qui ont pour objet de faire passer pour l'amour la comédie de l'amour. Méfiance à l'égard de la passion, réalité que l'homme ne maîtrise pas; méfiance à l'égard du langage, réalité que l'homme maîtrise trop bien: la voie est étroite pour le personnage marivaudien qui aspire à l'amour, mais ne veut s'y brûler, qui doute des paroles mais redoute encore plus le silence. "M'aimez-vous beaucoup?" demande la marquise à Dorante dans *Les Sincères*, "ne m'aimez-vous guère? faites-vous semblant de m'aimer? c'est ce que je ne saurais décider" (Sc. 11): tel est dans le théâtre bavard de Marivaux le tourment de personnages égarés dans un labyrinthe d'apparences et de mensonges, où celui qui se pique de sincérité n'est pas toujours celui qui ment le moins.

Pour Marivaux, la vérité, qui n'est au fond que de l'ordre du biologique, du physiologique ou du rapport de forces (rapports maîtres-valets, parents-jeunes gens), est donc décevante ou dangereuse; s'identifie-t-elle avec l'amour, elle n'apparaît pour ses héros, contemporains de Casanova, que comme la forme désenchantée du désir. Puisque tout est fini quand on sait et que l'on possède, il vaut mieux ne pas savoir et ne s'exposer ni à posséder ni à être possédé. La réalité ou ce qui en tient lieu, les héros de Marivaux ne cesseront de la tenir à distance, de la différer, voire de l'escamoter. Comment? Par le recours à un langage conçu comme le lieu d'un jeu et d'un enjeu: jeu d'apparences, de simulacres, d'énoncés en trompe-l'œil dont l'enjeu consiste à éprouver, à maîtriser, à sublimer le désir, à rendre séduisant ce qui ne l'est plus (l'amour dans *La Surprise*), ce qui ne l'est pas encore (l'amour dans *Le Jeu*), ce qui devrait n'avoir aucune chance de l'être (l'amour de Dorante pour Araminte dans *Les Fausses Confidences*). De là une dramaturgie de la séduction qui met en scène deux êtres au rôle bien défini: la femme, séduisante et séductrice, dont le cœur "se donne sa secousse à lui-même,"[11] et qui a mille manières naturelles et/ou artificielles de renouveler la réalité, de rendre au langage une incomparable virginité, "ici par une impatience, par une froideur, par une imprudence, par une distraction, en baissant les yeux, en les relevant, en sortant de sa place, en y restant"; l'homme, son contraire, qui a besoin d'être séduit pour exister: "eau dormante qui attend qu'on la remue pour remuer," l'être du sens et du bon sens, de la méthode et de la règle, faisant "l'amour réglément, tout comme on fait une charge . . . parce que c'est le devoir de [son] emploi," et pour qui la réalité — celle de son désir comme celle de l'objet désiré — ne serait sans le jeu de la femme que ce qu'elle est: quelque chose qui tend inéluctablement à se décolorer, voire à se nier. Que Marivaux, moraliste, ait cru voir dans la jeune fille qu'il surprit devant son miroir "les machines de l'Opéra"[12] et qu'il lui retirât aussitôt son amour, n'a guère d'importance; Marivaux, dramaturge, admet bien volontiers, semble-t-il, que la femme se définit par une indistinction de la surface et de la profondeur, de l'authentique et de l'artifice et que c'est justement cette indistinction qui compose la féminité naturelle de la femme, la rend séduisante aux yeux des hommes attendant d'être "remués" par son "aimable désordre d'idées," et lui permet, comme en se jouant, de retourner les situations et les êtres et de se soumettre les Lélio et les Arlequin.

Dans le théâtre de Marivaux, ce qui circule entre l'homme et la femme, sous les arabesques du dialogue, c'est un pathétique besoin de séduire, d'être séduit, d'apprivoiser et d'enchanter le monde qu'ils soupçonnent de ne pouvoir combler leurs désirs ou leurs rêves, dont ils redoutent la part d'inconnu, mais auquel ils sentent bien qu'ils ne peuvent échapper en dépit d'une peur ou d'une méfiance qui les pousse à d'éphémères tentatives de fuite. Comme cela apparaît dans *La Surprise de l'amour*, où, malgré leurs résolutions, Lélio et Arlequin devront bien finir par rentrer dans la société et y retrouver le commerce des femmes; dans *La Double Inconstance*, où, quoi qu'elle en ait, l'innocente Silvia ne peut empêcher que le Prince l'ait vue et remarquée; dans *Le Prince travesti*, où son expérience matrimoniale malheureuse et l'amitié de la Princesse ne sauraient fermer Hortense à l'amour de Lélio; dans *Le Jeu de l'amour et du hasard*, où Silvia craint que le mari que son père lui destine ne lui convienne pas; dans *Le Triomphe de l'amour*, où Léonide-Phocion veut faire oublier à Agis qu'elle est "née d'un sang qu'il doit haïr" (I, 1); dans *Les Fausses Confidences*, où l'amour de Dorante risque de se heurter chez Araminte à une "fierté" liée à sa richesse et à son rang; dans *La Dispute*, où quatre enfants qui ont été autoritairement retirés du monde, ignorants et innocents, vont avoir "la liberté de sortir de leur enceinte, et de se connaître" (Sc. 2).

Ces situations inconfortables, ces obstacles, contraintes, menaces, ce sont là les aléas obligés de la vie en société auxquels les personnages vont riposter par une stratégie de la séduction seule capable, sans violence ni drame, de résorber les antagonismes, de faire tomber les barrières de classe ou d'argent (*La Double Inconstance*, *Les Fausses Confidences*), de vaincre les aversions (*La Surprise*), de transmuer en amour l'hostilité ou l'indifférence (*Le Triomphe de l'amour*), de convertir en *oui* le *non* au mariage et de fondre dans un mari un homme raisonnable et un galant homme (*Le Jeu de l'amour et du hasard*). Ne s'agit-il pas toujours pour le personnage de séduire qui l'a déjà séduit? ou de séduire pour être séduit? "Franchement, je ne haïrais pas de lui plaire," dit la Silvia du *Jeu* de Dorante, ce futur mari qui l'inquiète en dépit de toutes les qualités qu'on lui attribue, "je ne serais pas fâchée de subjuguer sa raison, de l'étourdir un peu . . . si mes charmes font ce coup-là ils me feront plaisir, je les estimerai" (I, 5). Relever le défi du monde ou de l'autre par le défi du langage, c'est toute l'affaire de cette rhétorique de la séduction qualifiée naguère de marivaudage et devenue la matière même de l'action dramatique qui, dans le théâtre de Marivaux plus que dans tout autre théâtre, repose donc moins sur des actes que, pour reprendre un concept austinien, sur des actes de langage.

A l'origine du discours de séduction marivaudien, comme un principe générateur et moteur, il y a deux données essentielles — l'absence et le retardement — matérialisées par les différentes formes du masque. Qu'il soit réel (*Le Jeu*), verbal (*La Surprise*), ou psychologique (*Les Serments indiscrets*), le masque est toujours absence: absence du visage, donc d'être, absence de tout état civil, donc d'identité sociale, négation du temps, donc de l'enracinement et de la promesse, refus de la profondeur et du sens, primat du "hic et nunc," des apparences et du jeu sur la durée, le réel et le sérieux, triomphe de la simulation (Phocion) sur la production innocente, ridicule ou pathétique de ses désirs (Hermocrate et Lé-ontine): "Tant pis pour elle aussi, si elle me fait obstacle; je ne lui ferai pas plus de quartier qu'à son frère."[13] Comme tel, le masque est le premier élément d'un processus immoral, frivole, superficiel de l'ordre des signes et des apparences,[14] voué aux plaisirs et doué d'un immense pouvoir de séduction qui devient un tout aussi immense pouvoir de subversion. Mais avant d'exercer sa puissance, le masque se donne comme l'expression théâtrale d'un échec ou, ce qui revient au même, de la crainte d'un échec:[15] de là sa connotation tout autant sexuelle que sociologique. Si le masque que portent les héros de Marivaux traduit en effet leur difficulté à s'ajuster à la réalité, à centrer leur personnalité,[16] à se connaître, à se situer, à se fixer dans une société décrite depuis Dancourt comme un bal masqué, il nous introduit aussi dans la problématique du sexe et de l'érotisme chez Marivaux. S'il est vrai, comme le prétend Lacan, que "le ratage lui-même peut être défini comme ce qui est sexuel dans tout acte humain,"[17] le masque s'érotise de n'être qu'un acte manqué: le Prince n'ose avouer qui il est de peur d'échouer auprès de Silvia et de perdre quelque chose du plaisir que sa tendresse pouvait lui faire;[18] Silvia bronche devant un mariage qui la tente, puis s'irrite sous son masque d'être obligée à tout moment d'oublier qu'elle écoute avec tant de plaisir celui qu'elle prend pour un valet;[19] Léonide-Phocion et Léonide-Aspasie (dans *Le Triomphe de l'amour*) promettent à Léontine et Hermocrate ce qu'elles ne pourront jamais tenir . . . : je (Silvia) te suis promise, mais tu (Dorante) ne me possèdes pas; je jouis de t'entendre, mais je joue à me retirer; je (Phocion-Aspasie) t'appelle (Léontine-Hermocrate) et te conduis à la jouissance, mais tu ne jouiras jamais de moi qui joue avec toi: avec le masque s'ouvre l'espace du défi, l'espace non du désir, mais du jeu sur le désir. Jeu mouvant qui est tout autant de l'ordre du signe que du sexe, stratégie de détournement de la force du désir, de déplacement de la vérité du sexe, à travers laquelle s'exerce la souveraineté de la séduction:

La comtesse. Tout hérissé de rancune que vous croyez être, moyennant deux ou trois coups d'œil flatteurs qu'il m'en coûterait . . . vous m'allez donner la comédie.

Lélio. Oh! je vous défie de me faire payer ce tribut de folie-là . . .

La comtesse. Non, la partie ne me pique point, je la tiens gagnée.[20]

Portant dans ses plis les traces ou la peur d'un ratage, développant vis-à-vis de la réalité une stratégie d'avances et de replis, de provocations et de fuites, d'agressions et d'effacements, comme s'il craignait à tout moment d'être dévoilé, bloqué ou mis en déroute, le masque est tout pénétré d'un implicite sexuel qui, sans qu'on y prenne garde, diffuse un trouble érotique sur les comportements et les dialogues des personnages de Marivaux. Jouant et jouissant de cet implicite sexuel d'autant plus efficace qu'il demeure innommé et qu'on l'empêche d'éclater au grand jour, le porteur de masque est avant tout autre séduit par le masque qu'il s'est confectionné, car si ce masque, à l'origine, manifeste l'inquiétude de son désir, il est aussi ce par quoi ce désir, croyant ne pas être découvert, s'exprimera sans inquiétude: "Tiens, Bourguignon," déclare Silvia, déguisée en Lisette, "une bonne fois pour toutes, demeure, va-t'en, reviens, tout cela doit m'être indifférent, et me l'est en effet, je ne te veux ni bien ni mal, je ne te hais, ni ne t'aime, ni ne t'aimerai, à moins que l'esprit ne me tourne . . . Tu me parles, je te réponds, c'est beaucoup, c'est trop même, tu peux m'en croire, et si tu étais instruit, en vérité, tu serais content de moi, tu me trouverais d'une bonté sans exemple, d'une bonté que je blâmerais dans une autre . . . Le souvenir de tout ceci me fera bien rire un jour."[21] Langue érotique par excellence, car elle est celle d'un désir qui se cache pour mieux se désirer et qui désire son propre langage. Un langage conçu comme la périphrase du désir, où les dehors trompeurs dissimulent mais laissent entendre qu'ils dissimulent, où le sentiment qui n'ose s'avouer à lui-même redoute d'être déçu, se faufile au travers d'une rhétorique à double entente tout à la fois dévoilante et occultante qui devient le champ même de l'érotisme.

Même s'il lui arrive d'avoir honte de lui-même,[22] ce qui fait l'extrême séduction du masque, c'est cette manière ironique qu'il a de défier le monde et de l'inciter à se conformer à des désirs tapis sous sa surface spécieuse, dût-il pour y parvenir bousculer quelque peu l'ordre social et naturel.[23]

Dans la plupart de ses comédies, en effet, comme un principe moteur, Marivaux loge au creux de son discours le défi. Défi engendrant une parole qui à son tour semble avoir pour fin de l'entretenir et de le renouveler jusqu'à l'extrême limite. C'est dire que ce retournement du défi de la parole en parole de défi est lié à la technique du retardement. Procédant d'une absence, d'une négation ou d'un refus, impliquant toujours un écart par rapport à la réalité, le masque devient comme tel, du fait de son irréalisme, producteur non d'une action, mais d'une parole, ou plutôt d'actes de paroles — les railleries réciproques de Lélio et de la comtesse dans *La Surprise* ou les promesses de Phocion à Hermocrate dans *Le Triomphe de l'amour* — qui ont pour principal objet de retarder le plus possible, tout en les permettant, le passage à l'action, le contact avec la réalité. Dans la plupart des comédies de Marivaux, il n'est question que de l'amour. Mais qu'est-ce que l'amour pour Lélio trahi par sa maîtresse, pour Hortense "humiliée, rebutée, abandonnée"[24] par un mari qui fut pourtant un parfait amant? Désireux d'aimer et d'être aimés, ils vont différer jusqu'au bout le moment où ils devront se dire à eux-mêmes et avouer à l'autre leur amour.[25] "Que d'amour!":[26] tout le discours marivaudien fait de ce savoir une fête, mais plus important encore, le retardement calculé de ce savoir, jusqu'à l'excès (*Le Jeu*), jusqu'à la cruauté (*L'Epreuve*), fait aussi du discours une fête: en témoigne le délire verbal,[27] explosion de joie et de liberté, qui prend Silvia quand au troisième acte du *Jeu*, connaissant l'identité de Dorante, elle décide néanmoins, presque gratuitement, de poursuivre le jeu. Puisqu'elle sait et qu'elle n'a plus rien à craindre — "Dorante est vaincu; j'attends mon captif" (III, 4) — se développe alors seulement le jeu rituel de la séduction pure, au cours duquel Silvia, de ruses en surenchères, retarde le plus possible, pour sa jouissance personnelle, l'aveu que pourtant elle sollicite et brûle d'entendre. C'est que l'amour de Dorante n'est pas seulement l'enjeu de ce tournoi, il a toujours été, et il l'est encore bien davantage depuis qu'elle n'en peut plus douter, ce qui permet à Silvia de jouer: sous l'habit de Lisette, dont elle joue plus que jamais non sans cruauté comme d'un leurre, il ne s'agit plus uniquement pour elle d'aimer ou d'être aimée — ce qui est acquis — mais de séduire: c'est-à-dire de capter, par pur amour-propre de séductrice,[28] tout le désir de Dorante, de réduire par une surenchère de provocations toute volonté, toute résistance chez l'amant séduit, de soumettre par la force même de la séduction celui qui a toutes les raisons de résister — "il pense qu'il chagrinera son père en m'épousant, il croit trahir sa fortune et sa naissance" — de le rendre fou en l'obligeant à répondre à un défi et à surenchérir sur une surenchère: "il faut que j'arrache ma victoire et non pas qu'il me la donne" (III, 4). Portée tout entière en ce troisième acte par la joie exubérante et folle du jeu — "Ah! ah! ah! que ton cœur a de caquet ma sœur, quelle éloquence" (III, 4), lui dit Mario — Silvia oublie qu'en matière de séduction les jeux ne sont jamais faits, car dans ce mouvement irrésistible qui la pousse à séduire davantage Dorante pour être davantage séduite, il n'y a ni sujet, ni objet: tour à tour les deux jeunes gens sont emportés jusqu'au vertige dans un tournoiement de leurres, à la fois maîtres et victimes de leur mise en jeu d'actes de paroles: le savoir, appelé et différé, produit et producteur d'une stratégie d'incitation et d'excitation, est bien, comme l'écrit par ailleurs Shoshana Felman, "ce qui se donne à goûter dans un festin du langage."[29] Séduire, se séduire pour Silvia comme pour Don Juan, c'est donc "faire durer, à l'intérieur d'une parole désirante, la performance jouissive de la production même de cette parole";[30] c'est, en multipliant les antiphrases, les doubles ententes, les dérivations, les omissions, bref, en mettant en balance toutes les figures d'un discours oblique, exalter sa vie dans un présent toujours ravivé, réunir "dans un court laps de temps, une succession d'instants très rapprochés, de plaisirs presque enchaînés, si bien que la conscience ravie ne reste pas une seconde inoccupée"[31] et que le désir, dans ces jeux du langage et du hasard, ne cesse de se diversifier et de se renouveler.

Pas de meilleurs exemples de cette pratique ludique et érotique de la parole que *La Surprise de l'amour* et *Les Acteurs de bonne foi*. Ici et là, en effet, on ne se propose ouvertement, pour toute activité, que de produire un discours, mondain dans *La Surprise*, théâtral dans *Les Acteurs de bonne foi*: seul et même discours qui, devant n'être qu'un intermède, divertissant si possible, se donne à l'origine comme un jeu sans conséquence sur le discours: "Comme à la campagne il faut voir quelqu'un, soyons amis pendant que nous y resterons: je vous promets sûreté: nous nous divertirons, vous à médire des femmes et moi à mépriser les hommes,"[32] déclare la Comtesse. Quant à Lisette dans *Les Acteurs de bonne foi*, ce qu'elle aime de la comédie que ses amis vont jouer avec elle, "c'est, dit-elle, que nous la donnerons à nous-mêmes; car je pense que nous allons tenir de jolis propos" (Sc. 2). Mais quelles que soient les résolutions dans *La Surprise* ou les précautions dans *Les Acteurs*, le jeu n'est pas innocent, et la parole qui se voudrait conventionnelle, neutre, sans poids ni conséquence, s'enchaîne et tourbillonne avec allégresse sous l'effet d'une logique malicieuse qui sans cesse la relance jusqu'à faire perdre la tête à ceux qui croyaient la maîtriser — "Et moi je ne sais plus où j'en suis,"[33] se plaint Lisette dès le premier moment — et subrepticement, à l'insu du destinateur et du destinataire, elle se charge d'une épaisseur de vie propre à jeter le trouble: "Nous surprendrons,"[34] annonce Merlin avec quelque raison; et tout le monde est surpris! C'est qu'en effet le masque mondain, comme le masque de théâtre d'où cette parole est proférée, n'est pas vide. Sous l'indifférence ennuyée de Lélio et de la Comtesse dans *La Surprise* grouillent des peurs, des désirs, des frustrations et quelle que méfiances; sous les personnages stéréotypés de la comédie dans *Les Acteurs* et sous le vernis de leurs propos se cachent d'authentiques caractères (Sc. 2): de là l'équivoque, fascinante pour le locuteur même, d'un discours en porte à faux, qui, d'une part, veut apparaître comme un pur discours de comédie ou s'évertue à manifester le détachement ironique,[35] l'impersonnalité,[36] la superficialité et l'*insignifiance*[37] du parfait discours mondain, et qui, d'autre part, ne peut pas ne pas trahir les secrets du cœur, les palpitations de la sensibilité, les mouvements du désir. Sans doute le discours latent fait-il dire au discours manifeste ce qu'il ne veut pas dire, mais celui-ci ne dément-il pas en raison de son caractère fonctionnel ou ludique ce sens et ce sérieux qui semblent le traverser? Comme les héros de Beckett, plus de deux siècles plus tard, est-ce que, à ne rien vouloir signifier, les personnages de Marivaux ne sont pas en train de signifier? Ou bien à vouloir signifier quelque chose, ne sont-ils pas en train de signifier autre chose?

> *Blaise.* Pourquoi te hâtes-tu tant d'être amoureuse de Monsieur Merlin? Est-ce que tu en sens de l'amour?
> *Colette.* Mais vrament! je sis bien obligée d'en sentir, pisque je sis obligée d'en prendre dans la comédie. Comment voulez-vous que je fasse autrement?[38]

Charmes érotiques de l'équivoque, du miroitement de signes contradictoires où vient se prendre le désir, du jeu de cache-cache entre le mot et la chose sécrétant une délicieuse jouissance:

> *Merlin.* Allons, continuons, et attendez que je me déclare tout à fait, pour vous montrer sensible à mon amour.
> *Colette.* J'attendrai, Monsieur Merlin; faites vite.
> *Merlin, recommençant la scène.* Que vous êtes aimable . . .[39]

Le propre du langage marivaudien est de poursuivre le plus longtemps possible le jeu de l'indécidable, de livrer les personnages aux vertiges d'un discours spéculaire qui ne cesse de produire en lui-même des écarts, des distances intérieures, des dérivations par où l'amour se faufile sur le mode de l'apparition/disparition et dans son scintillement discontinu prend une conscience de plus en plus aiguë de lui-même. Le langage stéréotypé de la Comédie, dans *Les Acteurs de bonne foi*, se donne comme un simulacre ironique,[40] et de même que les désinvoltures de la Comtesse dans *La Surprise*, que les habiletés et les provocations de Flaminia dans *La Double Inconstance*, que les révélations calculées de Dubois dans *Les Fausses Confidences*, il fonctionne comme un leurre dessinant au-devant des protagonistes un espace linguistique ouvert et magnétique où les mots portés par leur propre ambiguïté, s'appelant l'un l'autre, tirant à eux, tirant avec eux, des désirs à peine conscients ou refoulés, des sentiments ignorés, des ébauches de gestes, créent progressivement un état tout à fait particulier — combien de "je ne sais où j'en suis," de "je ne sais ce que je lui réponds"![41] — propice au vertige et à l'aveu. Tout se passe comme si le signe verbal pourtant neutralisé — "ce n'est pas qu'elle m'aime tout de bon; elle veut dire seulement qu'elle doit faire semblant de m'aimer,"[42] dit Merlin de Colette — dégageait l'être de ses profondeurs, le remontait à la surface, donnait force et forme à un état latent inexprimable. Il joue en quelque sorte le rôle du rameau des mines de sel de Salzbourg, autour duquel s'opère un processus de cristallisation. Le miroitement des signes linguistiques dans le discours marivaudien — sans parler des autres signes que sont les jeux de regards, les fausses sorties, etc. — s'offre comme absence de profondeur, comme abîme superficiel; d'où l'accusation souvent portée (Voltaire, Palissot) contre ce théâtre de manquer de sérieux, d'épaisseur. Mais ces effets de surface ne doivent pas être seulement mis sur le compte d'une monotone et ennuyeuse affectation de style, d'une "subtilité épigrammatique de l'esprit"[43] et de l'écriture, qui défigurerait les pièces de Marivaux "comme une jolie femme se défigure par [ses] mines";[44] ils n'ont véritablement de sens que situés dans la perspective d'un discours séducteur qui semble se séduire lui-même pour mieux séduire autrui, et pour qui la réalité n'existe que mise en scène. Participant du cérémonial de la séduction, ils fonctionnnnent non comme des miroirs de réflexion, mais comme des miroirs d'absorption et deviennent source de vertige:

Blaise.   Cette comédie-là n'est faite que pour nous planter là, Mademoiselle Lisette.
Colette.   Eh bien! plante-moi là itou, toi, Nicodème! Eh bian! oui, je lui plais; je nous plaisons tous deux . . . il voulait de Mademoiselle Lisette, il n'en veut pus; il la quitte, je te quitte, il me prend, je le prends . . .
Merlin.   . . . Cela va à merveille, ces gens-là [Lisette et Blaise] nous aiment, mais continuons encore de feindre.[45]

Qui peut dire si les protagonistes sont les sujets maîtres de leur discours, l'utilisant à leur convenance comme un paravent, ou si le discours, à leur insu, ne se joue pas d'eux, ne se retourne pas d'abord sur ceux qui le tiennent, les enfermant dans sa logique, les entraînant par son propre dynamisme, les fissurant et leur faisant perdre la tête par des procédés de rhétorique qui semblent s'enchaîner et fonctionner quasi mécaniquement. Quelle que soit l'hypothèse retenue, ce qui se découvre dans le théâtre de Marivaux, c'est l'incomparable pouvoir de séduction du discours. Un pouvoir qui tient à l'ironie essentielle d'une parole postulant la réversibilité des signes — la comédie dans *Les Acteurs* devient la vie même et la vie se fait comédie — et cherchant par l'entremise de leurres séducteurs moins à délivrer la connaissance qu'à susciter le plaisir de glisser et de trébucher. Même s'ils prétendent l'être, jamais les signes verbaux ne sont neutres ni transparents: trop innocents pour ne pas être suspects, les plus anodins et les moins équivoques apparemment ne cessent de relancer la spirale des enjeux, le tourniquet de la séduction.

Sécrétée par une parole dont l'énonciation est toujours en excès ou en retrait sur l'énoncé, aspirée par le vide que crée ce décrochement, et se développant dans le monde irréel des signes, la vie des Silvia et des Dorante acquiert la mobilité de la fiction, la grâce légère de la poésie. Dans le monde de la représentation qu'est la société du XVIIIe siècle, le désir de plaire et d'être préféré, en même temps que la crainte d'être déçu, trompé ou rejeté, ne peuvent qu'emprunter les voies d'un discours de séduction par quoi les personnages, consciemment ou non, se constituent comédiens d'eux-mêmes, metteurs en scène d'un jeu théâtral chargé d'exorciser leur peur de l'autre et du monde et d'exprimer leur besoin de liberté et de domination.

En mettant en scène la séduction qui n'est que la forme mondaine de la théâtralité, Marivaux a fait du théâtre le sujet même du théâtre et il lui a demandé de devenir le lieu enchanté de la vraie vie.

Yves Moraud
Université de Brest

Notes

[1] C. Roy, *Lire Marivaux* (Neuchatel: Editions de la Baconnière, et Paris: Le Seuil, 1947), p. 55.

[2] *Le Paysan parvenu*, éd. F. Deloffre (Paris: Garnier, 1952), p. 52.

[3] *Le Cabinet du philosophe*, Septième feuille, in *Journaux et œuvres diverses*, éd. F. Deloffre et M. Gilot (Paris: Garnier, 1969), p. 390.

[4] *Journaux*, p. 390.

[5] R. Tomlinson, *La Fête galante: Watteau et Marivaux* (Genève: Droz, 1981), p. 160.

[6] *Les Sincères*, Sc. 11. Pour le théâtre de Marivaux nous renvoyons à l'édition de F. Deloffre, *Théâtre complet* (Paris: Garnier, 1968).

[7] Marivaux, *Théâtre complet*, p. 483.

[8] *Le Prince travesti*, I, 2.

[9] Tomlinson, p. 135.

[10] *La Surprise de l'amour*, I, 2.

[11] Cette citation ainsi que les suivantes sont tirées de *La Surprise*, I, 2.

[12] *Journaux*, p. 118.

[13] *Le Triomphe de l'amour*, I, 1.

[14] Pensons à la stratégie de séduction de Dubois dans *Les Fausses Confidences*.

[15] "*Silvia*: J'entretenais Lisette du malheur d'une femme maltraitée par son mari . . . Dorante arrive aujourd'hui; si je pouvais le voir, l'examiner un peu sans qu'il me connût" (*Le Jeu de l'amour et du hasard*, I, 2); "*Le Prince*: Je l'ai vue [Silvia] cinq ou six fois de la même manière, comme simple officier du palais . . . je n'ai pu la faire renoncer à Arlequin" (*La Double Inconstance*, I, 2); "Oui, Silvia; je vous ai jusqu'ici caché mon rang, pour essayer de ne devoir votre tendresse qu'à la mienne" (*La Double Inconstance*, III, 9).

[16] Cf. Tomlinson, p. 159.

[17] *Scilicet*, No. 6/7, p. 19. Cité dans Shoshana Felman, *Le Scandale du corps parlant* (Paris: Le Seuil, 1980), p. 156.

[18] *La Double Inconstance*, III, 9.

[19] *Le Jeu*, I, 1; II, 9.

[20] *La Surprise*, I, 7.

[21] *Le Jeu*, II, 9.

[22] "*Dorante*: Dans tout ce qui s'est passé chez vous, il n'y a rien de vrai que ma passion qui est infinie . . . Tous les incidents qui sont arrivés partent de l'industrie d'un domestique qui savait mon amour, qui m'en plaint, qui par le charme de l'espérance, du plaisir de vous voir, m'a pour ainsi dire forcé de consentir à son stratagème" (*Les Fausses Confidences*, III, 12).

[23] "*Dubois*: On vous aimera, toute raisonnable qu'on est; on vous épousera, toute fière qu'on est, et on vous enrichira, tout ruiné que vous êtes . . . Fierté, raison et richesse, il faudra que tout se rende" (*Les Fausses Confidences*, I, 2).

[24] *Le Prince travesti*, I, 2.

[25] Déjà D'Alembert écrivait que "cette guerre de chicane . . . que l'Amour se fait à lui-même dans les pièces de [Marivaux] . . . a fait dire . . . que ses amants s'aiment le plus tard qu'ils peuvent, et se marient le plus tôt qu'il est possible" (*Eloge de Marivaux*, in Marivaux, *Théâtre complet*, II, 985).

[26] Cri de bonheur de Silvia à l'avant-dernière scène du *Jeu de l'amour et du hasard*.

[27] "*Silvia*: Ah, Monsieur, si vous saviez combien je vous aurai d'obligation! Dorante et moi, nous sommes destinés l'un à l'autre, il doit m'épouser; si vous saviez combien je lui tiendrai compte de ce qu'il fait aujourd'hui pour moi, combien mon cœur gardera le souvenir de l'excès de tendresse qu'il me montre! si vous saviez combien tout ceci va rendre notre union aimable! Il ne pourra jamais se rappeler notre histoire sans m'aimer, je n'y songerai jamais que je ne l'aime, vous avez fondé notre bonheur pour la vie, en me laissant faire; c'est un mariage unique; c'est une aventure dont le seul récit est attendrissant; c'est le coup de hasard le plus singulier, le plus heureux, le plus . . ." (*Le Jeu*, III, 4).

[28] "Quelle insatiable vanité d'amour-propre," s'exclame M. Orgon (*Le Jeu*, III, 4).

[29] Felman, p. 142.

[30] Felman, p. 36.

[31] J. Starobinski, *L'Invention de la liberté* (Genève: Skira, 1964), p. 85.

[32] *La Surprise*, I, 7.

[33] *Les Acteurs de bonne foi*, Sc. 3.

[34] *Les Acteurs*, Sc. 1.

[35] "Ne vous gênez point, Monsieur, dit la Comtesse à Lélio. Tout ce que nous disons ici ne s'adresse point à nous, regardons-nous comme hors d'intérêt" (*La Surprise*, I, 7).

[36] Combien de tableaux, de portraits, de commentaires objectifs dans la bouche de la Comtesse et de Lélio! Cf. *La Surprise*, I, 5-7.

[37] Cf., dans *La Surprise*, *passim*, les propos sur le mariage de Jacqueline et du neveu du fermier de la Comtesse, mariage dont Lélio et la Comtesse se moquent bien.

[38] *Les Acteurs*, Sc. 4.

[39] *Les Acteurs*, Sc. 4.

[40] "J'oublie encore à vous dire une finesse de ma pièce; c'est que Colette qui doit faire mon amoureuse, et moi qui dois faire son amant, nous sommes convenus tous deux de voir un peu la mine que feront Lisette et Blaise à toutes les tendresses naïves que nous prétendons nous dire" (Sc. 1).

[41] *Les Fausses Confidences*, III, 12.

[42] *Les Acteurs*, Sc. 4.

[43] Abbé de la Porte, *Observateur littéraire*, article reproduit dans Marivaux, *Théâtre complet*, II, 973.

[44] Charles Palissot, article reproduit dans Marivaux, *Théâtre complet*.

[45] *Les Acteurs de bonne foi*, Sc. 5.

Religious Tolerance in Eighteenth-Century Drama:
Three Examples.

When they discuss *Nathan der Weise* as an outstanding statement about tolerance, which it is, Germanists are sometimes guilty of the unwitting implication that Lessing invented the concept, which of course he did not. Tolerance was a constant topic in Germany (as in England, and to a certain extent elsewhere in Europe) from the end of the seventeenth century onwards.[1] What Lessing did, using ideas debated for decades, was to cut through to the essentials and present on a solid philosophical basis a morally uplifting story. He made tolerance dramatic, moving and quotable.

While the bulk of the discussion in the eighteenth century is, as one would expect, in the form of expository prose, the subject of tolerance does crop up in the drama apart from Lessing's two contributions, the early comedy *Die Juden*, 1749, and *Nathan der Weise* thirty years later. For this article I have reached into the theatrical bran-tub and pulled out, to add to *Nathan*, Voltaire's *Zaïre* of 1732 and Richard Cumberland's *The Jew* of 1794: not, on the face of it, a promising trio from a comparative viewpoint. Cumberland, prolific author of moderate talent, model for Sir Fretful Plagiary in Sheridan's *The Critic* of 1779, finds himself indeed in exalted company alongside Voltaire and Lessing. The three works themselves are diverse. To begin with, while *Nathan* shows us representatives of the three great monotheistic religions, *Zaïre* portrays only Christians and Moslems, *The Jew* only Christians and Jews. *Nathan der Weise* is the supreme fusion of humane theory and practice, and *par-dessus le marché* a rather clever adaptation of the German Enlightenment's, and Lessing's own, comic convention to fit this new play of ideas.[2] *Zaïre*, arguably Voltaire's finest drama, his own favorite to the end of his life, while a skilfully constructed and innovative tragedy, an enormous success on the stage until well into the nineteenth century, is not in the final analysis a play of ideas, despite its labeling by Paris audiences as "tragédie chrétienne."[3] Cumberland's piece, on a par with his earlier plays such as *The West Indian* and *The Brothers* and in keeping with the English sentimental theatrical tradition, pulls out all the emotional stops; the plot is slight, the characters largely stereotypes. Yet for a decade or so *The Jew* was widely translated, often revived, and in the figure of Sheva not only produced a role coveted by actors, but must have touched some chords of tolerance in the audiences of its day. A "fairer" choice as a French expression of religious tolerance would have to be essayistic, not dramatic: perhaps Voltaire's *Sermon du Rabbin Akib*, or something by Montesquieu. Furthermore, Voltaire deals with religious questions in several dramas, for instance in *Œdipe*, *Alzire*, *Mahomet*; *Zaïre*, however, offers interesting parallels and contrasts to Lessing's *Nathan*.

Thus we have, in historical sequence, a love-tragedy with religious undertones, an uplifting but at times quite humorous drama of bigotry versus tolerance, and an out-and-out tear-jerker. Precisely this diversity — including an unevenness of quality — gives us a glimpse of the potential for dramatic exploitation in the philosophical/theological subject of tolerance.

The interest of *Zaïre* for this discussion lies primarily in its first scene. Fatime, a fellow-slave and fellow-European, notices Zaïre's new contentment with her lot. Has she forgotten the young Frenchman Nérestan, who was allowed by the Sultan two years ago to go to France to raise the ransoms for Christian prisoners and for Zaïre herself? Fatime hears with astonishment that Zaïre has joyfully accepted Orosmane's proposal of marriage and asks how she can ignore the supposition that she was born of Christian parents, though perforce brought up as a Moslem. Zaïre declares:

> Je le vois trop: les soins qu'on prend de notre enfance
> Forment nos sentiments, nos mœurs, notre croyance.
> J'eusse été près du Gange esclave des faux dieux,
> Chrétienne dans Paris, musulmane en ces lieux.
> L'instruction fait tout; et la main de nos pères
> Grave en nos faibles cœurs ces premiers caractères
> Que l'exemple et le temps nous viennent retracer . . .
> Prisonnière en ces lieux, tu n'y fus renfermée
> Que lorsque ta raison, par l'âge confirmée,
> Pour éclairer ta foi te prêtait son flambeau:
> Pour moi, des Sarrasins esclave en mon berceau,
> La foi de nos chrétiens me fut trop tard connue. (I, 1, 560)[4]

"L'instruction fait tout": one is not drawn to a faith in which one was not raised. Zaïre's words are a clear definition of the geographic determination of religious belief, of relativism. The dramatic discovery (II, 3) that Zaïre was captured on the very point of being baptized, is Nérestan's sister and daughter of Lusignan, last King of Jerusalem and also prisoner of Orosmane, might lead one to expect a stage set for a conflict in her between the claims of her new-found family and the deep roots of her Moslem upbringing. It is not so. "L'instruction" has left no permanent imprint after all, and the Moslem tradition can be discarded like a dress suitable for a foreign climate but out of place at home. Zaïre evinces little emotional attachment to the land in which she was brought up (V, 3). It was love that made her accept an "alien" faith (I, 1, 561), and love now is the moving force in her dilemma: a conflict between her devotion to the Moslem Orosmane and the stirrings of her Christian heritage. Nérestan states the problem bluntly as a conflict between Orosmane and God (III, 4), and Fatime tells Orosmane after Zaïre's death: "Tu balançais son Dieu dans son cœur alarmé" (V, 10, 616). For after the revelation Zaïre immediately identifies herself with Christianity and with European culture:

> Quoi? je suis votre sœur, et vous pouvez penser
> Qu'à mon sang, à ma loi, j'aille ici renoncer? (III, 4, 585)

There are several references to the call of her blood: "Songe au moins, songe au sang qui coule dans tes veines," urges her newly-discovered father (II, 3, 579), and her brother greets her simple admission that she loves the Sultan with an implacable "Opprobre malheureux du sang dont vous sortez" (III, 4, 586). In this impulse to identify with the Christians, Zaïre now sees the very hand of God which earlier she had seen in Orosmane's proposal (I, 1, 559; II, 2, 573). There is no sense that the God of Christians and Moslems is the same. In her first encounter with Orosmane after the relevation, Zaïre invokes the "Dieu de mon père" (III, 6, 589). She loves *in spite of* God, incurring perhaps eternal divine anger for the weakness of her heart (IV, 6, 605). The first scene of *Zaïre* thus simply serves (in the context of the whole drama) to heighten the heroine's subsequent inner turmoil. In fact, her volte-face has been prepared in this opening scene itself, with careful phrases interspersed in the exposition of the idea that faith is a matter of upbringing. For instance:

> . . . la main de nos pères
> Grave en nos faibles cœurs ces premiers caractères
> Que l'exemple et le temps nous viennent retracer,
> *Et que peut-être en nous Dieu seul peut effacer.*
> (I, 1, 560, my italics)

Zaïre is not intolerant, but the calm philosophic phrases of the first scene do not stand up in the face of the revelation of her origins and the importunings of her father and brother.

Orosmane shows a measure of tolerance and humanity, influenced by his love perhaps, but not originating in it. He is certainly not, like Lessing's Saladin, "Der Held, der lieber Gottes Gärtner wäre" (IV, 4, 312),[5] but while acknowledging the exigencies of war, fierce fighting and harsh imprisonment, he exhibits respect for his foes, and in turn, at least before the conflict arising out of the discovery, is addressed by Nérestan as "Respectable ennemi, qu'estiment les chrétiens" (I, 4, 564). He decides to end the tradition of the harem, in tribute to his respect for Zaïre (I, 2, 563); to make amends for his belief in the false report that Louis of France was about to mount a fresh attack; and, again under the influence of his love for Zaïre, he determines to free his old foe Lusignan (II, 2, 573; III, 1, 582-83); he plans to end at his court the exaggerated adulation and ritual "qui font de tant de rois des tyrans invisibles" (I, 3, 564). He asks only that the Christians acknowledge that Moslems are not without virtue (I, 4, 565 and III, 1, 582). Impressed by Nérestan's keeping of his word, he gives liberty, not to the promised ten prisoners, but to one hundred, and to Nérestan himself, who has no ransom (I, 4, 565). That he becomes prey to a murderous sexual jealousy is consistent with the deep and demanding passion that has been indicated from the beginning as characteristic of him (I, 2, 563 — "Je me croirais haï d'être aimé faiblement" — and I, 4, 567), and does not detract from his equally characteristic sense of honor. Zaïre keeps her promise to Lusignan and Nérestan not to throw herself at Orosmane's feet and reveal her origins, but against her better instinct — surely this "grand cœur" would be generous if told the truth? (IV, l, 596). At the end Orosmane, victim both of the Christians' contemptuous mistrust and of his own violent nature, is magnanimous:

Nérestan.   Qu'ordonnes-tu, barbare?
Orosmane. *(après une longue pause)*
            Qu'on détache ses fers. Ecoutez, Corasmin,
            Que tous ses compagnons soient délivrés soudain.
            Aux malheureux chrétiens prodiguez mes largesses;
            Comblés de mes bienfaits, chargés de mes richesses,
            Jusqu'au port de Joppé vous conduirez leurs pas. (V,10, 617)

Dying, his last words are a command for the safe conduct of Nérestan: "Respectez ce héros, et conduisez ses pas" (V, 10, 617).

In introducing French figures, and in Lusignan's case a historical personage, to the French classical stage, Voltaire took a bold step; at the same time, he presented his audience in Lusignan and Nérestan with a pair of bigots, characterized by "humeur altière" (I, 4, 566) and ill-placed contempt for those of another creed. Their language is full of the stock phrases of Christian fanaticism, the holy mission of the crusading knights. Brave they are without doubt: Lusignan has borne stoically long years of imprisonment, Nérestan has made a perilous journey to France to fetch his fellow-captives' ransom, but in raising money to release Zaïre and Fatime also, he has exhausted his resources, and delivers himself up to renewed and perpetual imprisonment, terming this sacrifice "d'un Français le devoir ordinaire" (II, 1, 568). The loyalty and honor of the Christians have long impressed Zaïre, to whom they seem "un peuple de frères" (I, 1, 560).[6] This brotherhood is a closed circle, however. The Christians' talk is full of references to their God, to their special relationship with him ("Dieu s'est servi de moi," II, 1, 568), their faith is "notre auguste foi," they praise the French, the chivalric code (II, 3, 574), heroic deeds, martyrdom. There is more than an implication of national superiority, and a clear conviction of the absolute sanctity of their faith before all others. That Zaïre has even contemplated marriage with Orosmane thus fills them with horror. She has betrayed her faith and her heritage in abandoning "her" God for a barbarian. Even before he knows she is his sister, Zaïre is for the returned Nérestan "une femme infidèle . . . qui lira sa honte écrite sur mon front" (II, 1, 572). Learning that his daughter is a Moslem, Lusignan brands her as "ennemie," betrayer and blasphemer of her God (II, 3, 578-79). The discovery that she is betrothed to Orosmane provokes Nérestan to declare she deserves to die (III, 4, 586). Only baptism can "te rendre à toi-même" (III, 4, 585) (a phrase which may remind us of Daja's linguistically convoluted hope in Lessing's play that Recha, married to a Christian and carried off to Europe, "Wird wieder was sie ist; ist wieder, was Sie ward" [IV, 6, 512-13]). Zaïre herself regards the baptismal rite as a kind of panacea for her inner pain. Orosmane calls Nérestan "ce généreux chrétien" (III, 1, 583), but for the Christians the Sultan is simply a barbarian, revealing for Fatime "l'âme d'un Tartare à travers ses bontés" (V, 3, 609). The Moslems are defilers of the holy places. Moralizing over the body of his sister, killed in a fit of mad jealousy by Orosmane, Nérestan sees divine retribution:

> Hélas! elle offensait notre Dieu, notre loi;
> Et ce Dieu la punit d'avoir brûlé pour toi. (V, 10, 616)

Voltaire uses differences of religion and the problem of a human being caught between and by two faiths as a basis for a psychological study of tragic love and jealousy. *Pace* Lessing in the *Hamburgische Dramaturgie*,[7] his play is highly effective, particularly in the scenes between the distraught Zaïre and Orosmane torn between love and suspicion. The basis or content of the faiths or of faith is not explored — Orosmane is shown in fact as tolerant because he is moving away from tradition is some ways, becoming less "Moslem." The "Epître Dédicatoire" to Falkener shows Voltaire's preoccupation with other more strictly dramatic considerations such as the depiction of love as the major theme, though he does make in it a deliberately equivocal passing reference to the religious question: "je pourrais vous dire pourquoi je n'ai pas donné à Zaïre une vocation plus déterminée au christianisme, avant qu'elle reconnût son père . . . mais les esprits sages . . . verront bien mes raisons sans que je les indique."[8] The statements of the first scene, the character of Orosmane and negative aspects in the portrayal of the Christians easily strike a modern reader, who can look back over the whole of the eighteenth century's and Voltaire's discussions about religion, and they cannot have been completely lost on the audience or reader of the 1730's, though the time was clearly not yet ripe for a play of theological ideas. Writing to Formont on May 29, 1732, Voltaire remarks: "Ou je suis fort trompé, ou ce sera la pièce la plus singulière que nous ayons au théâtre."[9] For the year 1732 it is indeed a remarkable play. Though the enthusiasm with which it was met and on which Voltaire comments in the "Epître Dédicatoire" — ". . . si [Zaïre] n'avait été que convertie, elle aurait peu intéressé; mais elle est amoureuse de la meilleure foi du monde et voilà ce qui a fait sa fortune"[10] — had little to do with theological questions, *Zaïre* contains some remarkable ideas which we know from later works to have been important for Voltaire. Zaïre's cry of "inhumaine vertu" (IV, 1, 595) at the sacrifice demanded of her, and her despairing question: what would Orosmane be *more* if he were Christian? (IV, 1, 595), well up from a human rather than a philosophical dilemma, but precisely in this can one view Voltaire's play as part of the larger theological questioning of the eighteenth century. In particular, the problem "what is faith that it demands we destroy a human relationship?" leads us to Lessing.

The gap of four and half decades between Voltaire's and Lessing's plays and the different politico-religious context in which they were written are, of course, significant. Conditions in France in 1732 prevented Voltaire from expressing more explicitly criticism of intolerance and praise of tolerance. Only a little further on, in Hamburg in the 1740's, H. S. Reimarus circulated his *Apologie oder Schutzschrift für die vernünftigen Verehrer Gottes*, with its radical deist views and rejection of the divinity of Christ, privately in manuscript form, for fear of serious consequences to himself and his family. Thirty years later, Lessing, believing himself to be living in a more tolerant intellectual climate, printed excerpts from it in a learned series to provoke academic discussion and found himself instead embroiled in the *Fragmentenstreit* with Protestant theologians and accused of attacking faith. In 1778 the Brunswick authorities withdrew his freedom from press censorship, imposing in effect a ban on further articles from him on religious matters (and, as a by-product, on the question of free speech). Turning back to drama, he wrote *Nathan der Weise*. That he could do so shows that, despite all his difficulties, there *was* a difference between France in 1732 and Germany in 1779 and that Lessing's sense of the strength of tolerance in his age was not, after all, mistaken. The directness with which he speaks out in *Nathan* not only is evidence of his own absolute courage of his convictions, but was bolstered by a tradition of decades of theological discussion in Germany and in particular by the freedom of expression allowed in religious matters in one of its larger states, Prussia (Lessing had previously lived for several years in Berlin, where *Nathan* was published).

In a very exact sense, Lessing's and Voltaire's plays are not comparable, for there is no figure in *Zaïre* to parallel Nathan in his role both as philosophical guide and practical example. There is also no Jew, and one would not expect one, given Voltaire's negative views on the race.[11] But the works touch at some points. In both the action is played out against the background of the enmity and cruelty of the Crusades, the full extent of which was beginning to be understood in Europe in the eighteenth century, modifying the traditional view of the campaigns as holy wars against the infidel.[12] In *Zaïre*, nothing changes: the racial and religious gap is as wide at the close as at the beginning. In *Nathan der Weise*, despite the account of the pogrom (IV, 7), despite all evidence of bigotry, despite Saladin's fears of a renewed conflict, despite the plan to assassinate him, despite the fact that he himself, on the occasion when he spared the Templar's life, cut short that of nineteen others, despite the Patriarch — the atmosphere is sunny, friendships are spontaneously concluded, tolerance never far away. The temporary armistice of the 1190's which provides the play's real setting may be seen metaphorically as a lull in the prevailing prejudices and tensions of Lessing's own time, giving us a glimpse of Utopia. In *Nathan* the co-existence of races and faiths is achieved, albeit in a small circle, for the *anagnorisis* here, unlike Voltaire's, leads not to conflict but to a sense of the interrelationship of mankind, and the curtain falls *"Unter stummer Wiederholung allseitiger Umarmungen."* In *Zaïre* the background of ineradicable differences simply adds piquancy and color to the old story of lovers' misunderstanding and jealousy.

There are thus some general parallels: the geographical and historical setting, the portrayal of children whose parentage is at first obscure and then revealed in highly dramatic fashion, some echoes of the dialogue of Fatime and Zaïre in the exchanges between Daja and Recha. However, the question of the role of upbringing, defined at the beginning of *Zaïre* and then put aside, is central to *Nathan*. What is in *Zaïre* a double and conflicting motivation is developed by Lessing separately in two characters, Recha and the Tempelherr. In Recha we have the full exposition of the idea that "l'instruction fait tout," in the Templar the notion that one's blood, one's heritage, however dimly felt, directs one's beliefs. But there, in both cases, the resemblance ends. For in the Templar what stirs is the broadmindedness of his father, the Moslem Assad who married a Christian and counted a Jew his friend.[13] Thus his strictly Christian upbringing in Europe is set aside and his vows to his Order prove untenable. Closer to the relativism of the first scene of *Zaïre* is, to be sure, the message of the "Ringparabel" that one receives one's faith, not as the absolute or only truth, but as a loving heritage from one's forebears and hence as geographically and racially determined. In Recha's case, "l'instruction" is not an established religion but the imparting of a humane fusion of heart and reason, of a natural religion that transcends the narrower claims of church/mosque/synagogue.[14] Throughout the play are passages which stress what Recha has become under Nathan's teaching. She herself, in the conversation in III, 1, which represents the closest parallel to Fatime's and Zaïre's first scene, says to Daja:

> Dich zieht dein Vaterland:
> Und meines, meines sollte mich nicht halten?
> Ein Bild der Deinen, das in deiner Seele
> Noch nicht verloschen, sollte mehr vermögen,
> Als die ich sehn, und greifen kann, und hören,
> Die Meinen? (III, 1, 26-31)

To quote Zaïre: "On ne peut désirer ce qu'on ne connaît pas" (I, 1, 557). In V, 3, the Templar, realizing how wrong has been his indignant reaction to Daja's revelation (IV, 8) that Recha was a Christian child adopted by Nathan, sums up the idea that "l'instruction fait tout":

Kein Kleiner Raub, ein solch Geschöpf! — Geschöpf?
Und wessen? — Doch des Sklaven nicht, der auf
Des Lebens öden Strand den Block geflößt,
Und sich davon gemacht? Des Künstlers doch
Wohl mehr, der in dem hingeworfnen Blocke
Die göttliche Gestalt sich dachte, die
Er dargestellt? — Ach! Rechas wahrer Vater
Bleibt . . .
In Ewigkeit der Jude . . . (V, 3, 92-100)

Yet, as Lessing presents it, this is not a mere philosophical/pedagogical concept, but part of the conflict of the drama involving the deepest feelings for Nathan and for Recha, the fear that they may lose each other. Recha's agonized cry to Saladin and Sittah, ". . . macht denn nur das Blut / Den Vater? Nur das Blut?" (V,7, 502-3), is the translation into living human terms of Zaïre's initial reasoned acceptance that she is what custom and upbringing have made her.

Since Richard Cumberland's *The Jew* is nowadays little read, a synopsis of its plot is in order. The play is set in London. Unbeknownst to her family and his, Frederic Bertram has secretly married Eliza, sister of his friend Charles Ratcliffe. Frederic's father, Sir Stephen Bertram, the better to sever his son's connection with the Ratcliffes (a respectable, once-wealthy family fallen on hard times), dismisses Charles, a clerk in his counting-house, and threatens to disown Frederic if he persists in his courtship of Eliza. Charles, a man of rigid honor, something of a philosopher, has protected, befriended and learned to respect Sheva, a rich but apparently miserly Jew, with whom Sir Bertram does business while at the same time despising him. Frederic, applying to Sheva for a loan to relieve the Ratcliffes, is surprised to find him willing to advance the money without security. Eliza, meanwhile, has disclosed her marriage to her mother, who blesses the couple; Charles, however, denounces her as dishonorable, a poor girl entrapping a prosperous husband against his father's wishes. Sir Stephen, now also aware of her marriage, learning of Sheva's loan to Frederic, upbraids and insults the Jew, but undergoes a change of heart when Sheva produces papers to show that Eliza has a private fortune of ten thousand pounds. Mrs. Goodison, former recipient of Sheva's generosity and now the Ratcliffes' landlady, discloses to Sheva that Mrs. Ratcliffe is the widow of the man who saved him from persecution and death in Spain. Charles' proud opposition to the marriage and his cruel words to Eliza provoke a quarrel between him and Frederic and lead to a duel. When Charles is slightly wounded, Frederic regrets his own part in the quarrel and the arrival of Sheva bent on preventing the duel helps to bring about a reconciliation. Sir Stephen, having presented himself to Eliza, who denies all knowledge of a fortune, is won over by her merit alone, but is now suspicious of Sheva. Frederic, Mrs. Ratcliffe and Charles with Sheva arrive in quick succession to produce the dénouement, in which Sheva is revealed as the "Jew of Cadiz," the secret donor of Eliza's fortune and a philanthropist hiding behind the miser's mask. He declares Charles to be his heir.

Both Lessing's and Cumberland's plays have a good Jew as the title-figure.[15] But significantly Lessing's title gives Nathan his name and adds the epithet "der Weise," bestowed on Nathan by his own people (II, 2, 261): he is an established, respected figure. Cumberland's title is simply *The Jew*, for the man's name is not important to the Christians who deal with him and he himself, hiding his generosity behind an exaggerated façade of the Jewish miserliness of popular tradition, has turned himself into a caricature, into — outwardly — what people expect him to be. Nathan has suffered in the past and fears he may suffer again, but he is in no way a pitiable figure, rather, in fact, a *Führernatur*, and certainly an articulate thinker who sets the philosophical tone of the play. Sheva is a rather comic figure, at least at the beginning, speaking English with a foreign flavor. In Charles' answer to Frederic's question about the cause of the mishandling from which the former has rescued Sheva — "I never ask'd the cause: There was a hundred upon one; that was cause enough for me to make myself a second to the party overmatch'd" (I, 5-6)[16] — we hear an echo of Lessing's declaration, "Auf den alle zuschlagen, der hat vor mir Friede." For Sheva is the eternal ready-made victim, the Wandering Jew. Frederic's reaction on the first mention of him in the play is to bait him. "My countrymen," says Charles, "with all their natural humanity, have no objection to the hustling of a Jew" (I, 5). Sheva lists the names Christians call him: "a miser . . . an uncharitable dog . . . a blood-sucker, an extortioner, a Shylock" (I, 6). He has no choice but to endure the abuse:

> We have no abiding place on earth, no country, no home: everybody rails at us, everybody flouts us, everybody points us out for their may-game and their mockery. If your playwriters want a butt or a buffoon, or a knave to make sport of, out comes a Jew to be baited and buffeted through five long acts for the amusement of all good Christians — Cruel sport, merciless amusement! hard dealings for a poor stray sheep of the scatter'd flock of Abraham! (I, 6-7)

In addition this Jew is alone and lonely: ". . . no sister, no broder, no son, no daughter: I am a solitary being, a waif on the world's wide common" (I, 12), "my very name will vanish out of memory when I am dead" (II, 22). Nathan adopts a child and creates a family household, he cultivates specific friendships, such as that with Al Hafi: Sheva compensates for his loneliness by adopting the world, concealing his kindliness behind a front of exaggerated parsimony.

Though not the only play of its time to portray a Jew positively, in this point, the endowment of Sheva with a universal benevolence, Cumberland shows originality. Otherwise the piece uses stock situations in very obvious ways, and the characters do not develop beyond stereotypes. There is no probing, as in *Nathan*, into questions of religion and tolerance, everything remains on the plane of sentimentality. But the author uses precisely this sentimental quality and simple, trite statements to urge audience or reader to throw off prejudice. The speaker of the *Prologue* speaks first of prejudice in general as a baneful parasitic creeper twined round the generous British Oak, adjures the audience to learn "this simple lesson of the heart — / Judge not the Man by his exterior part," and in the final section appeals directly in the particular case at hand

For a poor Client, for a luckless Wight,
Whom Bard ne'er favour'd, whose sad fate has been
Never to share in one applauding scene,
In Souls like your's [*sic*] there should be found a place
For every Victim of unjust disgrace. (n. p.)

Cumberland uses two methods to depict the problem. Firstly, his genteel Christian characters, while making frequent use of the Jews as money-lenders, are ever ready with callous insults: for Frederic, Sheva is "the meerest muckworm" (I, 4), for Sir Stephen Bertram he is "wretch, miser, usurer" (III, 39) and all Jews liars (III, 37). Sir Stephen rejects his clerk Saunders' defense of Sheva's honesty out of hand: "Yes, this you may believe, if you are disposed to take one Jew's word for another Jew's character: I am obstinate against both" (III, 38). Later Sheva, in his own defense, shows greater objectivity:

And what has Sheva done to be call'd villain? — I am a Jew, what then? Is that a reason none of my tribe shou'd have a sense of pity? You have no great deal of pity yourself, but I do know many noble British merchants that abound in pity, therefore I do not abuse your tribe. (III, 42)

Even the gentle Eliza, asked if she knows Sheva the Jew, exclaims:

Thank Heaven I do not: I can safely say I never to my recollection heard his name before. Some vile imposter, I suppose. (V, 69)

Secondly, Cumberland weaves into his text criticism of the Christians, their assumption of superiority and in general their social pride and empty traditions, mainly through scenes involving Sheva or conversations concerning him, but sometimes through the interchanges of these characters themselves. For instance, at the beginning of Act II, Mrs. Ratcliffe, in reduced circumstances, yet preserves snobbish attitudes developed in the days of her dead husband's prosperity, which demand she look down on the Bertrams, a shade lower in the same social class than she; Eliza, more realistically, says: "We must forget those days" (II, 16). In Act I, Charles Ratcliffe, fresh from an interview with the unfeeling Sir Stephen Bertram and comforted somewhat by Sheva's sympathy, declares to the Jew: "I'll call you Christian then, and this proud merchant Jew," to which is returned: "I shall not thank you for that compliment" (I, 11). In the final act, Sheva is astounded to find Charles and Frederic fighting a duel, the time-honored gentlemanly manner of settling a quarrel:

What a strange world is this! Are you not friends? Are you not brothers? Is that a reason you shou'd quarrel? And if you differ, must you fight? Can your swords argue better than their masters? You call that an affair of honor, I suppose; under your favor I do not think it a very honorable affair; 'tis only giving a fine name to a foul deed. (V, 65-66)

The prejudice portrayed in *Nathan der Weise* is often of a sophisticated order: for instance, the Tempelherr's contempt for Jews (II, 5), based on the idea that they passed on their élitist conception of a Chosen People to Christians and Moslems, was a fairly common stricture on Jews among eighteenth-century European freethinkers, who had, theoretically at least, a predisposition to tolerance.[17] In Cumberland's play, prejudice is more like that in Lessing's earlier comedy, *Die Juden* (1749), namely the general unthinking rejection by society of a whole race. The difference between *Die Juden* and *The Jew* is that the Gentile characters in the latter, in the true tradition of the sentimental play, are ready to make a complete about-face. After Sheva's appeal to Sir Stephen quoted above (". . . what has Sheva done to be call'd villain?"), the merchant immediately replies: "I am confounded and asham'd; I see my fault, and most sincerely ask your pardon" (III, 42). From about the middle of the play, trust grows so rapidly that Sheva can essay to interrupt the duel with "Let me in . . . I am Sheva, your friend" (V, 65). In the last scene of the play, Charles presents the Jew to the assembled company:

> This is the man — My benefactor; your's Eliza; Frederic's; your's, dear mother; all mankind's: The widow's friend, the orphan's father, the poor man's protector, the universal philanthropist. (V, 73)

Ifor Evans remarks of Cumberland's plays: "every human issue can be obscured in a welter of emotion."[18] In *The Jew*, however, emotion plays a role in clarifying the human issue. As an antidote to prejudice, Cumberland offers sentimental pity, in the sense of natural good feeling and concern for others (Nathan's "herzliche Verträglichkeit," perhaps). From the Prologue onwards an appeal is made to the heart. "Thou hast affections, feelings, charities," says Charles to Sheva, contrasting him with the stony-hearted elder Bertram (I, 11); ". . . take a little time to know my heart, before you rob me of my reputation," Sheva pleads to Sir Stephen (III, 39). Sheva, sometimes criticizing himself for his "weakness," indulges in a general love of his fellow-men: ". . . I love my monies . . . but I love my fellow-creatures a little better" (II, 21). Pity asks no questions. Defending Frederic to his own father, Sheva declares:

> I did see your son struck down to the ground with sorrow, cut to the heart: I did not stop to ask whose hand had laid him low; I gave him mine, and rais'd him up.
> *Sir S..*   You! you to talk of charity!
> *Sheva.*   I do not talk of it; I feel it. (III, 40)

Pity comes spontaneously, irrationally. Sheva refuses to let his actions be called generosity: ". . . if pity wrings it from my heart, whether I will or not, then I do give: How can I help it?" (IV, 51).

Tears — again in keeping with the sentimental literary tradition — are not shameful, but evidence of humanity. Weeping over the persecution of his race and the loss of his family, Sheva begs Charles' pardon, but the young man says: "I am more dispos'd to subscribe to your tears than to find fault with them" (II, 22). Later, gently chiding a penitent Sir Stephen for his treatment of his son, Sheva says: ". . . to look upon your son, and not to love him, I shou'd have thought had been impossible," and a line or two later the third Act ends thus:

> *Sir S.*   Farewell, friend Sheva! — Can you forgive me?
> *Sheva.*   I can forgive my enemy; much more my friend. (III, 43)

The theme of pity is reinforced in an even more sentimental fashion through the love-plot, which presents the idea of pure, true love going against strict conventions. When Eliza, trying to prepare her mother for the revelation that she is already married to Frederic, asks what her reaction would be were she to confess a crime, Mrs. Ratcliffe asserts: "Astonishment might keep me silent for a while, but my first words wou'd be to pity and forgive you" (II, 15). Later, Eliza refers to this maternal understanding when she begs her brother's forgiveness also — "in pity hear me" (III, 34). To Charles' interjection that their mother "is all pity; sorrow has melted her fond heart to weakness," she replies with a plea that he understand how her own "fond sorrow-melted heart" accepted Frederic's proposal (III, 35) and he is forced to leave in order not to give in to the "weakness lurking at my heart." The duel between Frederic and Charles is precipitated when Charles' intransigeance makes Eliza faint and Frederic "insults" him thus: "You've struck her to the heart — and that's a coward's blow" (IV, 56).

The happy ending of *Nathan der Weise* is realistic only in its own context and as a pointer to what human beings *might* attain. More true to the facts of Lessing's own times was the impasse of *Die Juden*, with the polite wistful exchange, expressed in the subjunctive, and altering nothing in the *status quo*:

Der Baron. O wie achtungswürdig wären die Juden, wenn sie alle Ihnen glichen!

Der Reisende. Und wie liebenswürdig die Christen, wenn sie alle Ihre Eigenschaften besäßen![19]

The Jew, having a contemporary setting forty-five years later (that is, inasmuch as it can be said to have any specific setting at all), ends with some hope for social progress — Sheva's generosity is brought into the open, he is revealed as the Ratcliffes' former benefactor in Cadiz, and Mrs. Ratcliffe urges Charles: "Remember, son, to whom you owe this happiness and emulate his virtues" (V, 74).

Zaïre adores God, but is confused about Heaven's will, which, says Nérestan, demands that she hate Orosmane and his race (III, 4, 585) and is guiding Louis of France in his campaign in the Holy Land to "délivrer ton dieu même" (III, 4, 586). For Zaïre, the conflict between apparently God-directed duty and her love cannot be solved so simply: "Inhumaine vertu!" she cries in her agony (IV, 595). *Nathan der Weise* develops the notion that "inhuman virtue" is a contradiction in terms: despite the Patriarch's sophistry,[20] villainy towards one's fellow-man is also villainy in the eyes of God, no religious duty exists which transcends one's duty to one's neighbor, and man's humanity to man is the chief means to express devotion to God. Recha's answer to Daja's remark about the Templar's fighting for "his God" is an answer to Nérestan also:

... 'Sein, sein Gott! für den er kämpft!'
Wem eignet Gott? was ist das für ein Gott,
Der einem Menschen eignet? der für sich
Muß kämpfen lassen? (III, 1, 39-42)

In *The Jew*, God and religion as such are hardly mentioned, but the speech with which Sheva closes the play implies the superior worth of natural over positive religion. Referring to "the treasure that integrity has collected," he says:

95

Notes

[1] See Harald Schultze, *Lessings Toleranzbegriff: Eine theologische Studie* (Göttingen: Vandenhoeck and Ruprecht, 1969), pp. 11-12 and 128-72.

[2] Among studies which deal with comedy elements in *Nathan der Weise* are Robert R. Heitner, "Lessing's Manipulation of a Single Comic Theme," *Modern Language Quarterly*, 18 (September, 1957), 183-98, and Wolf-Hartmut Friedrich, "Menander redivivus: Zur Wiedererkennung im *Nathan*," *Euphorion*, 44 (1970), 167-80.

[3] In a letter to Cideville on August 25, 1732, describing with a measure of false modesty how the audience at the fourth performance had acclaimed him as he sat in his box, Voltaire declared: "Il est doux de n'être pas honni dans son pays" (*Œuvres complètes de Voltaire*, ed. Louis Moland [Paris: Garnier, 1877-85], XXXIII, 289). *Zaïre* had nine performances when premiered in August 1732, and twenty-one at the reprise in November of the same year. A private performance was also put on at the house of Mme de Fontaine-Martel in which Voltaire played Lusignan. The play's success outweighed the inevitable criticism from some quarters and the parodies (on the latter, see *Œuvres complètes*, II, 536, footnote 1 to the "Avertissement des Editions de 1738 et 1742"). In the 1870's Sarah Bernhardt played the title role.

[4] References to *Zaïre* are to the Moland edition mentioned above, vol. II, and appear in the text, cited according to Act, Scene and page.

[5] References to *Nathan der Weise* are to Gotthold Ephraim Lessing, *Werke*, ed. Herbert G. Göpfert (Darmstadt: Wissenschaftliche Buchgesellschaft, 1971-79), vol. II, and appear in the text, cited according to Act, Scene and line.

[6] Lessing's Recha also admires the bravery and pities the sufferings of the Christians, though she expresses doubt about the heroic nature of their faith (III, 1, 69-73).

[7] In *Hamburgische Dramaturgie*, Nos. 15 and 16, Lessing criticizes *Zaïre* sharply, comparing Orosmane to his disadvantage with Shakespeare's Othello (*Werke*, IV, 298-303).

[8] *Œuvres complètes*, II, 538.

[9] *Œuvres complètes*, XXXIII, 272. This letter was written when Voltaire had completed one act of the play.

[10] *Œuvres complètes*, II, 540. Voltaire's article on his play in the *Mercure* (unusual, for the "Selbstrezension" was not yet in vogue) is in fact a lengthy résumé of the plot with emphasis on the love-interest ("Lettre de M. de Voltaire, à M.D.L.R. sur la tragédie de Zaïre," *Mercure de France*, August 1732, pp. 1828-43).

[11] See Arthur Hertzberg, *The French Enlightenment and the Jews* (New York: Columbia University Press, 1968), pp. 280-313, for a discussion of Voltaire's negative, but complex attitude toward the Jews and Judaism. Lessing, whose attitude toward Voltaire was, in its turn, largely negative, ends an early satiric poem, *Auf* —, based on the Hirschel affair of 1750, thus: "Warum die List, / Dem Juden nicht gelungen ist, So fällt die Antwort ohngefähr: / Herr V** war ein größer Schelm als er" (*Werke*, I, 46).

[12] See, for instance, Lessing's remarks in *Hamburgische Dramaturgie*, No. 7, in the course of his discussion of Cronegk's *Olint und Sophronia*, where he terms the Crusades "die unmenschlichsten Verfolgungen," "unselige Raserei" (*Werke*, IV, 263-64). The historical Saladin, who has a major role in *Nathan der Weise*, is briefly mentioned twice in *Zaïre*: I, 2, 562 and IX, 1, 596.

[13] See Ruth Angress, "'Dreams that were more than dreams' in Lessing's *Nathan*," *Lessing-Yearbook*, 3 (1971), 108-27, and my "'Zufall der Geburt' or 'Stimme der Natur': Upbringing versus Birthright in Lessing's *Nathan der Weise*," *Seminar*, 17 (September 1981), 181-95.

[14] The only place of worship mentioned in this play about religion is in fact the ruined "Christentempel" chosen by Daja as the setting off-stage between Acts IV and V for her revelation to Recha of the girl's Christian origins (V, 6, 464).

[15] Nathan is the only Jew in Lessing's play, but in addition to the central character Sheva, Cumberland introduces two members of his household, Jabal and Dorcas, who provide an interesting variation of the stock comic servant figures of eighteenth-century comedy. Possibly Mrs. Goodison is also Jewish (she once lived, like Sheva, in Cadiz), but this is not clear.

[16] References to this play are to Richard Cumberland, *The Jew: A Comedy* (London: C. Dilly, 1794), and appear in the text cited according to Act and page (the scenes being unnumbered).

[17] In his "Gegensätze des Herausgebers" to the second Reimarus *Fragment* of 1777 (on revelation), Lessing remarks of the Jews: "Dieses . . . Volk ist doch, in der ganzen Geschichte, schlechterdings das erste und einzige, welches sich ein Geschäft daraus gemacht, seine Religion mitzuteilen und auszubreiten. Wegen des Eifers, mit welchem die Juden dieses Geschäft betrieben, bestrafte sie schon Christus, verlachte sie schon Horaz . . . Die christlichen Völker, die den Juden in diesem Eifer hernach gefolgt sind, überkamen ihn bloß, insofern sie auf den Stamm des Judentums gepropft waren" (*Werke*,VII, 466). See also Henri Brunschwig, *Enlightenment and Romanticism in Eighteenth Century Prussia*, tr. Frank Jellinek (Chicago: University of Chicago Press, 1974), p. 286; H. G. Adler, *The Jews in Germany from the Enlightenment to National Socialism* (Notre Dame, Ind.: Notre Dame University Press, 1969); and Michael A. Meyer, *The Origins of the Modern Jew: Jewish Identity and European Culture in Germany, 1749-1824* (Detroit: Wayne State University Press, 1967).

[18] Sir Ifor Evans, *A Short History of English Literature* (Harmondsworth: Penguin, 1958), p.115.

[19] *Werke*, I, 414 (Sc. 22).

[20] The Klosterbruder, imparting to the Tempelherr the Patriarch's plan that the knight should lead an assassination attempt against Saladin, reports: "Nur — meint der Patriarch, — sei Bubenstück / Vor Menschen, nicht auch Bubenstück vor Gott" (I, 5, 686-87).

L'Anatomie d'un coup d'Etat ou la prise de pouvoir dans la tragédie *Mahomet* de Voltaire

En créant son personnage Mahomet, Voltaire se trouvait en présence de trois courants. La tradition orthodoxe, représentée par Baudier[1] et par Prideaux,[2] ne voulait voir en Mahomet, le Prophète arabe, qu'un imposteur et un vil débauché; le courant Boulainvilliers[3] soutenait que Mahomet était un grand homme et que sa religion était assez rapprochée du déisme; entre ces deux extrêmes, Bayle[4] et Reland,[5] prenant un juste milieu, reconnaissaient que Mahomet était un imposteur, mais jugeaient le mahométisme d'un œil moins sévère.[6] Au premier abord, le Mahomet de Voltaire semblait plus conforme à la tradition dévote. Les prélats et les ecclésiastiques de Lille ne trouvèrent rien à redire et plus tard le pape Benoît XIV permit à Voltaire de lui dédicacer sa tragédie. Cependant, quand la pièce fut jouée le 9 août 1742 sur la scène du Théâtre-Français, beaucoup de spectateurs du monde parlementaire furent choqués des "traits hardis contre la religion, le gouvernement et la morale établie,"[7] Jean Bernard Le Blanc fut surpris de ce que la police eût permis la représentation de la pièce: "La Politique y est pour le moins aussi maltraitée que la Relligion, c'est le triomphe du Déisme ou plustôt du Fatalisme" (Best. D2635).[8] Selon d'autres la pièce représentait "l'énormité en fait d'infâmies, de scélératesse, d'irréligion et d'impiété . . . Tout le monde dit que pour avoir composé une pareille pièce, il faut être un scélérat à faire brûler" (Best. D2638). Quel était le dessein de Voltaire en écrivant cette tragédie? En faire une pièce de combat? En voulait-il à la religion chrétienne? Ou voulait-il en faire un drame historique? Autant de questions que nous essaierons d'élucider.

Dans sa lettre dédicatoire à Frédéric, publiée pour la première fois en 1743, en tête de sa tragédie, *Le Fanatisme ou Mahomet le Prophète*, Voltaire, en réponse à ses ennemis, résumait l'intrigue de sa pièce en ces termes: "C'est un jeune homme né avec de la vertu, qui séduit par son fanatisme, assassine un vieillard qui l'aime, et qui dans l'idée de servir dieu se rend coupable sans le savoir d'un parricide; c'est un imposteur qui ordonne ce meurtre, et qui promet à l'assassin un inceste pour récompense" (Best. D2386). Certains critiques ont conclu que pour "l'auteur, le personnage principal n'est pas Mahomet, mais sa victime."[9] Cependant un examen plus attentif de la pièce nous pousse à soutenir que Voltaire, en réponse aux attaques de ses ennemis, n'a souligné qu'un aspect secondaire de sa tragédie au détriment d'un des événements les plus importants de la pièce et de l'histoire: la reddition de la Mecque, et la montée au pouvoir d'un homme d'Etat. Cet événement politique, d'une portée aussi considérable que celle de la chute de Rome ou de la prise de Constantinople, clôt l'ère du paganisme en Arabie et commence une nouvelle période: l'expansion de l'Islam et la conquête d'une partie du monde. Tel est le sujet que Voltaire a traité dans sa tragédie.

L'autorité de Mahomet, d'abord réduite à la région de Médine, s'étant étendue à une bonne partie de l'Arabie, seuls les Korachites de la Mecque s'opposaient farouchement à sa nouvelle religion. La réforme religieuse de Mahomet ne pouvait être solidement établie tant qu'elle n'était pas reçue dans la

Mecque, ville regardée de tout temps par les Arabes comme le centre de leur religion.

Pour soumettre la Mecque à la loi musulmane, la volonté de Mahomet se heurte à celle de Zopire, prince de la Mecque. Ce dernier représente un empêchement majeur au dessein du Prophète. Toutefois cet obstacle est complexe, car il ne s'agit pas d'éliminer un rival, mais plutôt de l'amener à exhorter ses sujets à suivre le nouvel ordre. Le seul recours à la force laisse à désirer sur le plan politique. D'une part, assassiner Zopire ne réussirait qu'à révolter ses sujets; d'autre part, occuper la ville et soumettre ses habitants par la force militaire n'aboutiraient qu'à en faire des esclaves; ce qui n'est pas dans les intentions de Mahomet, dont le but est précisément de rallier et d'unir toute l'Arabie sous le nouvel étendard. En homme d'Etat, rompu à tous les rouages du gouvernement et de la politique, Mahomet essaiera par tous les moyens d'avoir recours à la diplomatie et à la persuasion pour réaliser son dessein grandiose. Toute l'action dans les actes I et II consistera à montrer les vains efforts de Phanor, d'Omar et de Mahomet, qui se heurtent à l'entêtement de Zopire. Tous les moyens diplomatiques sont utilisés. Chacun, à tour de rôle, tentera vainement d'amener Zopire à changer d'avis.

Phanor, le premier, essaiera de convaincre Zopire que, dans les circonstances critiques, il faut agir en homme d'Etat, étouffer ses sentiments personnels qui le poussent à persévérer dans une lutte dont les conséquences seront la ruine et la dévastation de la cité. Ce qui importe avant tout, c'est de sauver l'Etat.

Les conseils de Phanor ne réussissent qu'à exciter la colère du chef de la Mecque. Comment peut-il s'allier à Mahomet? Trop de haine les sépare à jamais. Devant cette intransigeance du vieillard, Phanor le quitte pour remettre à Mahomet la réponse de son maître.

C'est alors que le Prophète envoie Omar, son ministre, pour essayer une seconde fois de fléchir la volonté de Zopire.

Introduit par Phanor, Omar commence par faire des propositions de paix à Zopire. Le Prophète, par pitié pour son âge, pour ses malheurs passés, serait disposé à épargner sa vie et celle des Mecquois, s'il se convertit à l'Islam. Zopire ne répond que par des imprécations, reprochant à Omar la honte d'être au service d'un tel maître. Ce qu'il reproche surtout à Mahomet, c'est sa basse origine sociale. Il ne peut comprendre qu'on puisse suivre un homme "sans honneur et sans bien."

Omar lui répond que ce n'est point la "naissance" qui compte, mais la "vertu":

> Il est de ces esprits favorisés des cieux,
> Qui sont tout par eux-même, et rien par leurs aïeux.
> Tel est l'homme, en un mot, que j'ai choisi pour maître:
> Lui seul dans l'univers a mérité de l'être;
> Tout mortel à sa loi doit un jour obéir,
> Et j'ai donné l'exemple aux siècles à venir.[10]

Zopire revient à ses arguments tirés du préjugé social. Il raconte à Omar toute l'histoire de Mahomet, sa basse origine, ses intrigues et ses perfidies. Il lui rappelle que, dans le passé, Omar lui-même avait combattu le Prophète.

Omar lui répond que ses actes passés n'étaient dictés que par son aveuglement et ses préjugés, mais que quand il a vu que Mahomet était né pour changer l'univers, il a associé sa vie au destin du Prophète:

Quand mes yeux, éclairés du feu de son génie,
Le virent s'élever dans sa course infinie;
Eloquent, intrépide, admirable en tout lieu,
Agir, parler, punir, ou pardonner en dieu;
J'associai ma vie à ses travaux immenses . . . (I, 4)

Omar termine son panégyrique par une seconde offre très généreuse: Mahomet serait disposé à l'associer dans ses grandeurs et à partager avec lui son empire. Devant le refus obstiné de Zopire, Omar le quitte pour aller se présenter au Sénat, et négocier une paix séparée sans avoir recours au chef de la Mecque.

Dans le second acte, c'est Mahomet en personne qui prendra l'initiative, et l'entrevue secrète entre lui et Zopire est une leçon de haute politique. Il lui parle en toute sincérité. Il lui explique ses vastes desseins; c'est la raison d'Etat, ce sont les circonstances historiques qui lui dictent ses actions. Il lui fait un exposé de la situation internationale. Le trône de la Perse est ébranlé, l'Inde esclave, l'Egypte abaissée; l'Empire romain d'orient se désagrège et tombe de toutes parts. C'est le moment ou jamais de profiter de cette décadence du monde: "Sur ces débris du monde élevons l'Arabie" (II, 5).

Mais pour unir le peuple arabe et libérer les peuples du monde soumis au joug politique et religieux de l'impérialisme romain, il faut renverser l'ancien ordre établi et offrir aux peuples de l'univers un nouveau culte et une nouvelle idéologie qui les ranimeraient:

Il faut un nouveau culte, il faut de nouveaux fers;
Il faut un nouveau dieu pour l'aveugle univers. (II, 5)

Peu importe que cette idéologie soit vraie ou fausse, ou qu'elle substitue un joug à un autre. La nécessité d'établir un nouvel ordre s'impose à la nation pour la rendre intrépide:

Ou véritable ou faux, mon culte est nécessaire . . .
Ma loi fait des héros. (II, 5)

Mahomet termine son discours en faisant appel à l'"aide" de Zopire, à sa participation à cette œuvre grandiose. Il a poussé les concessions jusqu'au bout; mais la voix de l'ambition soutenue par une sublime éloquence ne peut rien sur Zopire. Mahomet se voit alors dans l'obligation d'avoir recours au chantage, d'ébranler son rival en faisant appel à ses sentiments paternels. Il lui promet de lui rendre ses enfants qu'il regrette. Quand Zopire tout ébranlé demande le prix de leur salut, Mahomet revient à ses conditions généreuses: soumission à l'Islam et participation au pouvoir:

Annoncer l'Alcoran aux peuples effrayés,
Me servir en prophète, et tomber à mes pieds:
Je te rendrai ton fils, et je serai ton gendre. (II, 5)

Entre le choix de renier ses dieux ou de perdre ses enfants, Zopire refuse l'offre du Prophète.

C'est un échec cuisant pour Mahomet, car éliminer son rival par la violence ne servirait pas ses desseins. Mais à ce moment, Voltaire fair rebondir l'action. Omar arrive, il annonce de mauvaises nouvelles au Prophète. La moitié du Sénat vient de le condamner. Sa vie est en danger, il ne lui reste que le choix de répondre par la violence au crime qu'on prémédite. Comme le temps presse, la mort de Zopire est concertée sur le champ et il est question de choisir un officier fanatique capable d'obéir aveuglément aux ordres supérieurs, d'exécuter l'acte sans éveiller les soupçons des autorités mecquoises. Omar lui suggère Séide: "Pour un tel attentat je réponds de Séide" (II, 6). Omar énumère les avantages d'un tel choix. Il est le seul otage de Zopire qui peut aborder le vieillard en secret; il est jeune, simple, "aveugle avec courage," en "proie aux superstitions"; enfin: "C'est un lion docile à la voix qui le guide" (II, 6). Mahomet approuve le choix du meurtrier.

La décision de tuer Zopire ayant été prise, Voltaire, dans l'intention de prolonger l'action pendant deux actes, introduit un nouvel obstacle, d'ordre psychologique, qui consiste à pousser Séide au crime. Le dilemme du jeune homme pourrait être plus douloureux ou cornélien, s'il savait que sa victime est son père. Séide ne se trouve pas entre deux intérêts pressants et opposés, ou entre deux devoirs irréconciliables. Il lui est seulement difficile de comprendre que le sang versé d'un vieillard puisse plaire au ciel.

Quand Séide aura commis le crime et connu l'identité de sa victime, il en résultera pour Mahomet un nouvel obstacle extérieur en la personne de Séide qui finit par fomenter la révolte du peuple. Mais grâce à la mort de Séide, due au poison, et à l'opportunisme de Mahomet, ce dernier obstacle sera surmonté et la pièce sera dénouée.

La reddition de la Mecque est bien le sujet que Voltaire voulait traiter, événement historique qui inaùgurait la fondation d'une nouvelle religion et d'un nouvel empire, couronnant ainsi l'œuvre d'un grand homme. Le génie politique de Mahomet, selon Voltaire, c'est de s'être rendu compte que toute révolution sociale au sein d'une nation primitive, foncièrement religieuse et superstitieuse, ne peut se réaliser qu'à partir d'une idéologie basée sur la religion. Selon Voltaire, la religion est nécessaire au gouvernement d'un peuple. A ceux qui, comme Bayle, soutiennent qu'une société d'athées peut subsister, Voltaire donne raison théoriquement:

> Ceux qui ont soutenu qu'une société d'athées pouvait subsister ont donc eu raison, car ce sont les lois qui forment la société; et ces athées étant d'ailleurs philosophes, peuvent mener une vie très-sage et très-heureuse à l'ombre de ces lois: ils vivront certainement en société plus aisément que des fanatiques superstitieux. Peuplez une ville d'Epicures, de Simonides, de Protagoras, de Desbarreaux, de Spinosas; peuplez une ville de jansénistes et de molinistes, dans laquelle pensez-vous qu'il y aura plus de troubles et de querelles? (*Dictionnaire philosophique*, art. "Athée," XVII, 456)

Cependant une telle société de philosophes n'existe que dans l'imagination des utopistes, car, "si Bayle avait eu seulement cinq à six cents paysans à gouverner, il n'aurait pas manqué de leur annoncer un Dieu rémunérateur et vengeur" (*D.P.*, "Athéisme," XVII, 463). Un Etat fondé sur l'athéisme tomberait dans l'anarchie. "L'athéisme, à ne le considérer que par rapport à cette vie, serait très-dangereux chez un peuple farouche" (*D.P.,* "Athée," XVII, 456). Ce que Voltaire appelle avec dédain la "populace" a besoin du plus grand frein pour réprimer ses instincts, et seule la religion peut jouer ce rôle: "Il est donc absolument nécessaire pour les princes et pour les peuples que l'idée d'un Être suprême, créateur, gouverneur, rémunérateur et vengeur, soit profondément gravée dans les esprits" (*D.P.,* "Athéisme," XVII, 475). Pour Voltaire, comme pour son personnage Mahomet, l'Etat ne peut donc se passer de religion et il importe peu qu'elle soit vraie ou fausse.

Doctrinaire et révolutionnaire, Mahomet a la ferme conviction qu'une réforme sociale et politique s'impose à sa nation et à l'humanité: "Je viens après mille ans changer ces lois grossières" (11, 5). Le problème qui se pose à Mahomet est: comment réussir à persuader toute une nation d'abandonner une religion établie pour en adopter une autre plus conforme à des desseins grandioses de conquête? La tâche n'est pas aisée. Moins une société est évoluée, plus saintes sont la coutume, les mœurs, et les croyances. Plus les croyances d'une société sont stables et enracinées, moins le pouvoir politique est libre dans son action. Comme le peuple n'est pas encore arrivé à ce stade où seules la philosophie et la raison guident ses actes, Mahomet ne peut tenir au peuple ignorant et superstitieux le même langage politique et philosophique qu'il tient à Zopire et à Omar. Aux yeux du peuple, Dieu est l'auteur de la Loi. Qui d'autre que Lui oserait la corriger? N'est-Il pas le seul qui puisse changer ce qu'Il a édicté depuis des siècles? Tout chef d'Etat qui oserait commander quelque chose de contraire à la Loi établie y briserait son pouvoir et risquerait de se faire assassiner par un fanatique. Ce n'est pas Mahomet le fanatique de la superstition, c'est le peuple. Utiliser la contrainte ou la persécution religieuse n'aboutirait qu'à rendre le peuple plus fanatique, sans pour autant changer ses idées. Ce n'est pas Mahomet que le peuple craint, c'est Dieu. Il ne reste donc qu'une seule ressource à Mahomet, "faire parler le Dieu qui l'inspire," et s'ériger en Prophète. Mahomet n'est donc un imposteur que par la force des circonstances et dans ce qu'il croit être l'intérêt de sa nation:

> Ne me reproche point de tromper ma patrie;
> Je détruis sa faiblesse et son idolâtrie. (II, 5)

Cependant, si Mahomet trompe impunément le peuple, il ne se pose pas pour autant en prophète dans son entourage immédiat. Il fait une nette distinction entre le peuple et les maîtres. Il ne tient pas le même langage à Séide et à Zopire. Il traite ce dernier sur un pied d'égalité; sans chercher à le convertir à une religion donnée, son seul dessein est d'en faire un allié politique. Il en est de même d'Omar qui s'exprime devant Zopire comme un gouvernant:

> Le peuple, aveugle et faible, est né pour les grands hommes,
> Pour admirer, pour croire, et pour nous obéir. (I, 4)

Selon Voltaire, Abou Bakr, beau-père de Mahomet, était complice de l'imposture illustre de son gendre, "qu'il regardait comme nécessaire" (*Essai sur les mœurs,* XI, 210). Quand Mahomet mourut, il fut "regardé comme un grand homme par ceux même qui le connaissaient pour un imposteur, et révéré comme un prophète par tout le reste" (*E.M.,* XI, 207).

Voltaire a toujours été convaincu que l'Islam n'était qu'une arme politique aux mains de Mahomet pour la réalisation de ses propres ambitions. Mahomet impose à son peuple une théocratie dont le but serait d'unir toutes les tribus arabes divisées sous une seule autorité temporelle et spirituelle:

Sous un roi, sous un dieu, je viens la réunir. (II, 5)
Chargé des soins du monde, environné d'alarmes,
Je porte l'encensoir, et le sceptre, et les armes. (II, 4)

Quels sont les avantages d'un tel système politique? L'Etat ne risque plus d'être divisé ou affaibli par l'ingérence du pouvoir spirituel dans les affaires de l'Etat, comme c'est le cas pour les monarchies chrétiennes où le pape est le rival des rois. Dans le nouvel ordre établi par Mahomet, la religion est désormais subordonnée à la souveraineté du monarque. Détenant les pouvoirs du pontife et du roi, Mahomet réussit à imposer "silence au reste des humains" par "le glaive et l'Alcoran" (II, 5). Ses successeurs réussiront à maintenir un régime qui est à la source de la puissance nationale des Arabes. "Si jamais puissance a menacé toute la terre, c'est celle de ces Califes; car ils avaient le droit du trône et de l'autel, du glaive et de l'enthousiasme. Leurs ordres étaient autant d'oracles, et leurs soldats autant de fanatiques" (*E.M.*, XI, 213). Voltaire reconnaît que c'est grâce à ce mode de gouvernement que "les descendants d'Ismaël ont conquis une partie de l'Asie, de l'Europe, et de l'Afrique, ont établi un empire plus vaste que celui des Romains" (*D.P.*, "Abraham," XVII, 37). En disposant de la puissance temporelle aussi bien que spirituelle, les califes pouvaient fanatiser leurs troupes à leur guise et les mener à la conquête du monde pour une cause soi-disant religieuse.

Profondément différent des Pyrrhus, des Néron et des Oreste, Mahomet représente de la part de son auteur un nouveau type de héros plus conforme à la réalité politique. "Je n'ay pas prétendu seulement mettre une action vraye sur la scène mais des mœurs vrayes, faire penser les hommes comm' ils pensent dans les circonstances où ils se trouvent" (Best. D2386). Mahomet n'hésite pas à avoir recours au crime quand les circonstances politiques l'exigent. Ce n'est pas un Néron, mais, comme tout homme d'Etat digne de Machiavel, il éliminera ses ennemis chaque fois que son destin, son idéologie ou la sécurité de l'Etat est en jeu. Comme nous l'avons souligné, Mahomet n'avait pas l'intention de tuer Zopire, ce n'était pas dans son intérêt. Mais le vote du Sénat de la Mecque l'a forcé à prendre une décision rapide et décisive. Mahomet se distingue par son caractère viril, sa fermeté d'esprit, sa résolution dans sa conduite, son audace et son intrépidité.

Son caractère viril s'exprime dans son comportement envers les femmes. Plus tard, Voltaire réaffirmera ce point de vue à propos des mœurs de Mahomet: "L'amour, qu'un tempérament ardent lui rendait nécessaire, et qui lui donna tant de femmes et de concubines, n'affaiblit ni son courage, ni son application, ni sa santé" (*E.M.*, XI, 204). Sa passion pour Palmire n'entre pas dans le jeu de ses desseins politiques. Dans son entrevue secrète avec Zopire, il discute d'abord politique avec son rival, essaie de le convertir à sa cause, ce n'est qu'en dernier lieu qu'il propose de lui rendre ses enfants, mais il ne sera jamais question de sacrifier à l'amour de Palmire ses propres ambitions et la cause politique qu'il poursuit. Sa passion ne le domine pas en tyran, elle est d'une nature toute différente de celle de Rodrigue pour Chimène ou de celle de Pyrrhus, qui est disposé à abandonner ses alliés et à se lancer dans une guerre désastreuse pour un seul regard de sa maîtresse. Pyrrhus est peut-être un grand amant, mais sûrement pas un grand homme. Mahomet n'est ni un héros cornélien, ni un héros racinien; il n'existe aucun conflit intérieur entre le devoir et l'amour, aucune lutte contre une passion fatale et tyrannique dont il serait la victime. Il n'est pas un soupirant comme Pyrrhus ou Oreste cherchant par tous les moyens à conquérir le cœur de sa maîtresse; il ne désespère pas de se faire aimer d'elle. Que représente donc la femme aux yeux de Mahomet? C'est une possession. Les éléments caractéristiques de cette passion sont la sensualité, et un désir d'ascendant, de domination. Mahomet convoite Palmire parce qu'elle est la fille de son ennemi. En tant que souverain et conquérant, il dispose de Palmire au même titre que d'une province asservie; elle est sa propriété. Bien qu'il la préfère en secret à ses épouses, il n'a nullement l'intention de se contenter d'elle, et de répudier les autres. Il diffère d'Orosmane qui jure fidélité à Zaïre. Pourtant cet amour despotique de Mahomet n'est pas pour autant sanguinaire. Il n'est pas de ceux qui, comme Orosmane, tuent leur bien-aimée pour l'avoir crue infidèle. Sa jalousie est différente des héros de type racinien qui souffrent de ne pas se sentir aimés; qui, dans leur désespoir, finissent par tuer leur idole; qui sont amants avant d'être rois. La jalousie de Mahomet est intimement liée à l'amour-propre de l'homme d'Etat:

> Conçois-tu bien l'excès de mes fureurs jalouses,
> Quand Palmire à mes pieds, par un aveu fatal,
> Insulte à Mahomet, et lui donne un rival? (11, 4)

C'est le souverain qui est blessé et non l'amant. Quand Palmire se donne la mort devant lui et devant le peuple, il ne s'agenouille pas devant la victime, ne perd pas la raison comme Oreste, et ne se suicide pas à son tour.

Le Mahomet de Voltaire est un personnage que la scène française n'avait jamais connu auparavant. Différent des amants de la tragédie classique, il représente une tentative de la part de son auteur pour créer une tragédie d'un genre tout nouveau où l'ambition politique se substitue à l'amour comme ressort de l'action. Le temps et le soin que l'auteur mit à écrire son chef-d'œuvre, l'originalité de son héros Mahomet, tout concourt à nous convaincre que Voltaire avait la passion du théâtre, que son dessein n'était pas nécessairement de rendre le christianisme odieux, mais de faire une œuvre d'art originale par rapport à ses prédécesseurs, et comme disait Voltaire à son ami Cideville: "Ce Mahomet n'est pas comme vous croyez bien le Mahomet second qui coupe la tête à sa bien aimée, c'est Mahomet le fanatique, le cruel, le fourbe et à la honte des hommes le grand, qui de garçon marchand devient prophète, législateur et monarque" (Best.D2221).

Madgy Badir
University of Alberta

A Forgotten Eighteenth-Century French Translation of Shakespeare's *Julius Caesar*

The growth of French interest in Shakespeare during the eighteenth century has long been thoroughly documented. Both favorable and hostile attitudes towards Shakespeare were usually expressed in terms of literary values, but both were tightly bound to the non-literary phenomena encompassed in patterns of anglomania and anglophobia which developed after 1750. With Le Tourneur's translation of 1776-83 all of Shakespeare's plays became available to the French public, but a few, notably *Hamlet, Romeo and Juliet, King Lear, Macbeth,* and *Othello*, had been previously translated or adapted several times. Although not the most frequently translated, *Julius Caesar* was nevertheless, with Voltaire's *La mort de César* (1735), one of the first to be adapted to the French Stage.

The political implications of the struggle between monarchism and republicanism in *Julius Caesar* are clearly very great and yet it is perhaps not surprising that during the revolutionary period so little attempt appears to have been made to use a play which, while portraying tyrannicide and containing ringing speeches on liberty, ends with the defeat of the republic and the establishment of an empire after a struggle which Shakespeare portrays with great subtlety and without the clear division between the good and the bad that passionate times require.

Nevertheless there was one translation of *Julius Caesar* that did appear in the midst of the most turbulent period of the Revolution. This translation, produced and published by Nicolas de Bonneville,[1] has gone essentially unnoticed and is not mentioned in the various bibliographies and studies of Shakespeare in France.[2] It is of particular interest, however, for while Bonneville's translations of German plays are fairly well known, his concern with English literature is rather less well documented. Furthermore, the translation appeared at a moment of extreme political tension, in July 1793, the month in which Marat was assassinated and in which Bonneville himself was under threat of arrest. Although Bonneville's interest in *Julius Caesar* dates from the pre-revolutionary period, his publication of it in July 1793 was clearly motivated as much by political as by literary considerations.

Nicolas de Bonneville, friend of Thomas Paine, active revolutionary and pre-romantic writer, belonged to that generation which bridged the turbulent period between the reign of Louis XV and the beginning of the July monarchy. Born in 1760 at Evreux, Bonneville studied modern languages and became proficient in German and English. During the 1780's he undertook, with A.C. Friedel, to prepare and publish in French the main works of the German theatre. Bonneville appears to have done most of the work for this translation, which was published during the years 1782-85. It was essentially through this *Nouveau Théâtre allemand* that Bonneville was known before the Revolution. A project which he and Friedel had elaborated of publishing in French the major German novels did not come to fruition because of Friedel's death. Instead, Bonneville published in one volume a *Choix de petits romans imités de l'allemand* (Paris: Barrois, 1786). It is in this volume that he included some of his own poems and also the translation of scenes from two of Shakespeare's plays: the monologue from the beginning of *Richard III* and Hamlet's monologue "To be or not to be". In 1789 Bonneville began to participate more and more actively in public political life, both as a journalist and as a political figure.[4] He became an Elector of the city of Paris and gained some prominence almost immediately when he was made a commissioner responsible for the supplying of provisions to Paris. In the early period of the Revolution he allied himself with the more radical forces. With the abbé Fauchet he produced *La Bouche de fer* (1790-91) and then from 1791 until July 1793 he was editor of the *Chronique du mois* and with him were associated such names as Condorcet, L.-S. Mercier, and Collot d'Herbois. However, although in 1791 Bonneville's name was connected with the earliest republican tendency, by 1793 his association with the members of the Gironde (Dussaulx, Kersaint, Mercier, Roland, etc.) was placing him in that group which was to be eliminated as counter-revolutionary by the events of May 31-June 2. On May 18, during a session of the Convention Nationale, Levasseur referred to Bonneville as an aristocrat and Marat, who had already publicly attacked him in August 1792, joined in calling him "un aristocrate infâme. . . l'entremetteur de Fauchet."[5] With the fall of the Gironde, Bonneville's fate appeared sealed and indeed he was arrested, but was saved from the guillotine by the events of 9 Thermidor.[6]

Since the early months of the Revolution Lucius Junius Brutus had been a fashionable figure. His bust had been involved in a moment of drama at the May 28 session of the Commune when Hébert, recently arrested and released again as the Girondins began to lose control of the situation, entered the assembly: "Hébert entre dans la salle du conseil. De nombreux applaudissements retentissent de toutes parts. . . Chaumette lui remet entre les mains une couronne que lui avaient destinée des patriotes. Hébert la dépose sur le buste de J.-J. Rousseau . . . Une citoyenne des tribunes apporte une couronne qu'elle destine à être placée sur le buste de Brutus."[7] In July the Convention decreed that "les bustes de Marat, Michel Lepelletier, Dampierre et Brutus seront placés dans le lieu de ses séances."[8] Now, in the month in which Marat was assassinated, Bonneville seems to have decided that the public should be reminded of the story of another Brutus

Thus the translation of *Julius Caesar* which he had prepared appeared in the final number of the *Chronique du mois* (July 1793), preceded by a pretentious preface which nevertheless provides an interesting glimpse of Bonneville's ideas on translation in general and information on what he considered to be the value of this particular one. For, as Pierre Spriet has pointed out, "each approach to Shakespeare's text expresses a cultural commitment, some would say an ideology; the adoption of an archeological attitude is no less committed than the choice of a radical modernization of the original."[10]

Bonneville alludes to the theory that it was not Shakespeare but those who undertook after his death to publish his works who were responsible for dividing his plays into acts resembling thus in external form the French imitations of Greek tragedy. But according to Bonneville, the French did not really understand the nature of the Greek theatre in its unique naturalness, and, as the Greek theatre is unique, so the plays of Shakespeare form "un genre à part": "les Grecs ont un genre à part, on peut les égaler sans doute, mais non les surpasser en ce qu'ils ont de beau; c'est la nature elle-même, toujours simple et toujours belle. . . Shakespear a aussi un genre à part; ce qui forme son genre à lui, c'est l'art admirable qu'il emploie dans le développement *successif* d'un grand caractère."[11] Shakespearian tragedy, which Bonneville seems to consider progressive and dynamic in nature, rather than static and vertical as in the case of Greek tragedy, accords to time an active role and cannot therefore accommodate itself to the confines of the three unities. As a result, Shakespeare has "un nouveau moyen de présenter aux hommes la vérité," but one which is no less a depiction of reality than is the Greek tragedy.

Rather than a discourse on the merits of Shakespeare and the ignorance of his critics, Bonneville proposes to present one of Shakespeare's works to the judgment of his fellow citizens, "vous Républicains, qui ne voulez qu'être justes, et qui désirez aujourd'hui un nouveau spectacle, fait par des hommes libres" (p. 70).[12] His motive in publishing the translation is thus ostensibly literary although it is expressed in political terms.

But the timidity and conservatism which characterized previous attempts to translate Shakespeare into French are not overcome, even in the midst of this revolutionary period, for Bonneville adds: "Comme il ne faut rien brusquer cependant, j'ai d'abord cherché un plan qui vous convînt, qui ne blessât point trop les préjugés qu'on aime à caresser encore" (p. 70). Nevertheless, "près de Shakespear en liberté, je me suis trouvé parfaitement à mon aise," claims Bonneville, and so he has felt able to break the mold into which Shakespeare had been put. The bold tone returns and Bonneville proclaims: "J'ai senti que je pourrais. . . le suivre même, à volonté, dans ses écarts, souvent nécessaires pour le bien connaître. Si vous désirez connaître Shakespear, et ne pas couper les ailes du génie, craignez les censures minutieuses. . . " (p. 70). The new form that Bonneville has found, the way in which he proposes to release Shakespeare from the confines of forms which had been imposed on his theatre after his death, is to abolish acts and to replace them by an uninterrupted sequence of scenes. This sequence of scenes he considers to be "un genre absolument neuf pour notre scène" (p. 71)[13] and to correspond to "le plan primitif" (p. 71) of Shakespeare.

Bonneville's experience as a translator is evident in his remarks on the difficulties of translation. "Le style d'un ouvrage," he claims, "qui en est l'âme et la couleur ne se traduit pas" (p. 71). Thus the poetry of Shakespeare is presented as being at one and the same time central to the play and impossible to translate. Bonneville therefore returns to the general preoccupation of the translators of the period: the desire to render the idea, the general spirit of the original. Voltaire's failure is an illustration of the truth of this assertion. Any claims to translate style would be presumptuous, says Bonneville, before going on to claim, presumptuously, to have avoided slavish adherence to Shakespeare's text "en marchant à son côté, son égal. . . écrivant en homme libre, comme Shakespear, ce semble, eût écrit, s'il n'avait eu que notre langue en main. . . " (p. 71).

Obviously, the rhetoric of the period explains some of the apparently outrageous claims that Bonneville makes. And it is in the spirit of republican morality that he ends his introduction: "Je vous croirais, en vérité, bien peu Républicains, et bien peu dignes de sentir un bel ouvrage, si après avoir vu la *pièce dramatique* où Shakespear a peint son Brutus, vous ne preniez pas quelque plaisir à vous dire les uns aux autres: Voilà un homme, voilà un caractère, voilà un grand peintre du coeur humain" (p. 72). Bonneville's introduction, then, is a mixture of the rhetoric of the period, a few sensible but banal remarks on the difficulty of translation and evidence that he had some knowledge of the background and nature of Shakespeare's theatre as it was understood in the eighteenth century. An examination of the text of the translation reveals a not unexpected mixture of literary and linguistic conservatism[14] together with revolutionary republican influences. It is clear, from even a cursory examination, that "Bonneville worked from the text of Le Tourneur's translation, which he attempted to improve mainly from three points of view: the external structure, the political relevance, and the language (imagery and tone). The first and second of these categories result in systematic and generally superficial changes that can be described very briefly. The third is somewhat more complex and more interesting.

The change in external organization has already been noted: in place of five acts divided into scenes, Bonneville has chosen to use a division into scenes only. In his remarks on the act and scene division of *Julius Caesar,* Bonneville shows his awareness of a problem that had exercised such English critics as Pope and Samuel Johnson. In the case of *Julius Caesar,* the earliest known version, then as now, was that included in the First Folio of 1623. There, it is divided into acts but scenes are not indicated. In his edition of the works of Shakespeare in 1765, Johnson objected to this division, yet did not dare to reject it outright in practice. "I have preserved the common distribution of the plays into acts, though I believe it to be in almost all the plays void of authority. . . [Shakespeare's] plays were written, and at first printed, in one unbroken continuity, and ought now to be exhibited with short pauses, interposed as often as the scene is changed, or any considerable time is required to pass."[15] In the twentieth century, opinions on this matter still tend to be expressed with some degree of caution. One critic believes "that some, but not all, of Shakespeare's plays were composed in five 'acts.' But it seems best not to intrude this belief."[16] More assertively, T.W. Baldwin sees the existence of acts and scenes built into the structure of the plays, whether or not they were specifically indicated in the manuscript or printed versions: "The plays are certainly constructed in units, which contemporaries called acts. How the divisions between these units were discriminated, and whether these divisions were observed upon the stage are totally different matters . . . Whether the author himself discriminated the scenes by numbering, heading, centered entrances, etc., is of no real importance. According to Sir Walter [Greg], scenes are organic and functional on the Elizabethan stage, not merely external and mechanical. I take it, therefore, it is agreed that Shakespeare, like everybody else, wrote in scenes, whether or however he marked them, or wished them to be observed."[17]

Bonneville's departure from established tradition appears, at first glance, to be to some extent justifiable and to represent not so much an attempt to recreate the actual state of the play as written by Shakespeare as to find a form that would be in harmony with the nature and fundamental movement of the play. As usually edited, *Julius Caesar* is divided into five acts which are further subdivided into a total of eighteen scenes. Samuel Johnson's edition followed by Le Tourneur in his translation, maintains the act divisions, but adopts a division into a total of thirty-seven scenes, seven in every act except the fifth. Now Bonneville further subdivides to produce a total of seventy-one scenes. More than a century later, an English critic characterized *Julius Caesar* as being "of the panoramic, if not of the kaleidoscopic, order of drama — its appeal is of sequence rather than of composition."[18] Yet although Bonneville's idea might appear innovative at first glance, in the context in which he is working it is in fact traditionalist because, far from seeking to make the scene divisions correspond to an underlying structure, in the end the method he adopts for distinguishing scenes is merely the French classical practice of beginning a new scene each time a character enters or leaves the stage.

The political relevance in 1793 of a play such as *Julius Caesar* is obvious; at least, it is clear that it contains many lines which could easily be applied to the revolutionary situation and many sentiments which accorded well with the republican enthusiasm of the period. Bonneville made some attempt to emphasize these elements and to remove from the play certain forms of address that were out of fashion at that time. Thus the "My Lord" of Shakespeare, translated by Le Tourneur as "Seigneur," is variously replaced by the proper name or simply omitted: "Seigneur" is never used by Bonneville. "Madame" disappears in the same way. At times this betrays entirely the tone of the Shakespearian scene as, for example, in II, 4, when Portia questions the Soothsayer: "*Por.* Come hither, fellow: which way hast thou been? *Sooth.* At mine own house, good lady."[19] Le Tourneur renders the Soothsayer's reply: "Noble dame, de ma maison." Bonneville gives: "Femme! — de ma maison." Naturally, the word "noble" is expunged, even where quite clearly it is not used in the sense of "aristocratic." Thus the "bold or noble enterprise" (I, 2) becomes in Le Tourneur "quelque entreprise noble et hardie" (I, 5) and in Bonneville "une entreprise hardie" (Sc. 6). It would be fastidious to compile all the examples of the "purification," in the republican sense, of the language of *Julius Caesar*. The preceding examples are typical and illustrate the tone and, to some extent, the degree to which Bonneville's translation differs from Le Tourneur's.

However, although Bonneville's sympathies are republican, he is not favorably disposed towards the *mob*. Attention has frequently been drawn to the contemptuous tone of Shakespeare's treatment of the *mob* with its "stinking breath." In his translation, Bonneville uses various devices to heighten that hostility. It is in this connection that he reintroduces the word "noble" on one single occasion in order to add a sharpened ironic tone to the description of the mob. Thus where Shakespeare's word is "rabblement" (I, 2) and where Voltaire had used "canaille" (I, 5), Bonneville translates "noble assemblée" (Sc. 6).

At times, though only occasionally in the first three acts, Bonneville goes entirely beyond Shakespeare's text and adds lines of his own invention. At the beginning of Scene 43 (Shakespeare, III, 2; Le Tourneur, III, 2), immediately after Anthony has whipped the crowd into a riotous mood, Bonneville adds the following exchange:

Une voix.   Voyez-vous ces prêtres qui ne veulent pas recevoir le corps de César?

Une autre voix. Ils nous font des Dieux, qu'on n'en sait pas des trois quarts le nombre, et ils ne veulent pas que nous en fassions un, nous autres!

Une autre voix. Il faudra bien cependant en passer par là.

Once again the mob is shown in a hostile light, that of its unreasoning desire to deify its leaders. In effect the mob is portrayed as anti-republican and counter-revolutionary. Shakespeare reinforces his criticism by having the mob cheerfully kill Cinna because of his name. Bonneville goes even further and adds a short scene (Scene 46 between Shakespeare, IV, 1 and 2: Le Tourneur, IV, 1 and 2) in which Cicero, wounded and bleeding, is dragged by the raging mob into the Capitol, where he is rescued by Lepidus. Cicero exclaims before he collapses: "Et moi aussi, Triumvir, j'ai été porté en triomphe par le peuple!" Thus, as far as the early part of Act IV, the only major additions to or expansions of Shakespeare's text clearly have a political function and contain, as an underlying message, an attack on mob rule.

There are, however, other changes, mainly concentrated in the last two acts of Shakespeare's text. On the whole, Bonneville remains quite close to the original in the first three acts. The influence of Voltaire's translation[20] is clearly visible in this part of Bonneville's version. In Acts IV and V, however, precisely that part of the play that Voltaire had not translated, Bonneville omits passages and rearranges the text in such a way that he verges on adaptation rather than translation. The treatment accorded to the original, the basic presence of Le Tourneur's translation and the influence of Voltaire's translation can best be shown by three examples taken from various parts of the play.[21]

The first example is from the beginning of Act I, Scene 1:

Mar.	You, sir, what trade are you?
Sec. Cit.	Truly, sir, in respect of a fine workman, I am but, as you would say, a cobbler.
Mar.	But what trade art thou? answer me directly.
Sec. Cit.	A trade, sir, that I hope I may use with a safe conscience; which is indeed, sir, a mender of bad soles.
Mar.	What trade, thou knave? thou naughty knave, what trade?
Sec. Cit.	Nay, I beseech you, sir, be not out with me: yet if you be out, sir, I can mend you.
Mar.	What meanst thou by that: mend me, thou saucy fellow!
Sec. Cit.	Why, sir, cobble you.
Flav.	Thou art a cobbler, art thou?
Sec. Cit.	Truly, sir, all that I live by is with the awl; I meddle with no tradesman's matters, nor women's matters, but with awl. I am indeed, sir, a surgeon to old shoes; when they are in great danger, I recover them. As proper men as ever trod upon neats-leather have gone upon my handiwork.

Le Tourneur does not even attempt to translate the whole of this passage but reduces it to what he considers the essential idea:

Mar.	Et vous, je vous prie, quel est votre métier?
Sec. Pléb.	En vérité, Tribun, ce qui me fait vivre c'est mon aiguille: je ne me mêle ni d'affaires de négoce, ni d'intrigues de femmes; mais je fais revivre les vieux brodequins; quand ils sont en péril, mon art les sauve; le plus fier patricien a marché sur l'œuvre de mes mains. (I, 1)

Bonneville's version is in many ways more faithful and certainly more complete than Le Tourneur's.

Mar.   Et vous, je vous prie, quel est votre métier?
Une voix.   Mon métier, à moi, je suis comme qui dirait, sauf votre respect, Tribun . . . Je raccommode ce qui est usé.
Mar.   Je te demande quel est ton métier?
La même voix. C'est un métier que je puis faire en toute sûreté de conscience.
Flav. [sic] Ton métier, insolent? ton métier?
La même voix. Insolent? insolent? écoutez donc, ne vous fâchez pas, ne vous fâchez pas, savez-vous que je pourrais vous redresser, vous raccommoder?
Flav.   Que veux-tu dire par là?
La même voix. En vérité, Tribun, ce qui me fait vivre, c'est mon alêne; je ne me mêle d'aucune affaire, moi; ni d'hommes, ni de femmes; je fais revivre les vieux brodequins, quand ils sont prêts de périr, je les rétablis, moi, je les rétablis: les plus huppés de vos sénateurs ont marché sur l'œuvre de mes mains. (Sc. 1)

Bonneville's desire to remain close to the text is obvious. At the same time, the influence of Voltaire is clear in such matters as the not unsuccessful attempt to render into French the play on the word "cobbler," the omission of which by Le Tourneur had been strongly criticized by Voltaire. Bonneville also makes a much greater attempt than Le Tourneur to render the tone of popular speech.

The second example is also drawn from an early part of the play, but from a section in blank verse which is of a more evocative and poetic nature than the conversation of the opening scene:

Cic.   Why, saw you anything more wonderful?
Casca.   A common slave — you know him well by sight —
Held up his left hand, which did flame and burn
Like twenty torches join'd; and yet his hand,
Not sensible of fire, remained unscorcht.
Besides, — I ha'not since put up my sword, —
Against the Capitol I met a lion,
Who glazed upon me, and went surly by,
Without annoying me: and there were drawn
Upon a heap a hundred ghastly women,
Transformed with their fear; who swore they saw
Men, all in fire, walk up and down the streets.
And yesterday the bird of night did sit
Even at noonday upon the market-place,
Hooting and shrieking. (I, 3)

113

Le Tourneur's translation is complete and remains relatively faithful to Shakespeare's text:

Cic.   Eh Quoi! Qu'as-tu vu de si étrange?

Casca.   Un Esclave, vous le connaissez de vue, a levé sa main gauche en l'air; sa main a flambé soudain et brûlait comme vingt torches unies; et cependant sa main, sans en être offensée, restait insensible à la flamme. Bien plus, et depuis mon épée n'est pas rentrée dans le fourreau, devant le Capitole j'ai rencontré un lion; il me fixe d'un œil étincelant, et passe fièrement sans me nuire; et là s'est offert à moi un groupe de visages effarés; cent femmes que leur frayeur avait changées en statues; elles jurent qu'elles ont vu des hommes tout en flamme courir çà et là dans les rues; et hier l'oiseau de la nuit s'est abattu en plein midi, sur la place du marché, poussant des cris aigus et funèbres. (1, 6)

Bonneville on the other hand, while basing himself almost entirely on the Le Tourneur translation, omits part of the speech altogether:

Cic.   Qu'as-tu donc vu de si étrange?

Casca.   Un esclave, que vous connaissez de vue . . . Non, non, cela n'est rien encore. — Oui, tout à l'heure, devant le Capitole, et depuis mon épée n'est pas rentrée dans le fourreau, j'ai rencontré un lion, qui me fixe d'un œil étincelant, et passe fièrement sans me nuire. Et là, s'est offert à moi, sur un tertre élevé, un groupe de visages effarés, cent femmes que leur frayeur avait changées en statues. Elles jurent qu'elles ont vu des hommes, tout en flammes, courir dans les rues, et qu'hier le hibou sinistre s'est abattu en plein midi, sur la place publique, poussant des cris aigus. (Sc. 9)

In spite of this tendency towards omission on the one hand and extreme dependence on Le Tourneur on the other hand, Bonneville does try to render one or two details which he apparently felt Le Tourneur was mistaken to neglect. But his translation of *upon a heap* ("sur un tertre élevé") is merely proof of his sometimes imperfect grasp of the English text. What *is* clearly illustrated by this passage, however, is that Bonneville was not merely working with the Le Tourneur translation in an attempt to improve it as a French text, but was simultaneously using the English original as his basic text.

The omissions, expansions and examples of re-arrangement become more numerous particularly from Scene 55 to the end (*Julius Caesar*, V). The predominance of omission over expansion and the nature of the changes suggest that this last part of the translation was prepared in some haste.[22] In certain sections one can scarcely speak of translation, since although some lines are rendered accurately, in many cases Bonneville gives what is in effect a paraphrase. The following speech by Cassius is typical of Bonneville's technique towards the end of the play:

Cass.	Messala,
	This is my birth-day; as this very day
	Was Cassius born. Give me thy hand, Messala:
	Be thou my witness that, against my will,
	As Pompey was, am I compelled to set
	Upon one battle all our liberties.
	You know that I held Epicurus strong,
	And his opinion: now I change my mind,
	And partly credit things that do presage.
	Coming from Sardis, on our former ensign
	Two mighty eagles fell; and there they percht,
	Gorging and feeding from our soldiers' hands;
	Who to Phillippi here consorted us:
	This morning they are fled away and gone;
	And in their stead do ravens, crows, and kites,
	Fly o'er our heads, and downward look on us,
	As we were sickly prey: their shadows seem
	A canopy most fatal, under which
	Our army lies, ready to give up the ghost. (V, 1)

Bonneville:

Messala.	Que veut mon général?
Cassius.	Que tu saches que c'est malgré moi que je suis forcé, comme le fut Pompée, de confier aux hasards d'une seule bataille tout le dépôt de notre liberté. — Tu sais que j'ai toujours dédaigné ces vains présages; et je sens aujourd'hui que mon cœur, en dépit de ma raison, ajoute quelque foi à des pressentiments. Tu as vu ce matin ces deux aigles qui prenaient leur pâture dans la main de nos guerriers, comme ils ont disparu! Remarques-tu cette nuée de corbeaux voraces et de vautours, dont l'ombre impure couvre notre armée comme un cadavre expirant? (Sc. 57)

The weakening of the sense of personal doom and of the emotion felt by the spectator through the omission of references to Cassius' birthday and to the defeated Pompey, in a word the exclusion of many of those elements that Shakespeare used to give great density to Cassius' speech and to create a sense of the crushing weight of doom pressing down on Cassius, seriously mars the effect of the passage. What is left is tame and colorless, superficial and lacking in dramatic tension.

The weakness of the passage is particularly significant because it does not stem from any difficulty inherent in the translation itself. Cassius' speech does not contain images that would be particularly difficult to render into French or that would appear too strong or bizarre in translation.[23] Bonneville is compressing by omitting what he clearly believes are non-essential elements in the original and in so doing, he is demonstrating his inability to appreciate fully the richness of Shakespeare's text. What is noticeable is that the omissions are less likely to affect Brutus' speeches, for Brutus is clearly, for Bonneville, the central figure of the play.

The final scene (V, 5) of the original (Bonneville, Sc. 66-71) follows Shakespeare only loosely and in fact, is closer to Plutarch than to Shakespeare. Bonneville incorporates from Plutarch Brutus' answer when urged to flee: "Il faut fuir, mais avec les mains et non avec les pieds." In Bonneville's version, Brutus kills himself without an intermediary, the version of Brutus' death that Plutarch accepts as most probable.

After Brutus' death, Bonneville presents the final speeches of Anthony and Octavius with relatively little alteration, but reverses their order so that the play ends with Anthony's praise of Brutus.[24]

Finally, Bonneville adds an Epilogue suitable to the spirit of the times with clear reference to the events of May and June 1793:

> On lit en lettres de feu, au cœur de la scène, ces dernières paroles d'un proscrit:
> > Peuple, souvent trompé, garde-toi de proscrire;
> > Garde-toi de frapper sans un mûr examen.
> > Ouvre les yeux, si tu sais lire;
> > C'est l'histoire . . . Ouvre donc . . . C'est le peuple Romain.
> > Ils le flattaient pour le séduire,
> > Ils se proclamaient ses amis,
> > L'appelaient Peuple-Roi, pourvu qu'il fût soumis.
> > Plains un peuple puni de son cruel délire.
> > D'un franc républicain conserve les écrits;
> > Brutus et Cicéron dans Rome sont proscrits. (p. 168)

Bonneville was about to be arrested and the attacks on him by Marat and others left little doubt as to his probable fate. It is clear that he published his translation hurriedly and the Epilogue is testamentary in tone. Had he had more time, would Bonneville have been able to produce a better translation? There is little in his previous work that would justify such a supposition. Once again, the incompatibility of "the two most incompatible tongues of the Western world"[25] had overwhelmed the efforts of the translator.

Bonneville's introduction shows that his intention is close to that expressed by the Jansenists of Port-Royal in the seventeenth century in connection with Cicero: "il faut être extrêmement fidèle et littéral, et traduire comme Ciceron eût écrit s'il avait parlé notre langue."[26] But in practice he comes closer to the adaptive and modifying translation advocated by Houdart de la Motte in the first half of the eighteenth century. Bonneville's attempts to improve on Le Tourneur's translation fail, except in one or two minor instances. The clash and thrust of political ideas and the rapid evolution of the language during the revolutionary period did not find their echo in the timid and essentially colorless attempt by Bonneville to present Shakespeare's bold and vital tragedy to a politically aroused French public. Yet at the same time the fact that one of the more active journalists and writers of the period should choose to attempt to influence his public through the translation of *Julius Caesar* is a further illustration of the extent to which Shakespeare was present in France and was penetrating French consciousness at the close of the eighteenth century.

E.T. Annandale
University of Manitoba

116

Notes

[1] The only detailed study on Bonneville is Philippe Le Harivel's *Nicolas de Bonneville, préromantique et révolutionnaire, 1760-1828* (Strasbourg: Istra, 1923). Bonneville's translation of *Julius Caesar* is not mentioned.

[2] M. Horn-Monval, *Les Traductions françaises de Shakespeare* (Paris: C.N.R.S., 1963), does list "(Jules César) . . . Voilà un homme! (*Brutus!*) Scènes révolutionnaires, adapt. de N. Bonneville, extr. . . . 1793 (pp. 69-168). P. sans nom, 1793." This is, in fact, Bonneville's translation, but the reference is obscure and is incorrect in stating that this is a translation of extracts. There is a similar reference in A. Martin and G. Walter, *Catalogue de l'histoire de la Révolution française* (Paris: Bibliothèque Nationale, 1936-), V, 153, in connection with the July 1793 issue of the *Chronique du mois*: "Voilà un homme! Scènes révolutionnaires (traduction libre par N. Bonneville de quelques scènes de *Jules César* de Shakespeare)."

[3] Le Harivel, *Bonneville*, p. 130, states incorrectly that the quarrel between Cassius and Brutus in *Julius Caesar* is also included. Cf. also A. Génuist, *Le Théâtre de Shakespeare dans l'œuvre de Pierre Le Tourneur* (Paris: Didier, 1971), p. 256.

[4] See, for example, *Actes de la Commune de Paris*, 1ère série, II, 9, 12, 51; VI, 163; VII, 565-78, 585-96, etc.

[5] *Moniteur*, May 20, 1793, p. 420. Already in August 1792, Marat had called him a "flagorneur soudoyé de Bailly et Motier" (*Marat, ami du peuple, aux amis de la patrie*, Sept. 5, 1792).

[6] By January 1795, Bonneville's fortunes were improving and his name was included in the list of those "qui ont droit aux récompenses nationales" (*Procès-verbaux du Comité d'instruction publique, Convention Nationale*, V, 450).

[7] *Moniteur*, May 31, 1793, p. 506.

[8] *Moniteur*, July 27, 1793, p. 234. By February 1795 only the bust of Brutus remained in its place (*Moniteur*, Feb. 11, 1795, p. 421).

[9] Voltaire's *La Mort de César* had of course also performed this function.

[10] Pierre Spriet, "Beyond the limitations of translation," *Shakespeare Translation*, 2 (1975), 1-15.

[11] *La Chronique du Mois ou les Cahiers patriotiques des amis de la vérité*, July 1793, p. 69. Further quotations from Bonneville's Preface will be followed by the page number. Quotations from the translation itself will be identified by the scene number.

[12] Three years earlier, however, he had said: ". . . mais Shakespeare, avec toute la richesse de ses couleurs, la vérité de ses caractères et la majesté de ses tableaux, n'a pas fait un ouvrage dramatique dont l'ensemble soit supportable" (Preface to *L'Année MDCCLXXXIX ou les Tribuns du peuple* [Paris, 1790], p. viii).

[13] But L.-S. Mercier, for example, had already published *La Mort de Louis XI*, a play divided exclusively into scenes, in 1783.

[14] Bonneville's literary career is strewn with contradictory examples of, on the one hand, conservatism and, on the other, a willingness to go to bizarre lengths in the creation of spectacle. Thus, in spite of some neologisms, his translations of German plays are essentially conservative. But his own play, *L'Année 1789 ou les Tribuns du peuple* contains extravagances which are astonishing.

[15] S. Johnson, *Shakespeare* (1765), quoted by T. W. Baldwin, *On Act and Scene Divisions in the Shakespeare First Folio* (Carbondale and Edwardsville: Southern Illinois University Press, 1965), p. 18.

[16] C. Leech, "Message to the editor," in *Shakespeare Translation*, 1 (1974), p. x.

[17] T. W. Baldwin, *On Act and Scene Divisions*, pp. 25-26.

[18] *The Cambridge History of English Literature* (Cambridge: Cambridge University Press, 1910), V, 197.

[19] Our quotations from Shakespeare are taken from *The Complete Works*, ed. Peter Alexander (London: Collins, 1951).

[20] See Voltaire, *Jules César* in *Œuvres*, ed. L. Moland (Paris: Garnier, 1877-85), VII, 431-83. First published in 1764.

[21] Because Voltaire's *Jules César* is readily accessible, it is not quoted here. See *Jules César*, I, 1. The edition of Le Tourneur's translation used is that of 1776-83 in 20 volumes (Paris: Veuve Duchesne). *Jules César* is in vol. II, pp. 181-391.

[22] See, for the quarrel scene between Cassius and Brutus, Le Harivel, *Bonneville*, pp. 132-33.

[23] Cf. Le Tourneur, V, 3.

[24] "This was the noblest Roman of them all . . ." It is not surprising to find the word "noble" omitted and replaced by "grand."

[25] Jean Paris, "Translation and Creation," in *The Craft and Context of Translation*, eds. W. Arrowsmith and R. Shattuck (Austin: University of Texas Press, 1961), p. 58.

[26] J. P. Bénard and P. A. Horguelin, *Pratique de le traduction* (Montréal: Linguatech, 1979), p.12.

Les Représentations de Molière
à Paris pendant la Révolution
de la réunion des Etats généraux (mai 1789)
à la fermeture de la Comédie-Française (septembre 1793)

Quand on parle de la vie théâtrale pendant la Révolution française, on ne cite généralement que les pièces dites révolutionnaires, c'est-à-dire celles qui ont été écrites de 1789 à 1795 et, avec cette restriction importante, celles-là seules qui ont été "politiques." Du *Charles IX*, de Marie-Joseph Chénier (4 novembre 1789), aux *Jacobins aux Enfers*, d'Hector Chaussier (22 mars 1795), en passant par *L'Ami des lois*, de Jean-Louis Laya (2 janvier 1793), et par *Le Jugement dernier des rois*, de Sylvain Maréchal (17 octobre 1793), la liste en est longue. On néglige les pièces qui ont été écrites pour moraliser ou pour distraire, les deux n'étant pas incompatibles, et qui ne font aucune allusion ou peu d'allusion à la vie politique, comme *Le Vieux Célibataire*, de Collin d'Harleville (24 février 1792), qui figure pourtant encore en bonne place dans les anthologies "officielles" du théâtre du XVIIIe siècle, ou comme les plaisantes *Visitandines*, de Picard (7 juillet 1792). Mais surtout on ignore le répertoire, toutes les pièces à succès de l'Ancien Régime, qui avec des fortunes diverses ont continué d'être jouées, et non seulement à la Comédie-Française jusqu'à sa fermeture en septembre 1793, mais dans maints autres théâtres de la capitale depuis janvier 1791, date de la suppression des privilèges jadis accordés à certains théâtres (répertoire exclusivement attaché au théâtre qui avait créé les pièces).

Certes, et notamment à partir de la proclamation de la République (septembre 1792), Corneille, Molière, Racine, Marivaux et même Voltaire seront censurés, revus et corrigés: *roi* sera remplacé par *loi*, plus de nobles généreux, plus de trace de servitude. Le vers de *Tartuffe* (V, 7), "Nous vivons sous un prince ennemi de la fraude," deviendra ainsi: "Ils sont passés ces jours d'injustice et de fraude"; et, en décembre 1793, le vers du *Misanthrope* (III, 5), "Et mon valet de chambre est mis dans la Gazette," sera corrigé en: "Et l'homme le plus sot est mis dans la Gazette." Mais les meilleurs auteurs de l'Ancien Régime continueront d'être joués. Ils le seront devant un public neuf, avec le plus souvent des acteurs nouveaux: une vie nouvelle en quelque sorte, bien que difficile parce que soumise à une actualité fluctuante et contraignante. Il suffit de parcourir le répertoire des théâtres pendant la Révolution — et ces théâtres, peu à peu, vont être fort nombreux — pour se convaincre de la vitalité du répertoire "classique."

Dans ce vaste répertoire, l'auteur qui revient le plus souvent est Molière. L'homme qui avait fait rire Louis XIV et sa cour faisait encore rire les sans-culottes, et mieux qu'un autre!

Les faits et les chiffres le prouvent.[1]

Mon intention est de rapporter et de faire parler ici ces faits et ces chiffres, en procédant à un relevé systématique et, autant qu'il se peut, comparatif. Je suis conscient que de l'accumulation de ces données résultera une certaine sécheresse dans l'exposé. D'avance, je demande au lecteur de me le pardonner.

Pour des raisons pratiques, j'ai dû me limiter dans le temps en n'étudiant que les premières années de la Révolution.[2] Mais puisque le nom de Molière est associé étroitement depuis 1680 à celui de la Comédie-Française,[3] j'ai pensé qu'il serait déjà suffisamment concluant de montrer comment Molière s'est maintenu dans sa "maison" durant les premières années de la Révolution, puis comment, profitant des récentes libertés accordées au théâtre, il s'est échappé pour étendre son audience dans Paris, et avant même que la Comédie-Française ne fût fermée par Robespierre (septembre 1793).

I

Molière à la veille de la Révolution

Jusqu'à la Révolution, Molière reste l'auteur de la Comédie-Française, théâtre qui est, lui seul, conservateur légal du répertoire "classique" français joué avant et depuis 1680.

Durant les trois dernières années qui précèdent la Révolution (1786, 1787, 1788) et jusqu'à la réunion des Etats généraux (5 mai 1789), on joue et reprend à la Comédie-Française 17 de ses 34 pièces:[4] *Amphitryon*, *L'Avare*, *Le Bourgeois gentilhomme*, *La Comtesse d'Escarbagnas*, *Le Dépit amoureux*, *L'Ecole des femmes*, *L'Ecole des maris*, *L'Etourdi*, *Les Femmes savantes*, *Les Fourberies de Scapin*, *George Dandin*, *Le Malade imaginaire*, *Le Mariage forcé*, *Le Médecin malgré lui*, *Le Misanthrope*, *M. de Pourceaugnac* (déjà désigné parfois dans les affiches sous le seul nom de *Pourceaugnac*) et *Tartuffe*. Le total des représentations est pour Molière de 222, ses pièces le plus souvent représentées étant *l'Ecole des maris*: 37 représentations, *Amphitryon* et *Le Médecin malgré lui*: 26 chacune, *George Dandin*: 25, et *M. de Pourceaugnac*: 20.

Pour comparaison, les Comédiens-Français, durant le même temps, ont donné 52 représentations de Corneille, *Le Cid* l'emportant sur les autres pièces avec 12 représentations. Racine a 95 représentations, et ses pièces les plus jouées sont *Les Plaideurs*: 19 fois, et *Andromaque*: 14. Voltaire, mort depuis peu (1778) et qui va retrouver une certaine actualité avec la Révolution, ne parvient pas à surpasser Molière: 175 représentations, dont 24 pour *Zaïre* et 19 pour *Mahomet*. Quant à Marivaux, qui avait peu écrit pour les Comédiens-Français, il n'a que 18 représentations (*Le Legs*: 12, et *La Seconde Surprise de l'amour*: 6). Le Théâtre-Italien lui-même qui, en 1779, avait repris son propre répertoire de "pièces françaises," joue Marivaux de moins en moins; seules quelques pièces trouvent encore peu avant la Révolution un public accueillant: *Le Jeu de l'amour et du hasard*, joué jusqu'en septembre 1787; *Les Fausses Confidences*, dont les dernières représentations datent de juin 1788; à quoi il faut ajouter les comédies de *La Mère confidente* et de *L'Epreuve*, qui sont également à l'affiche en 1788. Mais en 1789 le Théâtre-Italien fait silence total sur Marivaux.

II

Jusqu'au décret du 13 janvier 1791

Pendant les vingt mois qui vont de la réunion des Etats généraux (5 mai 1789) au décret du 13 janvier 1791, qui supprimera les privilèges des grands théâtres, la situation est apparemment peu changée en ce qui concerne le répertoire des auteurs "classiques."

A la Comédie-Française, qui en décembre 1789 a pris le nom de Théâtre de la Nation, Molière continue d'être l'auteur du répertoire le plus joué: 15 pièces (les précédentes, moins *Le Malade imaginaire* et *Le Mariage forcé*), avec un total de 119 représentations. La comédie le plus souvent reprise est toujours *L'Ecole des maris*: 22 représentations; suivent *L'Avare*: 14 représentations, *Amphitryon*: 11, et *La Comtesse d'Escarbagnas*: 10. Ajoutons qu'en dehors de ces représentations, le souvenir de Molière se trouve entretenu par plusieurs pièces d'auteurs contemporains. Les Comédiens-Français en effet continuent de jouer *La Maison de Molière, ou la journée de Tartuffe*, comédie de Louis-Sébastien Mercier, créée le 20 octobre 1787 (on l'a jouée avec *Le Misanthrope* le 18 février 1789 "pour l'anniversaire de la mort de Molière"; le 12 septembre 1790, on en annonce la 22e représentation; et elle sera encore jouée le 24 juillet 1793, peu avant la fermeture du théâtre). Et s'ils ont monté sans succès le 19 novembre 1789 une pièce, dite historique, de Cubières-Palmézeaux: *La Mort de Molière*, on s'agite beaucoup, en revanche, depuis sa création, le 22 février 1790, autour de la comédie de Fabre d'Eglantine, *Le Philinte de Molière, ou la suite du Misanthrope*.

Durant le même temps, Corneille n'a que 5 pièces représentées avec un total de 18 représentations, dont 7 pour la comédie du *Menteur*, reprise le 18 mai 1789, et 5 pour *Le Cid*. Racine a 8 pièces représentées avec un total de 42 représentations, sa comédie des *Plaideurs* continuant d'être sa pièce la plus jouée (10 représentations). Voltaire, reconnu comme un des initiateurs du mouvement révolutionnaire, est souvent à l'affiche. Moins que Molière cependant: 13 pièces et 85 représentations; mais la reprise de sa tragédie de *Brutus*, le 17 novembre 1790, a fait grand bruit (le buste de Voltaire a même été apporté sur la scène) et va quelque temps au Théâtre de la Nation servir de point de ralliement aux révolutionnaires (13e représentation le 12 janvier 1791). Marivaux, là encore, fait piètre figure: le Théâtre-Italien continue de l'ignorer; et le Théâtre de la Nation, dans le répertoire qui lui appartient, ne lui concède que 17 représentations pour 4 pièces: *Le Dénouement imprévu, Le Legs, Le Préjugé vaincu* et *La Seconde Surprise de l'amour*.

III

De la liberté des spectacles à la proclamation de la République (13 janvier 1791 - 21 septembre 1792)

Au début de 1789, Paris comptait huit théâtres principaux: l'Académie royale de musique (l'Opéra); le Théâtre-Français (Comédie-Française); le Théâtre-Italien; le Théâtre de Monsieur, qui ouvrit dans la salle des Tuileries le 26 janvier 1789 et qui jouait des opéras italiens, des opéras-comiques français et des comédies françaises; le Théâtre des Variétés du Palais-Royal, plus connu sous le nom de Variétés amusantes; les Petits Comédiens de Beaujolais; les Grands Danseurs du Roi, qui jouaient des pièces et des pantomimes, spectacles agrémentés dans les entractes d'exercices de voltige et de danses; enfin, l'Ambigu-Comique, qui jouait toutes sortes de pièces. Ces théâtres se maintinrent en 1790, parfois en changeant de salle ou de nom (ainsi les Variétés amusantes, qui venaient de prendre le nom de Théâtre du Palais-Royal, s'installèrent en mai 1790 dans une nouvelle salle rue de Richelieu). Pièces nouvelles et pièces anciennes (précédemment créées dans chacun de ces théâtres) se partagent un programme qui, étant toujours à alternance, permet à un grand nombre de pièces d'être représentées dans un espace de temps limité. Chaque théâtre a son propre répertoire, le plus souvent spécialisé; et chacun se surveille jalousement.

Deux théâtres nouveaux ont été autorisés à ouvrir: le Théâtre de la Montansier, qui prit possession le 12 avril 1790 de l'ancienne salle des Beaujolais et qui jouait des pièces avec musique et des comédies; et le Théâtre-Français comique et lyrique, qui ouvrit rue de Bondy le 26 juin 1790.

Ce n'était là qu'un début. Avec le décret de janvier 1791 sur la liberté des spectacles, la vie théâtrale va se trouver en effet rapidement et complètement transformée. Désormais, tout citoyen pourra ouvrir une salle de théâtre, sous la seule réserve d'une déclaration à la municipalité; n'importe qui pourra jouer s'il en a le goût et s'il trouve une salle pour se produire. Plus de censure; n'importe qui pourra s'improviser auteur dramatique. Enfin, les "auteurs morts depuis cinq ans" pourront "être représentés sur tous les théâtres indistinctement." De là cette boutade rapportée en janvier 1792 par l'*Almanach des spectacles* de Froullé: "Bientôt on va compter dans Paris un spectacle par rue, un acteur par maison, un musicien par cave et un auteur par grenier."

Conséquence de cette liberté: les directeurs vont de plus en plus courir le risque de monter, dans des conditions peu propices à l'art, des œuvres nouvelles d'auteurs nouveaux, qui seront promises à une seule et unique représentation. La prudence leur conseille donc de profiter de la levée des interdits pour assurer leurs arrières, et de puiser dans le répertoire du passé, notamment dans l'inépuisable répertoire du Théâtre-Français et du Théâtre-Italien.

Ce théâtre du passé a fait ses preuves. Et comme il s'adressait autant sinon plus au public des villes qu'à celui des privilégiés, il est facile en procédant à un choix et après quelques aménagements de le faire apprécier d'un public populaire, d'autant qu'une grande partie de ce public, nouvellement acquise au

122

théâtre, ignore pour ainsi dire tout du théâtre du passé. Il ne s'agira plus de maintenir un répertoire pour le musée théâtral, comme le faisait le Théâtre-Français, mais de s'assurer un succès présent sur les succès passés, et de satisfaire le besoin, pour le nouveau public, de se cultiver. Il s'agira de distraire par ceux qui, dans le passé, l'ont su faire aussi bien et souvent mieux que la plupart des auteurs du temps présent. D'ailleurs, quand bien même ceux du présent pourraient le faire, ils ne sont pas assez nombreux pour garnir chaque jour les programmes des nombreux théâtres qui se sont ouverts ou s'ouvrent un peu partout dans Paris. Et on en revient à la nécessité de recourir au répertoire. Ajoutons que les œuvres du passé tombées dans le domaine public s'offrent comme une manne aux nombreux comédiens, venus des troupes de province ou comédiens improvisés, impatients de jouer à Paris dans les grands rôles réservés jadis à quelques-uns et qui font souvent la célébrité de ceux qui les interprètent.

C'est ainsi que Molière, par son théâtre comique, profond mais accessible à tout public, devient pour tous l'auteur providentiel.

1

Il l'était déjà, bien sûr, au Théâtre de la Nation, ex-Comédie-Française; et il l'est encore malgré une lente mais constante détérioration du prestige de ce théâtre, longtemps réputé pour être "le premier du monde entier."[5] Dans le vaste répertoire dont il était jusque-là le dépositaire exclusif (pour la seule période de janvier 1791 au 21 septembre 1792, 145 pièces de ce répertoire sont reprises), Molière tient toujours une place de choix: 15 pièces et un total de 93 représentations; soit, par ordre des pièces les plus représentées: *L'Ecole des femmes* et *L'Ecole des maris* avec 14 représentations chacune; *George Dandin*: 8; même total pour *Tartuffe*, comédie recommandée aux Parisiens comme une "peinture fidèle de l'hypocrisie et du fanatisme" (*Chronique de Paris*, 16 novembre 1791); *La Comtesse d'Escarbagnas* et *Le Médecin malgré lui*: 7 chacune; *M. de Pourceaugnac*: 6; *Amphitryon, Les Femmes savantes* et *Le Malade imaginaire*: 5; *Le Bourgeois gentilhomme* et *Le Misanthrope*: 4; *L'Avare*: 3; *Le Dépit amoureux*: 2; *L'Etourdi*: 1. Comparativement, c'est Voltaire qui talonne Molière: 15 pièces représentées et un total de 71 représentations: succès dû en grande partie au fait que de mai à juillet 1791 Paris a vécu à l'heure de Voltaire, avec le retour de son corps à Paris et sa translation, en "apothéose" (*sic*), au Panthéon. Viennent ensuite Racine: 7 pièces et 35 représentations; Corneille: 5 pièces et 21 représentations; Marivaux: 3 pièces et 21 représentations.

Mais depuis janvier 1791 l'ancienne Comédie-Française n'est plus le seul théâtre à transmettre l'héritage du passé. De plus, par son incapacité de se renouveler et de maîtriser les différents courants politiques qui l'agitent, elle se condamne elle-même et ses jours sont comptés. Elle commence par perdre son unité: le 27 avril 1791, les comédiens "rouges," qu'on appelait aussi les "démocrates" (Talma, Dugazon, Grandmesnil, Mlles Desgarcins, Lange, Vestris, et d'autres), se séparent de leurs camarades réputés "inciviques" et "aristocrates." Passant les ponts de la Seine, ils émigrent rue de Richelieu au Théâtre du Palais-Royal, inaugurant une nouvelle entreprise qui se donnera le nom concurrentiel de Théâtre-Français de la rue de Richelieu. Ils y reprendront d'abord les rôles qu'ils tenaient au Théâtre de la Nation; puis, en s'associant aux comédiens du Palais-Royal, ils feront revivre avec eux le meilleur du répertoire des XVIIe et XVIIIe siècles. Le 8 mars 1791, les comédiens du Palais-Royal avaient déjà donné l'exemple en montant, de Marivaux, *Le Jeu de l'amour et du hasard*, qui avait appartenu au Théâtre-Italien. Dans ce répertoire renouvelé, Molière occupe toujours la première place. Sur 128 pièces qui constituent jusqu'en septembre 1792 le répertoire de ce nouveau théâtre, on joue 11 pièces de Molière: *Le Médecin malgré lui*, avec 21 représentations; *L'Ecole des maris*: 11; *Le Dépit amoureux*: 10; *Les Fourberies de Scapin* et *Tartuffe*: 9 chacune; *L'Avare, L'Ecole des femmes, L'Etourdi* et *Les Précieuses ridicules*: 5; *La Comtesse d'Escarbagnas* et *Le Misanthrope*: 3; au total, 86 représentations.

Pour comparaison, c'est Voltaire qui vient ici encore en seconde position des "auteurs classiques," avec 10 pièces représentées et 45 représentations (dont 10 pour *Brutus* et 9 pour sa comédie de *Nanine*). A presque égale distance, Marivaux, dont le répertoire "français" s'enrichit maintenant du répertoire des Italiens, avec 8 pièces représentées et 49 représentations (dont 11 pour *Les Fausses Confidences* et 9 pour *Le Jeu de l'amour et du hasard*); puis, Racine: 4 pièces et 20 représentations (dont 11 pour *Les Plaideurs*); enfin, Corneille: 4 pièces et 13 représentations (dont 4 pour *Le Cid*).

2

Plusieurs théâtres qui existaient déjà en 1789 n'ont pas attendu la scission du Théâtre-Français pour lui emprunter son répertoire et introduire les pièces "classiques" dans leurs programmes. Certains l'ont fait systématiquement, d'autres occasionnellement.

L'ancien Théâtre de Monsieur, installé en janvier 1791 rue Feydeau et qui en juin prendra le nom de Théâtre de la rue Feydeau, paraît avoir été le plus hésitant: quatre pièces seulement sont empruntées au Théâtre-Français et au Théâtre-Italien, dont *Le Dépit amoureux* de Molière: 7 représentations.[6] C'est que ce théâtre se consacre essentiellement aux pièces nouvelles: 117, depuis son ouverture aux Tuileries en janvier 1789 jusqu'en septembre 1792.[7]

Dans les autres théâtres, l'ancien répertoire est mis abondamment à contribution. Et c'est Molière qui a le plus souvent la préférence. Ainsi Molière l'emporte à l'Ambigu-Comique avec 28 représentations de *L'Ecole des maris* et 26 de *George Dandin*; seul des autres "grands auteurs," Voltaire est mis au programme, mais il ne doit son succès qu'à une comédie jusqu'alors à peu près inconnue, *La Femme qui a raison* (42 représentations).[8] Le théâtre des Grands Danseurs du Roi, qui devient en juin 1791 Théâtre de la Gaîté, suit l'exemple et la mode, bien que les danses de corde, les pantomimes et ses loges grillées y soient plus prisées que les comédies classiques. Pour Molière, les Grands Danseurs ne retiennent que les comédies farcesques ou à quiproquo, ce qui convient au ton de la maison: 44 représentations du *Médecin malgré lui*, 42 des *Fourberies de Scapin*, 28 des *Précieuses ridicules* et 17 d'*Amphitryon*, comédie qui dans les programmes s'intitule parfois *Les Deux Amphitryons et les Deux Sosies* ou tout simplement, à la manière de Rotrou, *Les Deux Sosies* (les Grands Danseurs étaient réputés pour attirer les spectateurs en présentant la même marchandise sous des noms différents). Là, on le comprend, tant ce théâtre est éloigné du tragique, aucun Corneille, aucun Racine, aucun Voltaire. Seul, Marivaux est présent avec 33 représentations du *Jeu de l'amour et du hasard* (présenté lui-même sous différents titres) et 5 représentations de *l'Ile des esclaves*.

3

Quant aux théâtres qui n'avaient vu le jour qu'en 1790, le Théâtre de la Montansier et le Théâtre-Français comique et lyrique, ils ouvrent aussi leur scène à Molière, dès que le répertoire est devenu libre. Du 13 janvier 1791 au 21 septembre 1792, la citoyenne Montansier, dans sa salle du Palais-Royal, crée 38 pièces et reprend 105 pièces de l'ancien répertoire. Parmi celles-ci, 10 pièces de Molière avec un total de 45 représentations: *Les Précieuses ridicules*, pour lesquelles Devienne a composé une musique originale,[9] sont représentées 10 fois; *Le Dépit amoureux*: 9; *L'Ecole des maris* et *Les Fourberies de Scapin*: 6 fois chacune; *Tartuffe*: 4; *L'Avare* et *George Dandin*: 3; *Le Cocu imaginaire* (*Sganarelle*): 2; *L'Ecole des femmes* et *Le Misanthrope*: 1. La citoyenne Montansier fait cependant sa cour philosophique à Voltaire: 9 pièces et 71 représentations (dont 19 pour *Mérope*; mais aucun *Brutus*). Corneille et Racine, avec 5 pièces chacun, ont respectivement 19 (dont 8 pour *Rodogune*) et 26 représentations (dont 9 et pour *Iphigénie* et pour *Phèdre*). Marivaux, avec 2 pièces, a 8 représentations.

Le Théâtre de la rue de Bondy est plus modeste. Sur 15 pièces reprises à l'ancien répertoire après le décret de janvier 1791, on ne compte que deux Molière: *Le Dépit amoureux* (11 représentations) et *Tartuffe* (4 représentations). Mais c'est tout de même un succès pour Molière, si l'on sait qu'on n'y a joué aucune pièce de Corneille, de Racine, de Marivaux, ni aucun Voltaire.

4

Laborieusement, mais la recherche historique ne se fait pas sur des chemins faciles, il faut maintenant passer en revue des théâtres classés auparavant dans les "petits théâtres" et à ce titre négligés par les journaux, ou qui n'ont duré que peu de temps après leur création.

D'abord, les "petits théâtres" qui n'ont cessé, en marge des mondanités et des snobismes, de récréer les petites gens. Tel le Théâtre des Associés, boulevard du Temple, devenu en mars 1791 le Théâtre patriotique. On en connaît très insuffisamment les programmes. J'ai relevé néanmoins, pour la période qui nous intéresse, 5 pièces de Molière; par ordre alphabétique, *L'Avare*: 5 représentations; *Le Dépit amoureux*: 19; *L'Etourdi*: 4; *Les Fourberies de Scapin*: 12; *Le Médecin malgré lui*: 1; au total, 41 représentations. C'est relativement peu par rapport à Voltaire, dont on joua 9 pièces avec un total de 93 représentations (dont 22 pour *Brutus*). Marivaux n'est représenté que par *Le Jeu de l'amour et du hasard*: 21 fois. Aucun Corneille, aucun Racine. Mais compte tenu du peu d'information que nous avons sur ce théâtre, la prudence commande qu'on ne tire aucune conclusion de ces données.

On en dira autant du théâtre des Délassements comiques, situé lui aussi boulevard du Temple, et dont on ne connaît les programmes qu'à partir d'avril 1791; et encore, partiellement. Je n'ai relevé que 4 pièces de Molière: *Le Dépit amoureux* (21 représentations connues), *L'Ecole des maris*, *Le Misanthrope* et

Tartuffe. Là encore, Voltaire semble l'emporter avec 12 pièces (dont *Brutus*, avec 10 représentations). On trouve en outre deux Marivaux et un Racine: *Andromaque* (4 représentations).

Pour les nombreux théâtres ouverts après janvier 1791, qu'en dire? Certains ont fermé peu après leur ouverture, ou se sont transformés; peu ont duré. Molière s'est trouvé là engagé dans une vie théâtrale aventureuse, dont sa gloire se serait bien passée.

Le Théâtre de la Concorde, rue du Renard-Saint Merry, donna quelques représentations de mars à juin 1791. Dans le répertoire, on retrouve *Le Dépit amoureux*, *Le Médecin malgré lui* et *Le Misanthrope*, qu'accompagnent presque invariablement dans ce genre de théâtre *Adélaïde Du Guesclin* ou *Nanine*, de Voltaire; *Le Jeu de l'amour et du hasard*, de Marivaux; et quelques pièces passe-partout du XVIIIe siècle, comme *Les Fausses Infidélités*, de Barthe. Ce théâtre, pour quelques représentations du 3 novembre au 4 décembre 1791, s'appela Théâtre Jean-Jacques Rousseau; j'y relève encore une représentation du *Dépit amoureux*.

Le Lycée dramatique, boulevard du Temple, salle des élèves de l'Opéra, avait ouvert en mai 1791. Le répertoire devenu traditionnel est là, de l'inévitable *Adélaïde Du Guesclin* à *Zaïre*, de Voltaire, du *Cinna*, de Corneille, à l'*Andromaque*, de Racine; avec *Les Fausses Infidélités*; avec aussi *La Servante maîtresse* (1754), de Baurans, comédie mêlée d'ariettes venue du Théâtre-Italien et qui est en passe à son tour de s'infiltrer partout. On y a joué du Molière, bien entendu: *L'Avare*, *Le Dépit amoureux*, *L'Ecole des femmes*, *L'Ecole des maris*, *Le Médecin malgré lui*, *Les Précieuses ridicules* et *Tartuffe*. Le Lycée interrompit quelques mois au début de 1792 pour laisser la place à un nouveau Théâtre des Variétés ou Variétés dramatiques, qui, en février, joua 8 fois *Le Dépit amoureux*. Puis, le Lycée dramatique reprit le 29 avril 1792 avec *Les Femmes savantes*; on y joua en mai *Pourceaugnac, ou le gentilhomme limousin*. Mais on s'arrêta de nouveau en juin.

Le Théâtre d'Emulation, rue Notre-Dame de Nazareth, ancien théâtre de société du sieur Doyen, fut ouvert au public de mai à juillet 1791 par une "compagnie qui voulait y établir un spectacle où la jeunesse pût venir puiser des leçons de goût et de morale":[10] cinq pièces nouvelles, 14 pièces du répertoire, dont *Le Dépit amoureux* — encore lui —, *L'Ecole des maris* et *Le Médecin malgré lui*.

Chassés de leur salle par la Montansier, les Comédiens de Beaujolais, devenus en mars 1791 pour quelques jours les "Comédiens sans titre," donnèrent ou firent donner dans différentes salles, de janvier à mars 1791, quelques représentations pour lesquelles ils n'hésitèrent pas — ils étaient dans les premiers à le faire — à puiser dans le répertoire des théâtres ci-devant privilégiés. De Molière, ils jouèrent *Le Dépit amoureux* (6 représentations) et *L'Ecole des maris* (1 représentation). Pour Voltaire, on eut 3 représentations de *Brutus*, 2 de *Nanine* et 1 de *Mahomet*. Mais, ici encore, aucun Corneille, aucun Racine, aucun Marivaux.

Mentionnons également le Théâtre du Mont-Parnasse, boulevard d'Enfer, ouvert le 10 juillet 1791 avec *Le Dépit amoureux*, de Molière, et *Nanine*, de Voltaire, seule représentation connue en 1791. Il fit une réouverture le 9 avril 1792 avec *Le Dépit amoureux* et *L'Ecole des femmes*.

Nous retrouvons enfin Molière dans les salles de l'ancienne foire Saint-Germain: représentations intermittentes, dont les raisons d'être nous échappent le plus souvent. Ainsi dans l'ancienne salle de l'Ambigu-Comique, les élèves de l'Ecole dramatique donnèrent le 23 janvier 1791 *L'Ecole des maris* de Molière et le *Brutus* de Voltaire. Dans la même salle, en février 1791, une dame qui avait été directrice de troupe à Beauvais, fit jouer *Le Dépit amoureux*. Une autre troupe, qui se donnait le nom de Théâtre de la Liberté de la foire Saint-Germain, joua, de février à avril 1791, 4 nouveautés et 44 pièces du répertoire ancien et nouveau; on y retrouve *Le Dépit amoureux*, *Le Médecin malgré lui*, *Le Misanthrope*, *Les Précieuses ridicules* et *Tartuffe*. Le Théâtre des Variétés de la foire Saint-Germain joua, à partir d'octobre 1791, dans plusieurs salles de la foire et sous différentes directions; dans les pièces du répertoire, je relève encore *Le Dépit amoureux*, *L'Ecole des maris*, *Le Médecin malgré lui*, et *Les Précieuses ridicules*. Enfin, dans la salle qu'occupait précédemment à la foire le Théâtre de Monsieur, une troupe s'installa sous les noms prétentieux de "Théâtre lyrique" ou "Musée lyrique et comique" du faubourg Saint-Germain; de la fin mai à juillet 1791, elle monta un *Tartuffe* parmi quelques créations et une quinzaine de reprises du répertoire.

Quelle place avait l'art dans les représentations de ces théâtres plus ou moins improvisés? On l'ignore. A défaut de renseignements, je renvoie, pour le plus bas de l'échelle, à ce que l'*Almanach des spectacles* de Froullé, terminant la revue des théâtres de Paris en 1791, dit des deux théâtres situés l'un en face de l'autre "à l'entrée de la grande avenue des Champs-Elysées" et tous deux appelés "Théâtre de la place Louis XV": on y estropiait *Zaïre* et *Mahomet*, ou bien on y jouait des comédies à seule fin d'égayer les ouvriers du pont de Louis XVI et les marchands de tisane du quai des Tuileries. Et voici qui est significatif: "Le directeur, qui joue les premiers rôles, se présenta l'autre jour sur la scène et fit l'annonce en ces termes, d'une voix enrhumée: 'Messieux et Dames, d'main, drès les cinq heures du soir, j'aurons l'honneur que d'vous bailler la *Satyre* d'Voltaire et les *Fourberies d'l'Escarpin* d'Moyère'!"

5

On peut penser que ce genre de spectacle, qui se voulait populaire et qui n'était que bêtement médiocre, fut exceptionnel dans Paris.

Il est certain, en tout cas, que contrairement à ces théâtres de bateleurs fourvoyés dans le classique, plusieurs des théâtres créés en 1791 pourront rivaliser avec les "grands" théâtres, déjà solidement implantés dans la capitale. D'ailleurs ils réussiront, avec des fortunes diverses, il est vrai, à se maintenir assez longtemps pour que l'histoire du théâtre garde leur nom.

Tel le Théâtre de la rue de Louvois, ouvert le 16 août 1791 et qui, jusqu'au 18 août 1792, date de sa fermeture provisoire, donna 28 pièces nouvelles et reprit dans le répertoire ancien et contemporain 59 pièces, dont 7 Molière: *Le Dépit amoureux*, *L'Ecole des femmes*, *L'Ecole des maris*, *Le Médecin malgré lui*, *Le Misanthrope*, *Tartuffe*; à quoi il faut ajouter la première reprise à cette époque, le 11 octobre 1791, du *Mariage forcé*; au total pour Molière, 38 représentations. Pendant le même temps, Corneille n'a qu'une pièce et une seule représentation, Racine une pièce et 2 représentations, Voltaire 2 pièces et 6 représentations;

Marivaux a 3 pièces et 18 représentations, mais surtout grâce à la reprise de *L'Epreuve*, qu'on désignait alors sous le nom d'*Epreuve nouvelle* (11 représentations).

Tel encore le Théâtre du Marais, rue Sainte-Catherine, qui avait ouvert ses portes le 31 août 1791. Pour 12 créations, dont *La Mère coupable, ou l'autre Tartuffe*, de Beaumarchais, on compte 98 reprises. Là encore, Molière l'emporte: 8 pièces et 31 représentations: *Tartuffe*: 9; *L'Avare* et *L'Etourdi*: 5 pour chaque pièce, *L'Ecole des maris*: 4; *Le Misanthrope* et *Les Précieuses ridicules*: 3; *Les Femmes savantes* et *Le Médecin malgré lui*, une seule représentation. Pour comparaison, Marivaux a 6 pièces et 29 représentations (*Le Legs* est le plus joué: 12 fois), Voltaire a 10 pièces et 24 représentations (*Mérope* et *Nanine* l'emportent avec 5 et 4 représentations); Racine n'a que 2 pièces (*Les Plaideurs* et *Phèdre*) et 10 représentations chacune, Corneille 3 pièces (*Le Cid, Cinna* et *Le Menteur*) et une seule représentation pour chacune d'elles.

6

Mais pour Molière, l'intérêt se porte particulièrement sur un théâtre nouvellement construit rue Saint-Martin et qui ouvrit le 11 juin 1791, sous la direction de Boursault-Malherbe, ancien acteur-directeur du Grand-Théâtre de Marseille.[11] Ce théâtre prit en effet le nom de Théâtre de Molière,[12] bien que Boursault se soit dit le descendant du Boursault dont on sait le rôle joué contre Molière dans la querelle de *L'Ecole des femmes* en 1663. "La salle est d'une forme très agréable et décorée avec goût," note la *Chronique de Paris* du 21 juin 1791: "parmi les acteurs, il y en a quelques-uns qui ont du talent; et, en général, on y joue avec ensemble et avec intelligence." Boursault y tenait les rôles d'"acteur, administrateur, directeur, entrepreneur et régisseur"; sa femme jouait avec lui. Ils étaient secondés par le couple Scio: la femme était une actrice réputée et le mari était maître de musique (chef d'orchestre et compositeur). On y retrouvait aussi l'acteur Volange, dont on connaissait le talent pour interpréter plusieurs rôles (jusqu'à sept) dans une même pièce.

En fait, le Théâtre de Molière n'a eu de Molière que le nom, même si *Le Misanthrope* fut servi à l'ouverture du théâtre. Boursault avait promis à la barre de l'Assemblée Nationale de "ne laisser jouer dans son spectacle aucun ouvrage anti-patriotique"; "il fait plus, note la *Chronique de Paris* en juillet 1791, il tâche de représenter tous ceux qui peuvent fortifier l'esprit public et l'amour de la liberté." Les nouveautés "révolutionnaires" s'y succèdent en effet, depuis *La Ligue des fanatiques et des tyrans* (18 juin 1791), "tragédie patriotico-révolutionico-lanternico-nationale," comme la désigne l'*Almanach des spectacles* de Froullé, jusqu'aux *Trois ans de l'histoire de France* (29 avril 1792), "bigarrure" à grand spectacle, en passant par la *Revue des armées noire et blanche d'Outre-Rhin* (25 juillet 1791), mélodrame-parade, et maintes autres pièces de ce genre.

Quelle place Molière et les auteurs classiques du répertoire avaient-ils au milieu de toute cette mitraille? Une place modeste, le passé récent ou lointain servant surtout, semble-t-il, à compléter (ou à faire accepter) les nouveautés du jour. J'y relève jusqu'en septembre 1792 dix pièces de Molière: *Amphitryon, Le Dépit amoureux, L'Ecole des femmes, L'Ecole des maris, L'Etourdi, Les*

Femmes savantes, *Le Malade imaginaire*, *Le Médecin malgré lui*, *Le Misanthrope* et *Tartuffe*. Mais chacune de ces pièces n'a qu'une représentation ou deux; et c'est, là encore, *L'Ecole des maris* qui est, si l'on peut dire, la pièce la plus jouée: 6 représentations; au total, 21 représentations de Molière, pour vingt mois! alors que dans le même laps de temps le *Jérôme Pointu*, de Beaunoir (Variétés amusantes, 1781), obtient grâce à Volange 30 représentations. Voltaire n'est guère mieux traité que Molière: 7 pièces et 28 représentations (dont 13 de *Nanine*); Marivaux pour 5 pièces a 26 représentations (dont 10 pour *L'Epreuve*). Aucune pièce de Racine; deux de Corneille: *Le Cid* et *Le Menteur*, au total 5 représentations.

IV

Jusqu'à la fermeture du Théâtre de la Nation (septembre 1793)

A partir de l'abolition de la royauté (21 septembre 1792) et de la proclamation de la République (22 septembre), le théâtre aborde une période difficile, puisque la censure officieusement rétablie va constamment et étroitement surveiller le théâtre: on verra même à la fin de 1793 une pièce comme *Mérope*, de Voltaire, interdite. Le Comité d'Instruction publique contrôle le répertoire; et il faut "purger" les théâtres "de toutes les pièces propres à corrompre l'esprit républicain" (*Journal de Paris*, 2 avril 1793).

Molière peut-il encore faire entendre sa voix dans une kyrielle de pièces révolutionnaires, dont le plus souvent la platitude démagogique n'a d'égal que le style déclamatoire ou vulgairement poissard?

1

Le Théâtre de la Nation (ex-Comédie-Française) sera fermé par ordre de la Convention, sur arrêté de son Comité de Salut public, le 3 septembre 1793, et la plupart de ses comédiens emprisonnés.[13]

De la proclamation de la République à cette fermeture, pendant presque un an, les Comédiens-Français créèrent peu de pièces mais maintinrent le répertoire, du moins les pièces qui pouvaient encore trouver grâce auprès des autorités politiques.

Jusqu'au coup d'Etat du 2 juin 1793, qui, avec la victoire des Montagnards sur les Girondins, allait conduire au régime de la Terreur, les Comédiens-Français montèrent 9 pièces nouvelles, dont deux seulement traitaient d'événements ou de problèmes du jour: *L'Apothéose de Beaurepaire* (21 septembre 1792) et *L'Ami des lois* (2 janvier 1793). C'est par le répertoire surtout qu'ils gardent encore leur public; 103 pièces sont ainsi reprises par alternance pour quelques représentations. On relève dans ce répertoire 11 Molière, avec *L'Ecole des maris*: 7 représentations, *Tartuffe*: 5, *Amphitryon*, *L'Ecole des femmes* et *Pourceaugnac*: 4, *George Dandin* et *Le Médecin malgré lui*: 3, *L'Avare*, *La Comtesse d'Escarbagnas* et *Le Misanthrope*: 2, *Les Femmes sa-*

vantes: 1; au total, 37 représentations. *Le Dépit amoureux, L'Etourdi, Les Fourberies de Scapin* et *Le Malade imaginaire* ont maintenant disparu de l'affiche.

Pour comparaison, Voltaire a 10 pièces (dont la comédie de *L'Ecossaise*) et 38 représentations; Racine: 7 pièces et 12 représentations; Corneille: 4 pièces et 13 représentations (*Le Menteur* a lui aussi disparu) et Marivaux: 3 pièces et 8 représentations.

Après le 2 juin 1793 et jusqu'à la fermeture du 3 septembre, peu de chose; deux créations, dont la *Paméla*, de Neufchâteau, qui servira de prétexte à la fermeture du théâtre, et toujours le répertoire, avec cette particularité que les Comédiens-Français profitent à leur tour des libertés nouvelles pour faire une meilleure place à Marivaux: *L'Epreuve* et *Les Fausses Confidences* figurent désormais à l'affiche. De Molière, on ne joue, durant ces trois mois, qu'*Amphitryon, La Comtesse d'Escarbagnas, L'Ecole des maris, George Dandin* et *Le Médecin malgré lui*; au total, 6 représentations. Voltaire est mieux placé avec 8 pièces (dont *La Mort de César*) et 10 représentations; mais Corneille (*Le Cid*) et Racine (*Les Plaideurs*) n'ont chacun qu'une représentation.

2

La relève est assurée ailleurs. Notamment au théâtre rival de la rue de Richelieu, devenu l'officiel Théâtre de la République: de la fin septembre 1792 au début de 1793 on y jouera 11 pièces de Molière (dont *Le Malade imaginaire*, avec la réception des médecins); au total, 60 représentations.[14]

Pour simplifier et ne pas abuser plus longtemps de la patience de mon lecteur, compte tenu aussi de ce qui a été dit précédemment, je m'en tiendrai à une énumération des pièces de Molière jouées du début de la République jusqu'à la fermeture du Théâtre de la Nation (à peine un an de spectacles), avec référence aux théâtres de Paris qui les ont jouées.

Théâtres qui ont joué Molière durant ces douze mois (le Théâtre de la Nation exclu):

A. Théâtre de la République, rue de Richelieu
B. Théâtre de la rue Feydeau
C. Théâtre Montansier
D. Théâtre de Molière
E. Théâtre du Marais
F. Théâtre de la Gaîté
G. Ambigu-Comique
H. Théâtre patriotique
I. Délassements comiques
J. Théâtre de l'Estrapade
K. Foire Saint-Germain (salles du Théâtre des Variétés comiques, des Elèves du Théâtre-Français, Théâtre de Lazzari en février-mars 1793, etc.)
L. Salle des Elèves de l'Opéra, boulevard du Temple (différentes troupes, dites de Variétés)
M. Théâtre national, ouvert le 15 août 1793, rue de Richelieu, sur une portion de l'emplacement occupé précédemment par l'Hôtel Louvois.[15]

Pièces de Molière, par ordre préférentiel, la lettre renvoyant aux théâtres énumérés ci-dessus:

L'Ecole des maris: 61 représentations (A, B par la troupe du Marais, C, D, E, G avec 25 représentations, H, I, J, K, L).

Le Médecin de malgré lui: 47 représentations (A, B avec 7 représentations de la pièce mise en musique par Désaugiers en janvier 1792, D, F avec 20 représentations et parfois pour titre: *Le Fagoteur médecin malgré lui,* H, J, L, M).

Les Fourberies de Scapin: 37 représentations (A, C, E, F avec 18 représentations, I).

Pourceaugnac: 36 représentations (32 de la pièce mise en musique par Mengozzi au Théâtre Montansier en janvier 1793, et 4 au Théâtre de Molière).

Les Précieuses ridicules: 27 représentations (A, C avec 3 représentations de la pièce mise en musique par Devienne en août 1791, E, F avec 18 représentations, J).

Le Dépit amoureux: 22 représentations (A, C, D, H, I, J, K, L).

Tartuffe: 17 représentations (A, D, H, I, J, M).

George Dandin: 16 représentations (A, C, G).

L'Avare: 11 représentations (A, C, E).

L'Ecole des femmes: 8 représentations (E, H, I).

Le Misanthrope: 6 représentations (A, E).

Les Femmes savantes: 5 représentations (A).

Amphitryon: 3 représentations (F).

Le Malade imaginaire: 3 représentations (A).

L'Etourdi: 2 représentations (E).

La "maison" de Molière peut fermer ses portes. Il n'est guère de théâtres à Paris, on le voit, qui ne soient prêts à maintenir l'audience de Molière. Et non seulement à la maintenir, mais à l'étendre.

V

Bilan des représentations de Molière (1789-1793)

On peut maintenant procéder à une récapitulation des représentations de Molière à Paris plus d'un siècle après sa mort, de la réunion des Etats généraux à la fermeture de la Comédie-Française (52 mois), en prenant soin de distinguer les représentations données par les Comédiens-Français, longtemps propriétaires exclusifs de son œuvre, et celles données sur les autres théâtres de Paris à partir du décret de janvier 1791 qui libérait enfin le répertoire du passé.

L'ordre préférentiel se présente comme suit:

		Comédie-Française 5-1789 à 9-1793	ordre	Autres théâtres 1-1791 à 9-1793	ordre	TOTAL
1	L'Ecole des maris	45	1	146	3	191
2	Le Médecin malgré lui	17	8	164	1	181
3	Le Dépit amoureux	10	12	149	2	159
4	Les Fourberies de Scapin	5	13	106	4	111
5	Tartuffe	21	3	65	6	86
6	Les Précieuses ridicules	—	—	85	5	85
7	George Dandin	20	5	45	7	65
8	Pourceaugnac	12	10	37	8	49
9	L'Avare	18	7	30	9	48
10	L'Ecole des femmes	27	2	21	11	48
11	Amphitryon	21	3	21	11	42
12	Le Misanthrope	12	10	24	10	36
13	Les Femmes savantes	15	9	9	15	24
14	La Comtesse d'Escarbagnas	19	6	3	17	22
15	L'Etourdi	2	16	17	13	19
16	Le Malade imaginaire	5	13	5	16	10
17	Le Mariage forcé	—	—	10	14	10
18	Le Bourgeois gentilhomme	5	13	—	—	5
19	Le Cocu imaginaire	—	—	2	18	2
		254		939		1193

Parmi les réflexions et les remarques qu'on peut faire sur ce bilan, j'en retiendrai deux.

D'abord sur le choix. Les huit premières places reviennent à ce qu'on peut appeler des comédies "gaies," où se retrouvent plus particulièrement la tradition farcesque et l'esprit de la *commedia dell'arte*, et à une comédie condamnant l'hypocrisie religieuse: *Tartuffe*. Les théâtres autres que la Comédie-Française privilégient ce choix. Le *Bourgeois* qui veut devenir *gentilhomme* quand tant de gentilshommes cherchent à se faire oublier au milieu du peuple, n'a, cela va de soi, que quelques représentations, une en 1790 et quatre en 1792, et seulement au Théâtre de la Nation (Comédie-Française). Encore, ces représentations de 1792 s'expliquent-elles par des raisons qui n'ont probablement rien à voir avec un esprit de réaction: en 1792, sentant le public leur échapper et à défaut de créations de pièces révolutionnaires, les Comédiens-Français cherchaient le succès non seulement par le jeu d'acteurs aimés du public (Molé; retour de Préville, alors septuagénaire) et d'actrices nouvelles (Mlle Mézeray), mais aussi en jouant des pièces à grand spectacle: déjà en juin-juillet 1791, ils avaient remis la tragédie de Racine, *Athalie*, avec une musique nouvelle de Gossec, en associant pour le chant les Comédiens-Français et les Comédiens-Italiens. Quand *Le Bourgeois gentilhomme* fut repris le 4 février 1792 "avec sa cérémonie" et avec le vieux ménage Préville dans le rôle du ménage Jourdain, les Comédiens ne pensaient également que piquer la curiosité du public par un "spectacle" exceptionnel.

La deuxième remarque porte sur une comparaison entre le tableau établi ci-dessus et le tableau de fréquence des représentations de Molière à la Comédie-Française depuis sa création (1680) jusqu'en 1970.[16] Pour environ trois siècles de représentations à la Comédie-Française et pour les vingt pièces les plus jouées, l'ordre préférentiel est le suivant: 1) *Tartuffe*: 2851 représentations; 2) *L'Avare*: 2232; 3) *Le Médecin malgré lui*: 2115; 4) *Le Misanthrope*: 1895; 5) *Les Femmes savantes*: 1734; 6) *Le Malade imaginaire*: 1731; 7) *L'Ecole des maris*: 1568; 8) *L'Ecole des femmes*: 1435; 9) *Les Fourberies de Scapin*: 1260; 10) *Le Dépit amoureux*: 1246; 11) *Les Précieuses ridicules*: 1240; 12) *Le Mariage forcé*: 1181; 13) *Le Bourgeois gentilhomme*: 1115; 14) *George Dandin*: 1075; 15) *Amphitryon*: 1020; 16) *M. de Pourceaugnac*: 782; 17) *Sganarelle, ou le cocu imaginaire*: 761; 18) *La Comtesse d'Escarbagnas*: 579; 19) *L'Etourdi*: 573; 20) *L'Amour médecin*: 383. On voit quelle place privilégiée occupent dans cette liste ce qu'on considère dans nos histoires littéraires comme les "grandes" pièces de Molière, comédies de mœurs et de caractère: *L'Avare, L'Ecole des femmes, Les Femmes savantes, Le Malade imaginaire, Le Misanthrope, Tartuffe*. Mais il en est ici comme des goûts et des couleurs. Les circonstances peuvent faire varier les préférences du public; les comédiens et aujourd'hui les metteurs en scène peuvent, par leur talent ou leur goût personnel, imposer eux-mêmes au public certains rôles et certaines pièces. Pour en rester toujours à la Comédie-Française, voici un ordre préférentiel récent, celui des années 1961-1969: 1) *L'Avare*; 2) *Tartuffe*; 3) *Le Malade imaginaire*; 4) *Le Misanthrope*; 5) *Le Bourgeois gentilhomme*; 6) *Les Femmes savantes*; 7) *L'Ecole des femmes*; 8) *La Critique de l'Ecole des femmes*; 9) *Le Mariage forcé*; 10) *Le Médecin malgré lui*; 11) *Amphitryon*; 12) *Don Juan*; 13) *Les Fourberies de Scapin*; 14) *Le Dépit amoureux*; et en 16e position *L'Ecole des maris*, ces trois dernières pièces pourtant si prisées pendant la Révolution! Ce choix, lui-même, n'est pas, tant s'en faut, définitif. Et, durant la dernière décennie, quiconque par son métier a été amené à fréquenter les salles de spectacle à Paris, en France et aussi à l'étranger, a vu je ne sais combien de *Don Juan* et d'*Impromptu de Versailles*, pièces jusqu'au XXe siècle si souvent exclues de la scène! Quelle preuve de la vitalité de Molière dans la variété d'expression de son génie! Il y a toujours, quelles que soient les circonstances, un Molière pour faire rire. Et quand bien même on connaîtrait ses pièces par cœur, finira-t-on jamais d'en rire?

André Tissier
Université de Paris III

Notes

[1] Ce qu'on ne saura, au contraire, jamais, c'est comment on jouait Molière à cette époque (tout au plus signale-t-on un goût de plus en plus prononcé pour la "décoration") et comment il faisait rire. Les comptes rendus sont muets sur les réactions du public (hormis applaudissements, cris et sifflets) et ils se contentent de termes vagues sur le "jeu" de l'acteur: que signifie jouer une pièce "d'une manière très piquante" (*Petites Affiches*, 10 avril 1792) ou d'une "manière sublime" (*ibid.*, 27 décembre 1793)?

[2] Je me suis abstenu aussi de refaire l'histoire du théâtre de la Révolution; et je renvoie le lecteur à l'un des derniers-nés des ouvrages parus sur cette histoire: *The Theatre of the French Revolution*, par Marvin Carlson (Ithaca: Cornell University Press, 1966; traduction française: *Le Théâtre de la Révolution française* [Paris: Gallimard, 1970]), ouvrage de vulgarisation, qui rendra service au non-initié.

[3] En 1782, quelques jours après l'ouverture de la nouvelle salle située près du Luxembourg, faubourg Saint-Germain, le "patronage" de Molière est confirmé par une comédie de La Harpe, intitulée: *Molière à la nouvelle salle* (12 avril 1782; 15 représentations dans l'année).

[4] Parmi ces 34 pièces, 8 n'étaient pas entrées au répertoire de la Comédie-Française: *Don Garcie de Navarre, Don Juan* (cette comédie ne sera représentée à la Comédie-Française qu'au milieu du XIXe siècle; depuis 1680, lui est substitué *Le Festin de Pierre*, de Thomas Corneille), *L'Impromptu de Versailles, La Jalousie du Barbouillé, Le Médecin volant, Mélicerte, Les Plaisirs de l'île enchantée* et la *Pastorale comique*. En outre, 6 pièces n'étaient plus jouées, parfois depuis longtemps: *Les Amants magnifiques* (depuis 1705), *La Critique de l'Ecole des femmes* (depuis 1692), *Les Fâcheux* (depuis 1749), *La Princesse d'Elide* (depuis 1758), *Psyché* (depuis 1709) et *Sganarelle* (depuis 1754). Enfin trois pièces qui ne figurent pas dans ces listes, avaient été jouées peu auparavant: *L'Amour médecin* (10 fois de 1777 à 1781), *Les Precieuses ridicules* (37 fois de 1777 à 1782) et *Le Sicilien* (8 fois de 1777 à 1782).

[5] *Almanach des spectacles* de Froullé pour 1792, p. 213.

[6] Les trois autres pièces étant de Boissy, Piron et Framéry.

[7] Dont une comédie épisodique en un acte et en prose, *La Matinée de Molière* (anonyme; 23 avril 1789: échec) et une comédie en trois actes et en vers, *Alceste à la campagne, ou le Misanthrope corrigé* (de Demoustier; 5 décembre 1790: succès).

[8] Ses tragédies ont là peu de succès: *Mahomet*, 2 représentations, et *La Mort de César*: 1. A croire que Corneille, Racine et Voltaire ne soient pour certains que les auteurs (comiques) du *Menteur*, des *Plaideurs* et de *Nanine* (ou, exceptionnellement, de cette *Femme qui a raison*).

[9] La musique, les chants et la danse ont envahi le théâtre à l'époque révolutionnaire. Rien d'étonnant donc que Molière ait été mis en musique. Racine le sera lui aussi avec ses *Plaideurs* (Théâtre de la rue Feydeau, 23 juin 1792). Le commentaire des *Petites Affiches* du 25 juin est à ce sujet significatif: "Tout le monde écrit, tout le monde fait des vers, tout le monde veut faire des pièces de théâtre; et cependant la disette des bons [ouvrages] est si grande que, depuis quelque temps, on s'est avisé de toucher aux chefs-d'œuvre de nos maîtres . . . O grands hommes, vous seriez-vous jamais doutés qu'un jour viendrait où vos chefs-d'œuvre, qui devraient être sacrés, seraient retouchés, asservis à la froide mesure d'un trio, d'un duo ou d'un récitatif?"

[10] *Almanach des spectacles* de Froullé pour 1792, p. 273.

[11] Sur ce curieux personnage, le meilleur travail reste celui d'Ernest Lebègue: *Boursault-Malherbe (1752-1842)* (Paris: Alcan, 1935).

[12] Le Théâtre de Molière devint en novembre 1793 le Théâtre des Sans-Culottes. Mais le passage des Nourrices, qui bordait un des côtés du théâtre, a toujours gardé depuis 1791 le nom de "passage Molière."

[13] La Comédie-Française ne sera rétablie qu'en 1799. Voir mon article "Les Comédiens-Français pendant la période révolutionnaire (1789-1799)," *Revue d'histoire du théâtre*, 32 (1980), 142-59.

[14] Le Théâtre de la Nation n'avait donné dans le même temps que 43 représentations de Molière.

[15] Voir L[ouis]-Henry Lecomte, *Histoire des théâtres de Paris: Le Théâtre national, le Théâtre de l'égalité* (Paris: H. Daragon, 1907).

135

[16] D'après des tableaux publiés par Sylvie Chevalley dans les programmes de ce théâtre (l'année 1970 étant exclue). Ces tableaux font apparaître en outre que les pièces de Molière placées dans les sept premiers rangs sont aussi les sept premières de la liste générale des pièces les plus jouées à la Comédie-Française.